WOMEN, FAMILY, AND GENDER
IN ISLAMIC LAW

In what ways has Islamic law discriminated against women and privileged men? What rights and power have been accorded to Muslim women, and how have they used the legal system to enhance their social and economic position? In an analysis of Islamic law through the prism of gender, Judith E. Tucker tackles these complex questions relating to the position of women in Islamic society, and to the ways in which the legal system shaped the family, property rights, space, and sexuality, from classical and medieval times to the present. Hers is a nuanced approach, which negotiates broadly between the history of doctrine and of practice and the interplay between the two. Working with concepts drawn from feminist legal theory and by using particular cases to illustrate her arguments, the author systematically addresses questions of discrimination and expectation – what did men expect of their womenfolk? – and of how the language of the law contributed to that discrimination, infecting the system and all those who participated in it. The author is a fluent communicator, effectively guiding the reader through the historical roots and intellectual contours of the Islamic legal system, and explicating the impact of these traditions on Islamic law as it is practiced in the modern world.

JUDITH E. TUCKER is Professor of History in the Department of History and Center for Contemporary Arab Studies at Georgetown University, Washington, DC. Her previous publications include *Women in Nineteenth-Century Egypt* (Cambridge, 1985) and *In the House of the Law: Gender and Islamic Law in Ottoman Syria and Palestine* (1998).

THEMES IN ISLAMIC LAW 3

Series editor: Wael B. Hallaq

Themes in Islamic Law offers a series of state-of-the-art titles on the history of Islamic law, its application and its place in the modern world. The intention is to provide an analytic overview of the field with an emphasis on how law relates to the society in which it operates. Contributing authors, who all have distinguished reputations in their particular areas of scholarship, have been asked to interpret the complexities of the subject for those entering the field for the first time.

WOMEN, FAMILY, AND GENDER IN ISLAMIC LAW

JUDITH E. TUCKER

Georgetown University

CAMBRIDGE
UNIVERSITY PRESS

CAMBRIDGE UNIVERSITY PRESS
Cambridge, New York, Melbourne, Madrid, Cape Town, Singapore, São Paulo, Delhi

Cambridge University Press
The Edinburgh Building, Cambridge CB2 8RU, UK

Published in the United States of America by Cambridge University Press, New York

www.cambridge.org
Information on this title: www.cambridge.org/9780521537476

First published 2008

Printed in the United Kingdom at the University Press, Cambridge

A catalogue record for this publication is available from the British Library

Library of Congress Cataloguing in Publication data
Tucker, Judith E.
Women, family, and gender in Islamic law / Judith E. Tucker.
p.   cm.
Includes bibliographical references and index.
ISBN 978-0-521-83044-7
1. Women – Legal status, laws, etc. (Islamic law)
2. Married women – Legal status, laws, etc.
(Islamic law)   3. Divorce (Islamic law)
4. Domestic relations (Islamic law)   I. Title.
KBP526.3.T83   2008
340.5′9–dc22
2008019563

ISBN 978-0-521-83044-7 hardback
ISBN 978-0-521-53747-6 paperback

For Sue, Beth, and Prilla
my sisters

Contents

Acknowledgements

This book, in many ways both a synthetic and a reflective enterprise, is the product of many years of reading, researching, presenting, and listening on Islamic law and gender issues. It bears the marks of the many books and theses I have read, papers I have heard, and comments I have received. I have incurred so many debts along the way that I find acknowledging all those who have contributed to my understanding of Islamic law and gender in general and this book in particular a very daunting task. I cannot hope to recognize all the individuals and institutions that supported and influenced this project and therefore must resign myself to offering up a less than comprehensive accounting, with my apologies to all those whom I fail to mention.

The project would not have been possible without concrete support. Sojourns in Cairo were central to the beginning and the end of the process. I was fortunate to be the recipient of an American Research Center in Egypt/ National Endowment for the Humanities Fellowship in 2002–3 that allowed me to get the project in gear. I was also supported by a Georgetown University Senior Research Leave. The American Research Center in Egypt, its Interim Directors Jere Bacharach and Irene Bierman and staff, in particular Madame Amira Khattab, fostered an excellent environment for the scholars in residence. It was also my good fortune to be associated with the Cynthia Nelson Institute for Gender and Women's Studies (IGWS) at the American University in Cairo as a Visiting Research Scholar in the spring of 2007, when I was able (finally) to bring this book to completion. The spirit of my friend and collaborator, the late Cynthia Nelson, hovered close by, and her successor at IGWS, Martina Rieker, was a wonderful host, unstinting and creative in her encouragement of my efforts and, indeed, of gender and women's studies in general. I thank Martina and others of the IGWS associated faculty, including Soraya Altorki, Ibrahim Elnur, Feriel Ghazoul, Samia Mehrez, Hoda Lutfi, Hanan Sabea, Hania Sholkamy, and Mariz Tadros for conversations, comments, and the many benefits I derived from exposure to their ideas and knowledge.

Over the years I worked on this book, a number of other friends and colleagues gave me opportunities to present work in progress and otherwise shared information and insights. I want to thank several of them here, including Clarissa Burt, Farha Ghannam, Penny Johnson, Suad Joseph, Firoozeh Kashani-Sabet, Ziba Mir-Hosseini, Annelise Moors, Leslie Peirce, and Amira Sonbol. Georgetown University's Department of History and Center for Contemporary Arab Studies have been my intellectual homes, and my faculty colleagues in both units have played a major role in my ongoing education. I thank them all for their unparalleled collegiality, and mention in particular John Tutino, History Chair, and Michael Hudson, CCAS Director, for their support.

I have also been extremely fortunate to have worked with a number of exceptional graduate students over the years, several of whom were generous enough to read and comment on the entire manuscript. I want to thank Zeinab Abul-Magd, Aurelie Perrier, Nadya Sbaiti, and Sara Scalenghe for the gift of their time and attention. Much was clarified as a result of their careful readings. Dina Hussein and Aurelie Perrier also contributed greatly appreciated research assistance to this project, and Shady Hakim helped with the final preparation of the manuscript. The future of the field of Middle East history is in excellent hands.

My association with Cambridge University Press has been a happy one over the years, and I always welcomed the cheery "Cambridge Calling!" from Marigold Acland, who first solicited and consulted on this project. Elizabeth Davey and Sarah Green were helpful throughout the production process, and Frances Brown proved to be a very capable copy-editor. It was the Series Editor, Professor Wael Hallaq, who invited me to contribute this volume. I thank him for his confidence in me, although I must admit that this turned out to be a far more difficult project than he initially intimated. I also thank him for his close reading and criticism of a previous draft, which helped improve the manuscript. The shortcomings that remain are entirely my responsibility. I also want to thank Nancy Farley for her ever gracious assistance in the end game.

And finally I thank my near and dear ones who, even when a little weary of hearing about such projects, stayed interested. Karmah and Layth took absences and relocations in their stride, and always brought humor to bear on the situation. My husband Sharif was a wonderful companion in Cairo, took time out from his heavy schedule to help in the research and writing process, and even tolerated dinner conversation on the topic. They have my heart and my gratitude.

Every effort has been made to secure the necessary permission to reproduce the photograph used on the front cover of the book, however, it has proved impossible to trace the copyright holder. If any omissions are brought to our notice, we will be happy to include appropriate acknowledgements in any subsequent edition.

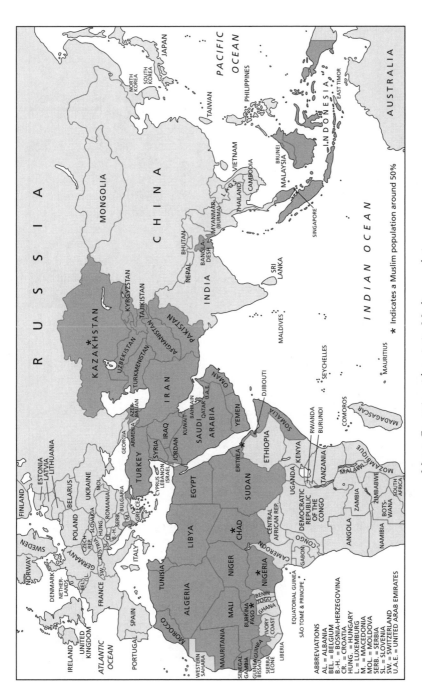

Map 1 Countries with majority Muslim populations

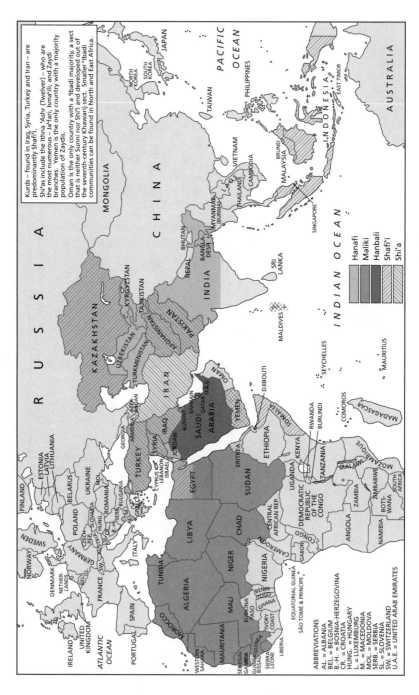

Map 2 Areas of predominance of Islamic legal schools (*madhhabs*)

Introduction

As I began to work on this book, I was the unhappy recipient of much bad news, forwarded on by friends and colleagues. A woman in Nigeria who had given birth out-of-wedlock faced a sentence of death by stoning as soon as her baby, whose father had been allowed to deny paternity, was weaned. The wife of a prominent entertainer in Cairo grew suspicious of her husband's behavior, followed him to an apartment, found him in bed with another woman, and made a huge scene, only to discover that the other woman was a legal second wife. Feeling was still running high in Saudi Arabia about the decision by religious police to prevent "uncovered" girls from leaving their burning school building, leading to the death of fifteen. A religious council challenged the minimum legal marriage age of eighteen in India, arguing that it violated the rights of community members to marry off their daughters as soon as they reached puberty. All this in the name of Islamic law. Of course, bad news travels fastest and farthest – these incidents cannot be taken to represent current doctrines and practices of Islamic law. Still, they demand our attention: how could a legal system that attempts to follow the will of God, a God who is compassionate and just, permit and even facilitate the expression of such rampant misogyny and unbounded patriarchal privilege? Why would many Muslim women, and their male allies, remain steadfast in their belief that Islamic principles are the fount of goodness and righteousness in this life and the hereafter, and Islamic practices, although perhaps in need of some review and revision, are the best guarantee of rights, privileges, and fairness for women?

The question was further complicated, for me, by the fact that my prior research interests, as a social historian of the Ottoman period in the Arab World, had brought me into contact with Islamic legal materials, including some of the juristic texts and records of legal practice that survive from the seventeenth and eighteenth centuries. I found it very difficult to reconcile the texture of these discussions and practices, imbued as they were by palpable concern for the rights of vulnerable members of society – the poor, the orphaned, the female – with the tone of current debates on matters like female dress and adultery. What was the relationship of the views of traditional jurists to those of the present? Are there enduring themes in the Islamic legal position on women and gender or do we see great variation over time? What are the basic premises of the Islamic legal constructions of women and gender and how have they been affected by historical contingencies? How have those constructions shaped and been shaped by the understandings and activities of ordinary people?

I raise these questions as a historian. I am not a Muslim and I am not exploring Islamic law from a faith-based perspective. My purpose is not, and cannot be, to engage in original interpreting of the law or to sit in judgment on how others have understood the rules of their religion. Rather, I approach the topic of Islamic law, women, and gender as a study of a multilayered history. It is part of the history of doctrinal development, the ways in which Islamic jurists, working with received texts and sophisticated methodologies, formulated rules about women, men, and their relationships. It is part the history of legal institutions and practices, how these rules were understood, implemented, and even modified by a range of legal actors, from individual judges to centralized state powers. It is also part the history of lay members of Muslim communities whose choices of doctrines to follow and legal avenues to pursue allowed the law to develop in rhythm with social needs, just as their legal inquiries and court appearances also served, at times, as contestation of legal discourse on women and gender issues. I try to address all three of these interwoven layers in the pages that follow as I consider how Islamic law and the Muslims who lived it constructed the relationship between law and gender.

LAW, WOMEN, AND GENDER

What is the relationship between law and gender? What role do law and legal institutions play in defining the male and the female in any given society? What kinds of limits based on the sex of a subject are set by the law and what kinds of liberations are made possible? In what sense can we talk about "gendered law" as a universal phenomenon, and what are the processes by which various systems of law are gendered? How do we mount challenges to a system of legal gendering that disempowers and impoverishes women as Women materially and emotionally just as it confers dubious privileges on men as Men? And is the law, in fact, a significant stage for struggle over basic issues of gendering in any society?

Feminist legal theorists in the West have debated such questions for the past few decades so that we now have a substantial body of literature addressing issues of the gendering of law and legal institutions in the West and its consequences for women in particular. They have developed a number of contending positions and approaches that, while by no means relevant in all instances to the issues and debates I will be considering in the context of Islamic law and gender, can be very helpful as points of comparison. In tracing some of the developments in feminist legal thought in the West, I am not intent on discovering a blueprint for subsequent discussion of Islamic law, but rather seeking out the questions and issues that may be of comparative interest.

The approach with the longest lineage, reaching from mid-Victorian times up to the present, is that of liberal feminist thinkers. The liberal tradition, particularly prominent in the Anglo-American context, accepts law and legal institutions as based on principles of rationality, objectivity, and fairness in their dealings with an autonomous legal subject. The problem, as far as women and gender are concerned, is that certain aspects of law have built-in, and often hidden, inequalities between men and women as a result of the evolution of the law in a patriarchal social environment. The feminist task, as far as liberal theorists are concerned, is to identify and correct those aspects of law that belie the liberal promise of equality and freedom of individuals before the law by discriminating against women. Examples of such discrimination include: disadvantaging women by allocating fewer material resources to them, as was long the case in property settlements in divorce cases; judging men and women's similar actions in different ways, as in criminalizing the behavior of the female prostitute but not her male client; and assigning men and women to distinct social roles, as in the sex-based classifications of "breadwinner" and "homemaker." Only with the eradication of such discriminatory laws and legal categories will women be able to realize the liberal promise of equal treatment as individuals with equal rights. The task is one of identification of such legal inequalities and their correction so that women can realize the promises of freedom and equality made by the liberal state and its legal institutions.[1]

The liberal project has not always proved to be so straightforward. Many who believe in calling upon the law and legal institutions of the liberal state

---

[1] For discussions of liberal feminist theory, see Hilaire Barnett, *Introduction to Feminist Jurisprudence* (London: Routledge-Cavendish, 1998), ch. 1; and Catharine A. MacKinnon, *Toward a Feminist Theory of the State* (Cambridge, MA: Harvard University Press, 1989), ch. 8.

to live up to their own terms of self-reference in regard to their female citizens are not entirely sanguine about the outcome. As Wendy Williams has pointed out, courts are not a source of radical social change; legal activism may succeed in extending male privileges to women, but it cannot change the fact that the law is fundamentally designed with male needs and values in mind. Equality is always comparative: in order to be equal to men, women must be the same as men, i.e. be ready to accept the standard of gender neutrality, the "single standard" that is based on male experience and male values. The only alternative under liberal thought is to accept that women do have certain differences from men and need protections and special benefits to compensate for this difference, although again the standard for difference, as with the standard for sameness, is that of the male. At a maximum, legal activism can recognize and redress past unequal treatment (by the law) by treating women in a special fashion (affirmative action) for a specific purpose and a limited time. But the larger project of achieving equality inevitably runs up against cultural assumptions that the law cannot directly challenge – that is the role of much broader social and political movements. Still, for Williams, the strategy of bidding for legal equality is an important one: women stake their claim to equal rights and a full share in their society by agreeing to the male norm, at least for the moment. On this basis, for example, Williams shied away from treating pregnancy as any different from other disabilities: viewing pregnant women as temporarily "disabled" allows them to receive benefits like men who are disabled without opening the Pandora's Box of special treatment for women as women.[2]

Questions about the limits of the liberal approach in general, and the insular, self-referential, and male-normed nature of liberal legal thought in particular, prompted the emergence of a contending approach that can be designated as "woman-centered" or "essentialist" depending on one's point of view. By way of positive assessment, Joanne Conaghan observed, "Such an approach lifts women from the wings and places them, their lives and experiences on centre stage."[3] Such centering has had a number of important results: Conaghan notes, for example, how attention to the ways in which women actually experience male violence was interjected into debates about the reform of criminal justice, and has in fact resulted in some changes

---

[2] Wendy Williams, "The Equality Crisis: Some Reflections on Culture, Courts, and Feminism," in *Feminist Legal Theory: Readings in Law and Gender*, ed. Katharine T. Bartlett and Rosanne Kennedy (Boulder, CO: Westview Press, 1991).

[3] Joanne Conaghan, "Reassessing the Feminist Theoretical Project in Law," *Journal of Law and Society* 27, no. 3 (2000): 363.

in the way courts handle these cases.[4] At a more comprehensive level, a woman-centered approach, according to advocate Robin West, addresses the harms to women that go unnoticed by the law because of the denial of women's experiences and, indeed, phenomenological existence:

Just as women's work is not recognized or compensated by the market culture, women's injuries are often not recognized or compensated *as injuries* by the legal culture. The dismissal of women's gender-specific suffering comes in various forms, but the outcome is always the same: women's suffering for one reason or another is outside the scope of legal redress. Thus, women's distinctive gender-specific injuries are now or have in the recent past been variously dismissed as trivial (sexual harassment on the street); consensual (sexual harassment on the job); humorous (non-violent marital rape); participatory, subconsciously wanted, or self-induced (father/daughter incest); natural or biological, and therefore inevitable (childbirth); sporadic, and conceptually continuous with gender-neutral pain (rape, viewed as a crime of violence); deserved or private (domestic violence); non-existent (pornography); incomprehensible (unpleasant and unwanted consensual sex) or legally predetermined (marital rape, in states with the marital exception).[5]

These "gender-specific injuries" that have been dismissed, trivialized, and ignored are all made possible, for West, by the female biological difference: women can be intimidated, raped, impregnated, and otherwise violated because of their biology. Female difference renders women vulnerable to special kinds of bodily harm, types of bodily invasion that men do not ordinarily experience and that the law, as a result, has not recognized. This same biological difference also shapes women in ways that undermine basic premises of the liberal legal system. The masculine bias of a legal system founded on the notion of an autonomous individual accords poorly with women's experience. Again, according to West:

Women, and *only* women, and *most* women, transcend physically the differentiation or individuation of biological self from the rest of human life trumpeted as the norm by the entire Kantian tradition. When a woman is pregnant her biological life embraces the embryonic life of another. When she later nurtures her children, her needs will embrace their needs. The experience of being human, for women, differentially from men, includes the counter-autonomous experience of a shared physical identity between woman and fetus, as well as the counter-autonomous experience of the emotional and psychological bond between mother and infant.[6]

---

[4] *Ibid.*, 365.
[5] Robin West, "The Difference in Women's Hedonic Lives: A Phenomenological Critique of Feminist Legal Theory," *Wisconsin Women's Law Journal* 3, no. 81 (1987): 82.
[6] *Ibid.*, 140.

The implications for law and legal institutions of such observations are far reaching. If we bring women, both as biology and experience, to the center, we immediately perceive the myriad ways in which law and legal institutions are dominated by male biology and experience. The woman-centered approach seeks to open up this system to the female as well, in terms of biology, experience, and even fundamentally different ethical sensibilities.

Not all critics of liberal feminist theory accentuate the positive in woman-centeredness. Catharine MacKinnon, for one, seems to caution against romanticizing the experience of women even as she embraces the position that the woman's point of view has been ignored in legal thought and practice. The fundamental problem, for MacKinnon, is that the legal system enshrines a gender hierarchy of subordination of the female by the male. This is not just difference, it is dominance. The law reflects and enables social and political institutions of inequality: women get unequal pay, do disrespected work, and are sexually abused. Such inequalities precede the law, which subsequently in the case of the liberal state legitimates the idea of non-interference with the status quo and the correction of only those inequalities actually created by prior legal action. Indeed, the liberal notion of privacy, that restrains the state and the law from entering into the "private" world of body and home, permits the oppression and abuse of women to proceed apace in the venue, the home, where it is at its most pervasive. Any appeal to abstract rights in such a context of social inequality can only authorize and reinforce male dominance.[7]

The history of women's experience, then, is a negative one which we draw on to reveal harms and abuses: there is little sense in MacKinnon's writing of a superior female ethics of connection that can serve as an alternate basis for legal development. Still, there is a very real role for feminist jurisprudence – MacKinnon critiques the "traditional left" view that law can only reflect existing social relations. Rather, a proactive feminist jurisprudence needs to push for substantive rights for women.

To the extent feminist law embodies women's point of view, it will be said that its law is not neutral. It will be said that it undermines the legitimacy of the legal system. But the legitimacy of existing law is based on force at women's expense. Women have never consented to its rule – suggesting that the system's legitimacy needs repair that women are in a position to provide. It will be said that feminist law is special pleading for a particular group and one cannot start that or where will it end. But existing law is already special pleading for a particular group, where it has ended.[8]

---

[7] See MacKinnon, *Toward a Feminist Theory*, 160–64, 187–92.   [8] *Ibid.*, 249.

Male dominance of the law, then, is to be replaced by female dominance. With women's experience of domination and abuse as the guide, feminist legal thinkers need to focus on developing laws and institutions that redress the harms done to women and establish the rights they need as *women*. One suspects that this is meant to be a transitional phase of legal activism but MacKinnon does not spell out her hopes for the final outcome.

Approaches like those of West and MacKinnon have been criticized as being "essentialist" in the sense that they tend to talk of women's experiences as if they were uniform across cultures, classes, and races, as if all women have some in-born attribute(s) that define them as women. Woman-centered approaches critique the "Woman of law" as a fiction created by law and legal institutions, but is the "Woman of legal feminism" equally fictional? Do the woman-centered theorists, in their claim to represent all women, actually erase the experiences of women different from themselves? There have been a number of responses to such criticism, including: an insistence on making very specific reference to women's experience in terms of class, culture, etc.; a self-conscious use of a "strategic essentialism" that is careful not to assume a single female identity; and, most often, a turn toward the study of the way law constructs gender and its social effects.[9] The last, exploration of the ways in which the law is productive of gender difference and is part of a society's gendering practices alongside other forms of knowledge like medicine, literature, etc., has probably captured the most attention among feminist legal theorists in recent years.

The major difficulty with woman-centered approaches, according to a legal theorist like Drucilla Cornell, is that they rest on the premise that there is a knowable woman's "nature." But how do we come to know this nature?

the deconstructive project resists the reinstatement of a theory of female nature or essence as a philosophically misguided bolstering of rigid gender identity which cannot survive the recognition of the performative role of language, and more specifically the metaphor. Thus deconstruction also demonstrates that there is no essence of Woman that can be effectively abstracted from the linguistic representations of Woman. The referent Woman is dependent upon the systems of representation in which she is given meaning.[10]

Thus the Woman and for that matter the Man of legal discourse are discursive constructs, only two of many contributions from various fields of knowledge that gender society. Since this discursive project permeates all

---

[9] Conaghan, "Reassessing," 366.
[10] Drucilla Cornell, *Beyond Accommodation: Ethical Feminism, Deconstruction, and the Law* (New York: Routledge, 1991), 33.

production of knowledge, we are not able to step outside language to ascertain the true nature of either the feminine or the masculine. At its most restrictive, the focus on deconstruction can lead away from giving any attention at all to women's lived experience – the danger here is that feminists will posit law as a "gendering practice" and concentrate only on unveiling its "gendered narratives" without any reference to women's lived experiences, and therefore without any sense of prospects for change in the system.[11] In fairness to Cornell, this is not her position. On the contrary, she thinks that the project of deconstructing legal (or other) discourse can be done using imagination and metaphor to produce alternate visions, feminine ways of seeing a world in which gender plays out very differently – she believes in the power of utopian thinking. In this more activist deconstructive mode, an exploration of the ways in which law and legal institutions construct gender takes its place as part of the larger project of examining gendering practices in the society as a whole with an eye to change. The law is just one small site of possible contest over gendered power relations, of course, and gender-neutral law, or rather law that realizes the full potential of both the masculine and the feminine, could only emerge in the context of a transformation of the entire society.

All the foregoing discussions of law and gender rest in part on the premise that law and legal institutions are created and controlled by a state or other power cluster, and that the discourses and practices of the law play their part in the perpetuation of prevailing power relationships, from the fairly benign liberal idea of a tainting of the law by patriarchal influence to the more intractable postmodern notion that legal discourse is thoroughly implicated in the construction of gender hierarchies. Across the spectrum there is a sense that the law is something that happens to individuals, that through its claims to abstraction, rationality, and neutrality it imposes its gendered version of power. Even for those theorists who embrace Foucauldian skepticism when it comes to the relevance of juridical frameworks to modern forms of power, legal institutions are part of the disciplining process. The question is primarily one of focus: most feminist legal theorists have concentrated on exploring the formal law that has come to monopolize the meaning of "law" in the West.

Legal theorists who have turned their attention to other areas of the world, where modern and postmodern forms of power in general and formal law in particular have less claim to total hegemony, have tended to approach the question of law and gender somewhat differently. Many in the

[11] Conaghan, "Reassessing," 369.

field of legal anthropology, for example, assert that the model of legal centralism, the system in which state law is the normative order and all other sources of norms are illegal or unimportant, applies rather poorly in large areas of the world, particularly those with a colonial past. We are more apt to encounter legal pluralism, the existence of more than one system of law or legal discourse (customary, tribal, religious, colonial, etc.), possibly including as well a number of "semi-autonomous social fields" that generate rules drawing on any of the above systems of law as well as norms derived elsewhere.[12] Different social fields (families, community groups, village or tribal councils, local courts, etc.) participate in the process of legal gendering in a society, and are characterized by a high level of interaction among parties in a process that privileges negotiation over rote application of rules. The law, in this context, is a fairly fluid and open system, subject in its interpretations and rulings to considerable ongoing input from those involved in the negotiating process. Such an analysis shifts our focus from formal rules and the ways they are applied to women in the courts to the array of actors in the legal system – jurisprudents and judges, community elders, the litigants themselves – who are continually gendering the law through their selective use and interpretation of different sources.

I must be careful not to overstate the case here: this is not a version of the Weberian theory of the evolution of law and legal institutions that describes a "primitive" legal system that is irrational with no solid basis in intellectual reasoning (rather than rational like that of the West) and substantive with no fixed rules (rather than formal with abstract rules like that of the West).[13] The kind of pluralist legal system described above may, in fact, have elaborate and multiple intellectualized legal cultures and a high degree of consistency and predictability in its legal discourse. The salient point is that the system allows for, in fact mandates, a fairly high level of lay participation in the unfolding of various legal processes. While one can argue that women, for example, might still experience considerable difficulty in representing themselves in any terms other than those of the dominant discourse, the availability of multiple discourses and the process of negotiation entailed in the system at least introduces the possibility of a more active subversion of some of the harmful aspects of gendered discourse and practice.

---

[12] See Agnete Weis Bentzon *et al.*, *Pursuing Grounded Theory in Law: South–North Experiences in Developing Women's Law* (Oslo: TANO Aschehoug, 1998), ch. 2, who draws from the work of Sally Falk Moore as well.

[13] For a helpful summary of Weber's legal theories and a discussion of their (in)applicability to Islamic law, see Haim Gerber, *State, Society, and Law in Islam: Ottoman Law in Comparative Perspective* (Albany: State University of New York Press, 1994), 27–30.

Susan Hirsch, in her study of legal processes and gender discourses in Swahili coastal Kenya, is interested in the ways in which gender is constituted and negotiated through speech in the legal arena.

In Bourdieu's terms, some discourses are authorized as official by those with institutional standing, and others are marginalized, silenced, or ignored. Such authorizations, which are sometimes expressed through explicit ideological statements, have significant impact on speakers' abilities to constitute gender. Institutional regimes of language combine with legal definitions of persons to construct those who enter court, shaping their discursive possibilities for indexing and reconfiguring gender. Paradoxically, law "genders" individuals in ways that define their positions both in society and in legal contexts, while also affording space for contesting those positions. [14]

Hirsch explores the ways in which women, in particular, work within the confines of a gendered law (specifically the Islamic regulations for marriage and divorce) on the one hand and the social conventions of female speech and behavior on the other to bend rules in their favor. While women are supposed to be obedient to their husbands, for example, such obedience does not prevent them from going to court to complain about their treatment by their husbands: they present themselves as obedient and persevering wives using a standard female narrative style even as their very presence in court and their public airing of their husbands' shortcomings send quite a different message. They are able to use conventional forms of gendered speech (women's story telling) in court, a venue that ordinarily privileges speakers (men) who are more at ease in public institutional settings, to contest and help redefine social expectations of female tolerance in a marriage.[15] They are operating within the terms of the dominant legal discourses, but the interactive and negotiable aspects of legal practice allow them to shift those terms to their advantage.

Another highly relevant aspect of Hirsch's study is the fact that the parties to these marital conflicts are able to draw on an array of legal discourses. Islamic law is one such discourse, or rather it should be said set of discourses open to a certain amount of interpretation when it comes to the rules governing marital relations. In addition, in the pluralist legal atmosphere of the Swahili coast, disputants may also have recourse to what Hirsch terms "Swahili ethics," a version of the ethical life that colors community views of how one should act based on Swahili *mila* or custom. Although many

---

[14] Susan F. Hirsch, *Pronouncing and Persevering: Gender and the Discourses of Disputing in an African Islamic Court* (Chicago: University of Chicago Press, 1998), 20.
[15] *Ibid.*, 20–22.

elements of ethical marriage reflect Islamic legal concerns, the discourse of Swahili ethics also includes additional rules and understandings about matters of love and propriety. A third discourse that can be activated in legal settings is that of the Swahili spirit world: possession by *jini*, or spirits, can be identified as the source of marital conflict and exorcism as the resolution. Last, and least prominent in Hirsch's view, is the secular law of the state, an artifact of the colonial experience. For coastal Swahili people, the postcolonial state is remote and alien, much as the colonial state was, and thus the rules and conventions of the official legal discourse are little known or trusted. Although Swahili people rarely resort to official secular law in marital disputes, it does exist as a possible last resort in intractable cases. Hirsch is careful to note that these legal discourses do not exist as hermetically sealed systems, but rather merge and overlap. The ideology of the official secular discourse, for example, is that all the others (Islamic, ethical, spirit world) are subordinate: they claim jurisdiction only at the pleasure of the state.[16] What happens on the ground suggests that something very different is going on as disputants choose their venues and have selective recourse to a variety of discourses. It is this possibility of choice and manipulation of various discourses that seems to present opportunities that are not found in systems of legal centralism.

As I explore Islamic law and legal institutions in relation to women and gender, I want to be attentive to the ways in which law and legal spaces are gendered by rigid definitions of male and female, by hidden harms done to women through the norming of the male experience, and by the strictures of dominant discourse that set limits on how women can even think about themselves and their relations to others. I also want to open the discussion to the possibility of female agency in legal systems, to the ways women have found in the past and present to maneuver within and between different legal discourses and practices. Feminist legal theorists and legal anthropologists, through a variety of different approaches, have raised many relevant questions about the nature of law and legal struggles that will help direct our attention, I hope, to both the shared and unique features of gendering in Islamic law.

ISLAMIC LAW

Before we address Islamic legal discourse and related practices as implicated in larger projects of gendering in Islamic societies, we need to consider however briefly the nature of the law, what "Islamic law" has been

---

[16] *Ibid.*, 85–90.

understood to mean over the past 1,400 years of Islamic history, and how various Muslim thinkers and communities have institutionalized Islamic legal practices. Islamic law, perhaps most importantly, is held to be divine law. Most Muslim and non-Muslim scholars of the law would agree with the significance of Coulson's remark: "Law is the command of God; and the acknowledged function of Muslim jurisprudence, from the beginning, was simply the discovery of the terms of that command."[17] Islamic law or the shariʿa, as the path or way of God, was to be comprehended (insofar as humanly possible) and implemented as part of individual submission to God's will and as vital to the wellbeing of the Muslim community as a whole. Once we move beyond this basic agreement on the centrality of the shariʿa as a guide to both personal and community life, universal consensus tends to erode.

First, there is the epistemological question of how Muslims should go about discerning God's commands. There was, and still is, widespread concurrence that the single most important source of knowledge about the shariʿa is the revelations recorded in the Qurʾan. Roughly 10 percent of Qurʾanic material legislates human behavior, although much of this has to do with religious duties and ritual practices and only a small fraction with rules for social relations and community life. Some topics, such as marriage and inheritance for example, receive fairly detailed treatment but many other issues are dealt with in a general fashion or not at all. Muslim intellectuals developed techniques for reading and interpreting Qurʾanic verses the meanings of which were not always transparent: this science of *tafsir* was an important component in the development of Islamic jurisprudence or *fiqh*. Not all interpreters agreed on the meanings and implications of the rules for human behavior laid down in the Qurʾan, however, so that there were divergences in juristic opinion from early on.

A second important source for legal guidance was the hadith, the narratives of the *sunna*, the practices and sayings of the Prophet Muhammad during his lifetime that were passed down by his associates. The hadith were eventually gathered into a number of canonical collections, but there was some disagreement concerning the authenticity of certain of the narratives despite the development of a rigorous and sophisticated methodology of hadith authentication. Still, the hadith played a very important role in the development of the law because they were a source often employed to help with the interpretation of opaque verses of the Qurʾan on the one hand, and to fill in the many silences of the Qurʾan on issues of legal import on the

[17] Noel J. Coulson, *A History of Islamic Law* (Edinburgh: Edinburgh University Press, 1964), 75.

other. The Shiʿi branch of Islam was more restrictive in its use of the hadith, accepting only those narratives recorded by one of their own leaders or imams. Among Sunnis, questions of authenticity and legal relevance were never definitively settled and continue to fuel disagreements right up to the present.

A third recognized source of law was *ijmāʿ*, consensus, following the Prophet Muhammad's reported remark that "My community will never agree in error." Although originally conceived of as the consensus of the Companions of the Prophet, those who actually shared in the early mission of Islam, over time such consensus came to be defined by most as agreement among the great jurisconsults of an age as to the implications of the Qurʾan or hadith for a given legal doctrine, or even their consensus on matters that were not explicitly discussed in either of the sacred sources. In its reach outside the boundaries of the sacred texts, *ijmāʿ* had a potential similar to that of the fourth source of law, *qiyās*, or analogical reasoning. *Qiyās* allowed jurists to address "new" situations not covered explicitly by the Qurʾan, hadith, or a pre-existing consensus by deducing a legal rule by way of analogy to an existing point of law or principle found in any of the three prior sources.[18]

The types of mental effort and techniques that legal thinkers employed in this process of using textual guidance, consensus, and their own powers of deduction to discern the shariʿa were termed *ijtihād*, the exercise of one's reason to interpret the law. Western scholarship once differed in its understanding of the role that *ijtihād* played over time in the development of the law because some of the pioneers of Islamic legal history had embraced the idea that, after a period of legal development, "the gate of *ijtihād*" had been effectively closed in the late ninth century by which time the major legal doctrines had been put in place.[19] This is no longer the predominant scholarly view; rather we now have broad consensus that *ijtihād* continued to be a widely accepted practice across the Islamic centuries, as clearly witnessed by ongoing doctrinal developments in a rich legal literature, and scholarly attention has turned to various subtleties in the development of hermeneutical methods.[20]

---

[18] For standard discussions of the sources of Islamic law, see *ibid.*, chs. 3, 4; J. N. D. Anderson, *Law Reform in the Muslim World* (London: University of London Athlone Press, 1976), ch. 1; Jamal J. Nasir, *The Islamic Law of Personal Status*, 2nd edn (London: Graham & Trotman, 1990), 18–28.

[19] This is the view of both Coulson, *A History*, and Anderson, *Law Reform*.

[20] See Wael B. Hallaq, "Was the Gate of Ijtihad Closed?," *International Journal of Middle East Studies* 16, no. 1 (1984); Baber Johansen, "Legal Literature and the Problem of Change: The Case of Land Rent," in *Islam and Public Law: Classical and Contemporary Studies*, ed. Chibli Mallat (London: Graham & Trotman, 1993), 29–47; Rudolph Peters, "Idjtihad and Taqlid in 18th and 19th Century Islam," *Die Welt des Islams* 20, no. 3/4 (1980): 131–45.

The vitality, and indeed the flexibility, of Islamic law is attributable, in part, to the fact that the shariʿa was not, throughout most of its history, a fixed legal code. The process of interpretation of the Qurʾan and hadith, and the use of consensus and analogy, was an ongoing and open-ended affair. Legal schools (*madhhab*, pl. *madhāhib*) with a degree of doctrinal consensus did emerge. The Shiʿi branch of Islam evolved a distinct approach to many legal issues, with some important ramifications for gender issues as we shall see below. The four major Sunni schools, the Hanbali, Hanafi, Maliki, and Shafiʿi, developed a certain degree of internal consistency as reflected in their core canonical writings so that we can talk of doctrines that are characteristic of a particular school, although these Sunni schools operated on the basis of mutual respect for each other's rulings. The production of legal texts continued apace, however, so that we are by no means dealing with completely fixed or frozen positions. Islamic legal thinkers continued to write works of *fiqh* (or jurisprudence), either textbooks that summarized the doctrine of a school or commentaries on legal doctrine that explored the relevance of legal source material to issues of substantive law. Jurists known for their learning and wisdom (muftis) were also called upon to issue legal opinions (fatwa, pl. *fatāwa*) in response to questions about concrete legal situations. Their responses might then be collected and those of the better known constituted texts of importance and reference.

Although the shariʿa, in the strictest sense, is the law of God that human-kind attempts to reveal, over time the term shariʿa came, in popular under-standing, to encompass this textual tradition – works of *fiqh* and *fatāwa*, various treatises on special legal topics of interest, handbooks for judges outlining proper procedure and comportment, etc. All these products of the intellectual endeavor to apprehend God's law constituted the shariʿa along with the legal materials of the Qurʾan and the hadith. A jurist of a particular school would focus, of course, on the texts of his own legal tradition, but certainly a Sunni thinker would be expected to be familiar with the key doctrines of other schools as well. The possibilities for flexibility and change in a system of law that was not codified, that harbored several different legal schools of mutual legitimacy within each of which there were, in fact, both majority and minority opinions, and that furthermore retained a system for the delivery of juridical opinions in response to new issues that might crop up should be readily apparent.

I do not want to underplay some of the constraints and fixed parameters of this legal system. We can discern a drive for consistency and certainty of doctrine in juridical writings, a search to identify the authoritative position on any particular issue. As Wael Hallaq notes:

If legal pluralism was there to stay – a fact which the jurists never questioned – then it had to be somehow curbed or at least controlled, for, as a matter of consistency and judicial process, doctrinal uncertainty was detrimental. Which of the two, three, or four opinions available should the judge adopt in deciding cases or the jurisconsult opt for in issuing fatwas? The discourse of the jurists, in hundreds of major works that we have at our disposal, is overwhelmingly preoccupied by this problem: Which is the most authoritative opinion?[21]

In an attempt to answer this question, the jurists developed the science of *tarjīḥ*, a methodological approach to dealing with conflicting legal opinions through a systematic examination of their sources, modes of transmission, and reasoning. While the practice of *tarjīḥ* can be understood as a remedy for the proliferation of opinions produced by the practice of *ijtihād*, it did not lead to agreement on authoritative opinions in all or even most cases because of the complexities and indeterminacies of the methodology itself. It has been argued, however, that it did help impose a certain discipline within each school, although it was a discipline that stopped far short of anointing a particular set of opinions as the uncontested and monolithic doctrine of a specific school.[22]

The sharīʿa was not only a matter of doctrinal debates. It was also, throughout much of its history, a body of substantive law that took institutional form under a series of political powers. When we talk of Islamic law, we are referring as well to a system of Islamic courts that operated at varying levels of autonomy over the centuries. A comprehensive history of the Islamic court system has yet to be written, however, and we lack detailed information about the courts in most eras of Islamic history. The Islamic courts under the Ottoman Empire are perhaps the most studied, thanks in large part to the availability of court materials as a result of the Ottoman focus on record keeping. We cannot assume that the organization and practices of these courts necessarily reflect those of Islamic courts in other times and places. On the contrary, the changing nature of polities and empires across Islamic history surely influenced a number of key elements, including the degree of centralized control of the courts' procedures and personnel, the presence or absence of officially sanctioned schools of law, the relationship between a "secular" law of political design and the sharīʿa, the influence of local or customary rules and practices, and, perhaps most importantly, community perception and utilization of the court venue for

---

[21] Wael B. Hallaq, *Authority, Continuity, and Change in Islamic Law* (Cambridge: Cambridge University Press, 2001), 126.
[22] See *ibid.*, ch. 5.

daily business activities as well as disputes. The Ottoman case, although we cannot assume it is representative, certainly suggests the very important role the court might play in the development of Islamic law and society.

There is much to suggest that the Ottoman Empire kept a firm hold on the Islamic court system that operated within its boundaries. The Empire appointed the qadis of all the major courts and moved them to new posts every few years, and the Hanafi legal school was given official legal standing in the Empire. The Ottomans developed secular codes of law to deal with matters of taxation and public order critical to the prosperity and security of the Empire, but such codes coexisted with the shari'a and the Empire sought to reconcile these codes with the religious law and make sure they were recognized in the courts. As possessors of a far-flung Empire with an enormous rural hinterland, the Ottomans were compelled to tolerate a certain level of legal pluralism: nomadic peoples applied tribal law and peasants in many rural areas had their own customary practices, but in the cities and towns of the Empire there was a surprising degree of consistency in rules and practices. But the shari'a was by no means completely captured by the Ottomans. The qadis and muftis were the heirs of a long legal tradition with recognized principles, procedures, and substantive content. They were the lynchpin for the continuity of this tradition while at the same time they worked in the service of the Empire. What role did these men, and the ordinary members of the population who brought their legal business to qadis and muftis in the court system, play in the development of Islamic law and Islamic society?

We have some divergent answers to this question. In his study of Ebu's-su'ud, the holder of the position of Mufti of Istanbul in the sixteenth century, the highest judicial office of the time, Colin Imber asserts that the court was marginal indeed to the development of the law:

The judges were at the center of the Ottoman, or indeed of any Islamic legal system, in that they were responsible for the day-to-day application of the law. Nevertheless, they played no part in its development since, although a judge's decree is binding and irrevocable in a particular case, it cannot serve as a precedent in the future. Ottoman judges, it is true, kept detailed records of court proceedings, but for administrative rather than juristic purposes.[23]

In this view, the daily business of the court is effectively sealed off from the intellectual tradition that is the "law." The judges' role is to apply established legal doctrine to the individual cases that come before them, and

---

[23] Colin Imber, *Ebu's-su'ud: The Islamic Legal Tradition* (Stanford: Stanford University Press, 1997), 7.

there is no possibility that their decisions or the activities of litigants in the court can alter that doctrine. Although this is strictly speaking perfectly true in the sense that Islamic law is not case law, and court decisions have no value as precedent, it overlooks the role that the courts might play by way of the fatwa. People often solicited an opinion from a mufti before they took their case to court and this opinion could be introduced as a supporting statement in their case: questions of current social and economic concern were thus injected not just into the courts, but also into the arena of general juristic discussion. Imber's conclusions about the extreme conservatism of the law are thus belied in part by his own work on the mufti Ebu's-su'ud, inasmuch as he concludes that the contribution of this brilliant legal thinker included the introduction of some new ideas and practices into Islamic law even if Ebu's-su'ud himself did not openly admit their novelty. From Imber's point of view, however, this mufti is the exception: in general, the courts, the muftis whose views were often presented as part of a case, and the litigants who chose to come to court and present themselves in certain ways all belong to the epiphenomenal field of social history, not to the history of the law, which is portrayed as a remarkably inert discourse. We cannot hope to learn much of anything about the "law" from the study of practice in the courts where rote application of doctrine held sway.

Wael Hallaq sharply contests the notion that Islamic law in the Ottoman period, or any other period for that matter, suffered from the effects of inertia. On the contrary, Hallaq argues, change was a structural feature of the law, as amply illustrated in the Ottoman period through the work of Ibn 'Abidin (1783–1836), a mufti and "jurist-writer" from Damascus. Hallaq traces his development of a very original contribution to doctrine, namely the idea that custom could serve as a source of law, even to the extent of overriding material from the Qur'an and the hadith. The salient point here is that Ibn 'Abidin was not a maverick thinker, but rather was "entirely loyal to the hermeneutical imperatives of the Hanafite school," which provided the methodologies and multiplicities of opinion that allowed him to turn "the ladder of doctrinal authority right on its head."[24] Jurist-writers of the Ottoman and earlier periods were also quite comfortable incorporating recent fatwas that offered new interpretations into their juristic treatises, citing the importance of attending to the contemporary needs of society. Not all fatwas were equally valid, of course, and the jurists chose those that both were doctrinally sound and spoke to issues of current concern. Still, as treatises expanded to include this new material and authoritative collections

---

[24] Hallaq, *Authority, Continuity, and Change*, 232.

of new fatwas joined the legal canon, substantive law was developing in rhythm with social change.[25] Many of these fatwas were issued, of course, in response to cases that came from or were on their way to the courts, thus drawing the court system into the dynamic of legal change.

Haim Gerber, in his study of Ottoman law between the sixteenth and the early nineteenth centuries, takes a more anthropological approach to Islamic law in which formal law takes it place alongside the equally important legal processes of self-presentation and negotiation. There is a shift in focus here from doctrine to the actors in legal systems who give the law its meaning. In a random sample of 140 cases of litigation in the Ottoman Islamic courts, he found a striking contrast between the functioning of law courts in colonial New England (New Haven), where "the court was mainly used by the aristocracy to regulate and control the lower classes," and the Ottoman situation:

in all but a few cases, it was the social underdog who initiated the case – women versus men, non-Muslims versus Muslims, commoners versus members of the elite. The court is seen mainly as a tool of the common people to defend a modicum of legal rights … Whereas in colonial New Haven the upper class had a clear advantage, this is distinctly not so here. Women won seventeen of twenty-two cases against men; non-Muslims won seven of eight cases against Muslims; commoners won six of eight cases against *askeris* [members of the official elite].[26]

Here the emphasis is placed on how ordinary members of a society understand the rights they enjoy by way of legal doctrine, and how they act on their own behalf to secure these rights which are always under pressure in a stratified society. As Gerber and all other researchers who have looked at the Ottoman court records will testify, people went to the courts in droves, for notarial purposes but also for claims and disputes of various kinds. In the case of Gerber's study, the ways in which they resorted to the legal system had significant implications for society: they were leveling the hierarchical playing field. Islamic law provided the doctrines and institutions that made this possible – that is a remarkable fact that surely belongs in any history of the law. But did all this activity on the part of ordinary people make a dent in legal doctrine? Was the formal discourse of Islamic law susceptible to influence from below, from the ways in which local institutions and ordinary people understood and availed themselves of legal doctrines? It is difficult to arrive at definitive answers to these questions because of the bifurcation in the literature on Islamic law. On the one hand, we have

---

[25] See *ibid.*, 188–94.   [26] Gerber, *State, Society, and Law*, 56.

studies of formal legal doctrine like those of Imber and Hallaq, who differ dramatically in their understanding of the degree of dynamism in the law but focus in the main on doctrinal discussions among jurists of various types. On the other hand, we have works focused on legal institutions and practices like that of Gerber in which social actors and the social and political setting have pride of place and doctrinal positions remain a very secondary concern.

In the following review of Islamic law and gender issues I will try to treat the law, doctrine and practice, as a whole. I submit that it is not just what the shari'a "says" about women and gender that matters (and that is well nigh impossible to distill given the large number and complexity of relevant legal texts), but also how the shari'a has been understood and lived by Muslims, jurists and laypeople alike. Islamic law as a dominant discourse was not just preserved and transmitted legal doctrine, but was also the ways in which doctrines were applied or not by the courts, interpreted in specific cases by the muftis, and used as the basis for legal strategies by ordinary people. Nor should we neglect the role of the state. The extent to which Islamic law has been implicated in legitimating and controlling projects of state power has implications for gender hierarchies.

I have been discussing, up to this point, Islamic law from its formative years in the ninth and tenth centuries up to the late nineteenth century. When we consider the history of Islamic law over the past 100 or 150 years, however, the role of the state, and the jurists as well, changes rather dramatically. The modern "reforms" of Islamic law constituted an epistemological break in the legal system that must inform any discussion of the law in the twentieth century. Initially, the state powers of the nineteenth-century Islamic regions sought to rationalize their legal systems as part of a series of moves to resist the pressures of European encroachment. In some respects, the assertion of direct state control over law making and legal institutions was not altogether a novelty: beginning in the late fifteenth century the Ottoman Empire, for example, had developed legal codes (the *qanūn*) enforceable by its officials to deal with matters of tax collection and some public security, and had reserved the right to intervene in various ways in the Islamic court system by appointing judges and official muftis. But in the nineteenth century, there were two significant changes. First, the jurisdiction of certain legal institutions, those which were under the direct control of the state and applied legal codes of western inspiration, was greatly expanded to cover most commercial affairs. Second, the state took upon itself the task of codifying Islamic law in a striking departure from previous practice. As noted in the Ottoman case:

This represented a complete reversal of the position previously occupied by the Shari'a – as an uncodified, divine law which had an authority, inherent in itself, over every Muslim, from Caliph to slave. Not only so, but the law in question, commonly known as the Majalla, did not take the form of a straightforward codification of those opinions which had come to prevail, on this matter or that, in the school of law which was accepted as official in the Ottoman Empire (that is, the Hanafi school), but represented an eclectic choice from among the wide range of opinions which had at any time been advocated by a Hanafi jurist ... selected on the basis of their apparent suitability to the exigencies of modern life.[27]

In the course of the later nineteenth and early to mid twentieth centuries, this process of codification reached into matters of what came to be called personal status – marriage, divorce, family obligations, etc. – not only in the Ottoman Empire but in Egypt, Sudan, areas of sub-Saharan Africa, and Iran. In the place of a shari'a of great textual complexity being interpreted and applied by muftis and judges, modern states instituted singular shari'a-based legal codes to be enforced by state officials in state courts. The logic of the growth of the modern state in the twentieth century was to thereby take control of the rump Islamic judicial system, to centralize, standardize, and otherwise assert full authority over all judicial processes. The first of what was to prove to be a long series of such state reforms was the Ottoman Law of Family Rights (OLFR) of 1917, a codified law regulating marriage and divorce. The framers of the OLFR employed the method of *takhayyur* (selection), described above, whereby they studied both majority and minority opinions in the Hanafi school, or dominant doctrines in any Sunni school, to choose the rule on any given issue that best seemed to suit modern needs and concerns. Subsequently, the successor states of the Ottoman Empire and others followed a similar course when they promulgated personal status laws. Algeria, Egypt, Indonesia, Iraq, Jordan, Kuwait, Lebanon, Libya, Morocco, Pakistan, Syria, Tunisia, and Yemen all produced distinct personal status codes, and periodically reformed them, from the 1920s right up to the present.

The pioneers of Islamic legal history in the West tended to view the modern reform of Islamic law, particularly in the areas of personal status, as indicative of a "resurgence of legal moralism,"[28] a series of attempts to redress some of the hardships people had experienced under the law as a result of legal formalism. They often pointed to the case of the deserted wife under Hanafi law, who, in the absence of proof of divorce or her husband's

---

[27] Anderson, *Law Reform*, 17.
[28] Noel J. Coulson, *Conflicts and Tensions in Islamic Jurisprudence* (Chicago: University of Chicago Press, 1969), 95.

demise, was condemned to remain legally married for ninety-nine years until her spouse could be presumed dead. The standard narrative holds that the authorities in various Islamic countries were prevailed upon by their own populations to correct such abuses and institute just rules and predictable practices by a judicious selection and then codification of rules from all four major Sunni legal schools. The resulting codes were distillations of the true intent of the shariʿa and its realization in the modern context. In general, legal historians have applauded the efforts of the reformers who employed eclectic choice from different opinions and schools as well as a return to basic sources of law to fashion modern codes.[29]

Not all jurists interested in legal reform worked within the context of state control and the codification project. A number of Islamic modernists, like Muhammad Rashid Rida, al-Tahir al-Haddad, Mahmud Shaltut, and Muhammad al-Ghazali, from the early twentieth century on, endorsed the principles of reform and paid particular attention to issues of methodology that the independent jurist might employ in the project of modernization (but not necessarily codification) of the law. In his review of the progress of "modernization" of Islamic law relevant to women's issues, Fazlur Rahman held that one of the major thrusts of the program of social reform outlined in the Qurʾan was to improve the position of women. "To be effective, a realistic reformer, however, cannot go beyond a certain limit in his legal reform and can only lay down certain moral guidelines according to which he hopes his society will evolve once it accepts his legal reforms."[30] It is to these moral guidelines, as developed in the Qurʾan, that the reformer returns in order to understand the full intent of the original Islamic project and decide how it might best be realized today. Rahman himself thought that Qurʾanic material, for example, pointed to the prohibition of polygamy under most circumstances and the restriction of the male right of unilateral divorce. In these and other matters affecting women's position he was an advocate of sweeping reform. Muslim reformers, in their own terms, are justified in their approach not simply or even primarily because they improve people's lives in the modern world, but because they are engaged in the vital task of helping with the evolution of society as envisioned in the Qurʾan. This kind of return to the Qurʾan for moral guidelines is fully consonant with a new or rather renewed approach to Islamic law based on a close and educated reading of Qurʾanic revelation.

[29] See, for example, Anderson, *Law Reform*, 42–82; Coulson, *Conflicts and Tensions*, 96–116; and Joseph Schacht, *An Introduction to Islamic Law* (Oxford: Clarendon Press, 1964), 106–07.

[30] Fazlur Rahman, "A Survey of Modernization of Muslim Family Law," *International Journal of Middle East Studies* 11, no. 4 (1980): 451.

Some contemporary scholars are not so sanguine about the motivations and outcomes of the reform project. As part of the modern state's bid for heightened control of its citizenry, legal reform entailed the application of standard national norms, an emphasis on formal process and written records, and the cultivation of an impersonal legal culture. Did this always result in greater rights and freedoms for individuals? What was lost in the transition from the "traditional" Islamic court that applied an unbounded shari'a to the state court that applied a formal shari'a-like code? Certainly the state gained in its powers of surveillance and discipline in the process, and there is a sense that the local communities have lost out. The poor, the female, the ill-educated may have faced greater hurdles as the rules and the venues of law become unfamiliar to them. On the other hand, many of the substantive aspects of reform did work in favor of the disadvantaged in society, as we shall see in the case of women. The extent to which these gains were offset by the loss of the leeway built into the traditional Islamic legal system, in which flexibility was afforded by the very absence of a code, is an area I will further explore below.[31]

In the late twentieth century we began to see another brand of reform with the "Islamization" of legal systems. As a number of political regimes faced crises of legitimacy as a result of failing social and economic policies, their strategies of modernization and westernization were called into question. In Iran, for example, the overthrow of the Shah and the triumph of the Islamic Revolution in 1979 entailed a rejection of western models and an attempt to institute a new Islamic order. In Pakistan, the military regime of Zia al-Huq emerged in the same period and embarked on a campaign to "restore" Islamic society. In both these cases, the legal system was to receive special attention. Programs of Islamization inevitably took a critical look at prior legal reforms that seemed to be implicated in the overall project of westernization: both new regimes first abrogated many of the laws that had been produced by reformist currents, and then instituted laws based on their versions of what constituted an unadulterated Islamic approach. Such Islamization programs have not usually addressed all aspects of the legal system in equal measure: there has been a distinct tendency to focus on the showier (and easier in the sense of less disruptive to basic economic and political interests) areas of penal law and personal status law. The introduction of "Islamic" penalties for certain crimes (amputation for theft or

---

[31] For a summary discussion of recent evaluations of the reform project, see Annalise Moors, "Debating Family Law: Legal Texts and Social Practices," in *Social History of Women and Gender in the Modern Middle East*, ed. Margaret Lee Meriwether and Judith E. Tucker (Boulder, CO: Westview Press, 1999), 150–55.

stoning for unlawful sexual intercourse) allows the state to display cultural legitimacy and punitive power at the same time, while the introduction of dress codes and other kinds of restrictions on women have the virtues of high visibility and minimum threat of serious opposition (since they tend to have the greatest impact on poorer females).[32] We should not overlook the fact that these Islamization programs, from the legal point of view, are less a restoration than an innovation. For the state to make "Islamic" rules and then use modern means of repression to apply them to its population as part of a legitimating process does not, in terms of substance and procedure, find much support in traditional Islamic legal thinking.

Official state projects are not the only late twentieth-century developments in Islamic law. The popular engagement with Islam as both a religious and a cultural identity that modern regimes are trying to exploit has also found expression in non-official circles. The legal writings, including fatwas, of present-day religious leaders are an increasingly popular genre: in many cases they discuss current issues of political concern but also matters of personal behavior – dress, comportment, ritual observance, etc. They are particularly prevalent in Shi'i communities where the seeking of guidance from qualified 'ulama' is a basic plank of religious observance: Khomeini's fatwas have been hugely popular for the past forty years or so, as are those of Shaykh Fadlallah of Lebanon today. Even among Sunnis, there has been considerable interest in the legal guidance of prominent Islamic thinkers whose books and radio and television shows are doing well. Muslims who live in predominantly non-Muslim societies have also been taking advantage of the many internet "fatwa sites" where individuals can obtain answers to questions about living a good Muslim life. It is worth noting that this phenomenon, the individual search for direction from those learned in the law, feels strongly akin to the way Islamic legal procedures were conceptualized, if not always followed, over the centuries. Whether in fact the methods and substance of much contemporary juristic activity can lay any real claim to the Islamic legal heritage is, as we shall see, a hotly debated topic.[33]

Such echoes should not obscure the basic fact that the Islamic legal discourse, or rather Islamic legal discourses, has not had a continuous history. Intellectuals of varying views and abilities, state powers with

[32] See Ayesha Jalal, "The Convenience of Subservience: Women and the State of Pakistan," in *Women, Islam, and the State*, ed. Deniz Kandiyoti (Philadelphia: Temple University Press, 1991), 77–114; and Afsaneh Najmabadi, "Hazards of Modernity and Morality: Women, State and Ideology in Contemporary Iran," in *ibid.*, 48–76.

[33] See the discussion of this question in Khaled Abou El Fadl, *Speaking in God's Name: Islamic Law, Authority and Women* (Oxford: Oneworld, 2001), ch. 2.

different agendas and capacities, ordinary people with distinct interests shaped by class, race, and gender, have all contributed to the evolution of Islamic law. It is difficult to characterize this law and its institutions as the expression of one particular form of domination – of a state, or a class, or a gender. In the discussion that follows, however, we are most interested in how the law intersected with, and molded, gender hierarchies in the societies in which it has played a significant role.

ISLAMIC LAW AND GENDER

How has Islamic law constructed gender and what kinds of limits, suppressions, or even possibilities has it set for the gendered subject? I want to approach these questions from four different angles. First, to what extent has the law discriminated against women as women using the liberal standard of equality, and what is the pattern of this discrimination? Second, has the law employed male norms and measures that marginalize the female experience? Third, what kinds of linguistic representations of women and men do we find in law and how have they bounded discourse on gender? And fourth, what room has there been for female agency in legal institutions and processes, and what has been the effect of this agency over time?

We can begin with the standard liberal question of how the law has discriminated against women, how it has permitted practices and indeed legislated rules that treat men and women differently in a way that disadvantages women. In many cases, we are not dealing here with the hidden discrimination of western liberal thought, but rather with a law and set of legal institutions that are forthright in the privileging of men in certain areas of economic and social life.

Islamic legal thought has assigned women and men, in many instances, distinct social roles. Jurists drew on material from the Qur'an and hadith to argue that men were meant to be the providers in a family and therefore enjoyed legal rights of authority within (and outside) the household. Although in general the Qur'an deals with women in an egalitarian and non-discriminatory fashion, there are verses that have provided the basis on which to build gender hierarchies. Out of a total of 6,660 verses in the Qur'an, it has been argued that only six establish some kind of male authority over women.[34] One of the most critical Qur'anic passages is found in chapter 4, verse 34:

---

[34] These verses are: 2:221, 2:228, 2:282, 4:3, 4:34, 24:30 as identified by Shaheen Sardar Ali, *Gender and Human Rights in Islam and International Law: Equal before Allah, Unequal before Man?* (The Hague: Kluwer Law International, 2000), 43.

Men are the managers of the affairs of women
For that God has preferred in bounty
One of them over another, and for that
They have expended of their property.
Righteous women are therefore obedient,
Guarding the secret for God's guarding.
And those you fear may be rebellious
Admonish; banish them to their couches,
And beat them. If they then obey you,
Look not for any way against them; God is
All-high, All-great.[35]

This verse has provided the most powerful basis for the legal elaboration of Man as breadwinner and Woman as obedient dependent within the family. As we shall see below, jurists developed a number of discriminatory rules for marital relations, including the concept of the *nāshiza* or the disobedient wife who forfeits her rights to marital support and, in the opinion of some jurists, is also subject to corporal discipline by her husband, in reference to this verse and other selected hadith narratives. The legal responsibilities men bore for the material support of wives, parents, and children were part of this package, as were the rights to this support that a man's relations acquired. The relevant issue here is the gendering of the social role of provider with consequent authority over dependents. Although this was interpreted strictly speaking as a familial relationship, with no necessary implications for social roles outside the household, the construction of financial responsibilities as male and financial dependence as female, domestic authority as male and domestic subservience as female, inevitably resonated in the world outside the domestic sphere.

This is not to suggest that women as women were systematically discriminated against in other areas, such as that of control of material resources. Certain aspects of Islamic law in the pre-reform period strike us today as very progressive. Once a woman came of age (signaled by reaching puberty), she, like a man, was to have complete and independent possession of her property; no man, neither father nor husband, had any right to the ownership, enjoyment, or disposal of her property. She had full legal capacity as far as her private property was concerned. The absence of discrimination against women as property-holders contrasts with the situation in Europe well into the modern period. A woman in Renaissance Florence, for example, was legally required to have a male guardian for her property and her person

---

[35] Here and elsewhere I am using the translation by Arthur J. Arberry, *The Koran Interpreted*, trans. Arthur J. Arberry (London: Allen & Unwin; Macmillan, 1955).

without whom she could not enter into any legal agreement. Her property typically consisted of her dowry, given to her by her natal family in the understanding that she would have no further claim on family property, and her husband could use the dowry as he liked as long as he obtained her passive consent.[36] By way of contrast, the prevailing substantive rules of the Islamic legal system designated the dowry as the private property of the bride over which her husband had no claim whatsoever. Furthermore, a female was entitled to a set portion of the estate of a number of her relatives, and although in general she was only entitled to one half the share of her male counterparts, this inheritance was also her inviolate private property. The kind of naked discrimination against women that we find in the marital relationship, where most rights (to divorce, child custody, etc.) are strongly gendered in favor of the male, does not characterize the law when it comes to matters of access to the material goods of society.

Another standard liberal concern has been with the way the law judges similar actions in different ways depending on the sex of the perpetrator, such as the criminalizing of prostitution for the female prostitute but not for her male client. In pre-reform Islamic law, we do have some stark distinctions drawn between the sexes in terms of license: men can lawfully seek sexual variety, for example, through polygamy and concubinage while women are held to the standard of monogamy in a display of discrimination based on the construction of difference in male and female sexuality. When it comes to sexual crimes, however, specifically that of unlawful sexual intercourse, i.e. sexual intercourse outside a licit relationship of marriage or concubinage, legal doctrine, based directly on Qur'anic material, does not discriminate. As long as force is not involved, both male and female parties are equally culpable and subject to draconian punishments. Discrimination again creeps into penal matters when we consider the matter of the *diya*, financial compensation in case of accidental death: those held responsible for the death of a woman were required to pay one-half the *diya* of a man. In the case of injury, the same rules applied: a female's loss of a limb or an eye was usually calculated at half the indemnity of that of a male.

Islamic jurists of the pre-reform period did not apologize for such discriminatory laws: they viewed them as based on sound legal sources and fully appropriate to gender differences in their societies. During the reform period there was some nibbling around the edges of some of the rules that clearly discriminated against women in the areas of marriage

---

[36] Thomas Kuehn, *Law, Family and Women: Toward a Legal Anthropology of Renaissance Italy* (Chicago: University of Chicago Press, 1991), ch. 9.

arrangements, divorce, and child custody, and many of these discriminatory laws are the objects of campaigns for legal change today. Islamic modernists like Fazlur Rahman are of the opinion that such discriminatory laws are passé, out of step with the true intentionality of Islam:

The conservative holds that this statement of the Qur'an [about the man as manager of the affairs of women, is normative, that the woman, although she can possess and even earn wealth] is not required to spend on the household, which must be solely the concern of the male and that, therefore, the male enjoys a certain superiority. The modernist liberal, on the other hand, argues that the Qur'anic statement is descriptive, that, with the inevitable change in society, women can and ought to become economically independent and contribute to the household and hence the spouses must come to enjoy absolute equality.[37]

The modernist liberal position, which takes the traditional liberal stand against all such forms of legal discrimination, has yet to carry the day. On the contrary, the author of a recent study of the Qur'an and hadith as guides to our understanding of women's rights and position, published in 2000, organized his book into two parts: (1) matters in which Islam gives men and women full equality, including the right to life, ritual obligations and religious rewards, and competence in economic transactions and (2) matters of "distinction" between men and women, a much longer list which includes divorce, inheritance, polygamy, guardianship, dress and ornamentation, upbringing and education, witnessing, etc. These distinctions may serve to "honor and protect" women, but there is no pretense that they serve the cause of equality.[38] It is important to note, as a result, that unlike in the West where liberals have had to ferret out hidden forms of discrimination in a legal system that lays claim to treating all individuals equally, the Islamic legal system has always recognized, and justified, this differential treatment of women and men. Indeed, many of the current campaigns for legal reform focus on aspects of such legal discrimination, seeking adjustments and ameliorations that could soften, and eventually eliminate, differential treatment.

Second, if certain aspects of Islamic law are clearly discriminatory, is the law also normed male to the exclusion of the female experience? In a sense, the female experience is very present in the law: if a woman-centered perspective is one that takes account of the particularities of the female experience of reproduction, childbearing and child nurturing, then Islamic

---

[37] Rahman, "A Survey," 453.
[38] Muhammad Bultaji, *Makanat al-Mar'a fi al-Qur'an al-Karim wa-l-Sunna al-Sahiha: Dirasat Mu'assala Muqarana Mustaw'iba li-Haqiqat Manzilat al-Mar'ah fi al-Islam* (Cairo: Dar al-Salam, 2000).

law and legal institutions have involved themselves intimately with female issues. There is little "private" in Islamic law in the western legal sense of a realm of intimacy that is off limits for the state and its legal institutions. A quick look at any standard legal treatise or collection of fatwas makes this point very clearly. In the *Al-Hidaya* of al-Marghinani, a work of Hanafi legal commentary composed in the twelfth century and frequently cited by subsequent legal thinkers, the rules for rituals, buying and selling, business partnerships, etc. are juxtaposed to detailed regulations on matters such as the material maintenance a wife can require from her husband, the expectations for conjugal sexual activity, and the responsibilities of a nursing mother and father to the baby and to each other.[39] Collections of fatwas, like that of the renowned jurist Khayr al-Din al-Ramli, a seventeenth-century mufti from Palestine, also waded right into intimate territory in responses to questions about when a girl was physically ready for sexual intercourse, the various ways in which a woman could lose her virginity, or what a man should do if he were sexually aroused by the sight of a pretty boy.[40] Nor are such topics relegated to some obscure reach of the work: juridical commentaries and collections usually gave these family matters pride of place, just after the requirements for religious rituals at the beginning of the volume. The long arm of the law did not stop at the bedroom door, and the woman's physical comforts and sexual experiences within marriage, the legitimacy of her pregnancy, and her special needs as a nursing mother were all well within its purview.

But is this inclusion of the female body and its difference an inclusion of the woman's experience of this difference? The authors of canonical legal treatises, up until the very recent past, were to the best of my knowledge all men. And although there is a tone, at least among some, of concern for women and their rights in the areas of reproduction in the context of legal marriage and concubinage, this is certainly not the same as hearing the woman's voice and having the female experience. One could argue that Islamic law does, indeed, have a feminine vision of connectedness: the family is knit together by numerous reciprocal rights and obligations, most of which privilege the wellbeing of the family and the community over any individual right to liberty or privacy. The elaboration of rules for the responsibility a given individual bears to support other family members

---

[39] Burhan al-Din ʿAli ibn Abi-Bakr al-Marghinani, *Al-Hidaya: Sharh Bidayat al-Mubtadi*, 1st edn, 4 vols. (Cairo: Dar al-Salam, 2000).

[40] Khayr al-Din ibn Ahmad al-Ramli, *Kitab al-Fatawa al-Kubra li-Nafʿ al-Birriyya*, 2 vols. (Cairo, Bulaq: n.p., 1856–57).

is a good example of the ways the law constructs the family. Al-Marghinani, for instance, covers the following obligations of material support created by family relationships: husbands for wives and children, parents for adult daughters, adult male and female children for indigent parents and grand-parents, brothers and sisters for their minor or indigent siblings, nephews and nieces for their indigent aunts and uncles and vice versa, first cousins for their indigent counterparts, owners for slaves, and, in addition, a man has to help anyone who is needy from among certain of his relatives through marriage, including his mother-in-law, his daughters-in-law, and step-children.[41] These are legal obligations, enforceable in court, and a judge could assign specific payments to recalcitrant individuals and/or attach their assets.

But even if women's special physical and emotional needs are attended to in this connected family that recognizes male–female difference, the law ultimately speaks in the voice of male experience. While a woman's relation-ship with her infant and her role in its early nurturing are honored by special provisions for support, for example, there is no question in all schools of law but that children are part of the father's lineage. Any point of conflict between the mother's desire to nurture and hold her child close and the father's right to assert possession of the child for his family in the wake of a divorce is resolved in favor of the child's father. Thus the mother has temporary rights of custody (*ḥiḍāna*) of her child, but the natural guard-ianship of the child and custody once the child has reached a certain age (which varies from one school of law to another) is vested in the father.[42] Here the mother's role in reproduction is, in fact, limited to childbirth, nursing, and the nurturing of young children; the intense and lifelong attachment of a mother to her child gets no legal recognition. As we shall see below, women and children (and some men as well) developed ways of working within or around these rules, but clearly the male drive for progeny trumped female sensibilities as far as the rules for child custody were concerned. Thus, I would argue that although the female experience is present in Islamic law at least in a refracted fashion and we do not face the same barriers of privacy that served to obscure it in the modern West, this female experience has often been a secondary consideration, hostage to male patriarchal priorities. It should come as no surprise that current discussions

---

[41] Al-Marghinani, *Al-Hidaya*, 2:653–59.

[42] For a review of the position of various legal schools on child custody, as well as some of the modern reforms, see Nasir, *The Islamic Law*, 181–89. See also, with particular reference to India and Pakistan, David Pearl, *A Textbook on Muslim Law* (London: Croom Helm, 1979), 83–87.

of the need for further legal reform in female circles often focus on the rules governing issues of child custody and possession of the marital domicile after divorce, two issues of critical importance to the experience of divorced women.

Third, I want to consider in an initial fashion the kinds of linguistic constructions of the Female within which much of Islamic legal discourse takes place, that is, the ways in which legal discourse is reflective of and contributes to a process of gendering that permeates the societies in which it is located. I will consider other aspects of this Woman of legal discourse over the course of the book (Woman as domestic, as disruptive, as inferior), but I begin here with Woman as silent, arguably a key construction from which most others flow. The problem of silence has struck many of those, particularly women, who have written about Islamic law, as in the following:

> History abounds with examples that indicate that whenever silence was imposed on women, or any other group for that matter, it has led to erroneous and self-contradictory views about them, which in turn has led to the build-up of traditions as well as laws detrimental to them. Similarly, Islamic legislators have opted for an interpretation of Islam that gives a capricious and unrealistic portrayal of the female nature and diminishes the rights Islam allocates to women, ignoring not only the dictates of common sense, but also the spirit, and sometimes the explicit sense, of the Qur'anic text as well as the generally accepted facts about the life of the Prophet. In order to perpetuate such an interpretation, the voices of women jurists, and those who engage in dialogue about Islam, were progressively silenced.[43]

Hamadeh goes on to note that the women of the time of the Prophet and the first Caliphs in the early Islamic community were outspoken participants in their society and in the interpretation of the meaning of Islam. The process of quieting and then silencing them in the following centuries represented a historic defeat for women: the development of the law was left in the hands of male interpreters of the shari'a for whom, in one extremist version, the very sound of the female voice was a provocation to be forbidden in public space.

The Woman as silent both shaped and was shaped by Islamic legal discourse. Imposed silence meant that few women jurists had any impact on the development of the law: the female voice is largely missing from legal discourse. A cursory glance at any standard bibliography of legal works will confirm the fact of the absence of women writers.[44] In the biographical

---

[43] Najla Hamadeh, "Islamic Family Legislation: The Authoritarian Discourse of Silence," in Yamani and Allen, *Feminism and Islam*, 333.

[44] See, for example, the bibliography in Schacht, *An Introduction*, 215–85; and Hossein Modarressi, *An Introduction to Shi'i Law: A Bibliographical Study* (London: Ithaca Press, 1984).

dictionaries that recorded the lives of prominent Muslim intellectuals over the centuries, women appear, in diminishing numbers as the centuries go by, primarily as transmitters and scholars of hadith, not as interpreters of the law.[45] Although the women of scholarly families were often well educated and no doubt conversant with the major works of the legal canon, they apparently were not encouraged or thought able to make any contribution to the ongoing evolution of legal thought. To what extent were the rules for marriage, divorce, and child custody the outcome, in part, of this elimination of the female voice and therefore the female experience?

The construction of the Woman as silent, however, was not without its contradictions. Women had equal rights to property and full legal capacity to enter into contracts (the Qur'an is clear on these points), so how could these activities be reconciled with female silence? A business contract, for example, is only valid with the active consent of the parties to the contract, so to exercise the rights they were given to manage and dispose of their property, women had to have a voice. The voice might be muted through the employment of agents to represent women in business dealings and in litigation of all kinds, a common practice particularly among upper-class women. Such an agent had to be appointed by the woman herself, however, and his conduct was subject to review if he did not adhere strictly to the instructions he had received from the woman who appointed him.[46] So the voice of the woman inevitably intruded, however indirectly, into the sphere of business dealings.

The female voice seemed to be even more problematic in the case of the marriage contract, for which the jurists worked out special rules. Although the marriage contract was, in principle, a contract between the bride and the groom, and thus needed the voice of the bride for its validity, the jurists found various ways for a woman's relatives to speak in her name. With the exception of the Hanafi school, all other legal schools required a woman to have a marriage guardian, her father or closest other paternal relative if her father were not available, whose task it was to conclude the marriage contract, including the expression of her consent. For a female in her legal minority, the guardian had the right to conclude a valid contract without the consent or even knowledge of the bride, a bride rendered not only voiceless but sightless as well. A woman in her legal majority should not be coerced into a particular marriage, however, so that most women retained

[45] See Ruth Roded, *Women in Islamic Biographical Collections: from Ibn Saʿd to Who's Who* (Boulder, CO: L. Rienner Publishers, 1994).
[46] Al-Marghinani, *Al-Hidaya*, 3:1131.

the right to refuse a marriage.[47] But how did a woman signal her consent? In the case of a virgin, the absence of a clear sound or sign of refusal upon learning of the contract signified her approval: a woman's silence is her agreement, her acquiescence. In using female silence as the legal measure of her participation in what was no doubt one of the most important moments of her life, legal discourse constructed Woman as the passive and inert partner to masculine arrangements. I discuss the complexity of the rules for marriage contracts, their formalities and effects, in more detail below; for the moment I want to point out that this very complexity suggests some struggle on the part of the jurists to square their proclivities for female silence with some of the basic principles of female capacity embedded in the legal sources. In brief, the construction of Woman in legal discourse has not been all of a piece; on the contrary there are many cracks and tears that lend themselves, as we shall see, to ongoing disputation. A number of Islamic feminists today are reviewing some of the man-made constructions of Woman in legal literature on the basis that they contradict clear indications of God's will found in the Qur'an and authentic hadith.

Finally, I want always to keep in mind the fact of female agency, the many active ways in which women themselves, and their male allies, have influenced the development of Islamic law. It is true that, up until the recent past, women were not part of the intellectual discussions, debates, and individual efforts that went into the development of the law over time. Nor were women usually muftis, judges, or other official actors in the court system, with the exception of their role as expert witnesses in areas related to "women's" matters. But all studies of Islamic court systems, particularly in the Ottoman period and later when we have the required source materials, conclude that women were very active participants in many of the cases that came before the courts.[48] Women used the Islamic courts, like their male

---

[47] See Nasir, *The Islamic Law*, 50–53.

[48] See, among others, Mary Ann Fay, "Women and Waqf: Toward a Reconsideration of Women's Place in the Mamluk Household," *International Journal of Middle East Studies* 29, no. 1 (1997): 33–51; Haim Gerber, "Social and Economic Position of Women in an Ottoman City, Bursa, 1600–1700," *International Journal of Middle East Studies* 12, no. 3 (1980): 231–44; Hirsch, *Pronouncing and Persevering*; Ronald C. Jennings, "Women in Early 17th Century Ottoman Judicial Records: The Sharia Court of Anatolian Kayseri," *Journal of the Economic and Social History of the Orient* 18, no. 1 (1975): 53–114; Abraham Marcus, "Men, Women and Property: Dealers in Real Estate in 18th Century Aleppo," *Journal of the Economic and Social History of the Orient* 26, no. 2 (1983): 137–63; Margaret Lee Meriwether, *The Kin Who Count: Family and Society in Ottoman Aleppo, 1770–1840*, 1st edn (Austin: University of Texas Press, 1999); Ziba Mir-Hosseini, *Marriage on Trial: A Study of Islamic Family Law: Iran and Morocco Compared* (London: I.B. Tauris, 1993); Annalise Moors, *Women, Property, and Islam: Palestinian Experience, 1920–1990* (Cambridge: Cambridge University Press, 1995); Leslie P. Peirce, *Morality Tales: Law and Gender in the Ottoman Court of Aintab*

counterparts, for notarial purposes: they registered sales and purchases of property, they recorded business partnerships and loans, they endowed waqfs (entailing property for religious or charitable causes) in large numbers, and they entered into contracts of marriage. The record of this activity, at least for the Ottoman period, has established beyond question the fact that urban women knew about their independent rights to property and exercised them in the court setting. Many of these women, particularly those from the elite, sent agents to court to conduct their business, but women of more modest backgrounds often came on their own to make arrangements in matters of petty trade, small purchases, or humble waqfs. The Islamic court was, then, a space where women belonged in the sense that its notarial functions were available, and essential, to the conduct of their economic and social lives.

The court was also the venue for litigation. Women pursued debtors, accused assailants, questioned the legality of marriage contracts, sued former husbands for dowers, protested unfair divisions of inheritance, and argued about child support. Such recourse to the court in significant numbers (and the court records of the Ottoman period at least suggest a staggering number of people, men along with women, took their business to the Islamic court) demonstrated their knowledge of a number of rights in the area of community and family relations, and their belief that the courts were likely to hear them out and provide redress. And, at least for the periods for which we have some systematic information, their trust was not misplaced: if they could demonstrate that their rights had indeed been violated, the judge was likely to find in their favor.[49] The apparent ideological commitment of the court and its personnel to upholding rights thought to be inscribed in the shariʿa, regardless of the social power of the plaintiff, made sure that those rights remained part of the collective memory of the community. We can ask to what extent women's assertions of such rights were vital to this process: by going to court and getting a hearing and/or by posing a question to a local mufti, women were a central part of a process of review and implementation of their legal rights. They worked within the

(Berkeley: University of California Press, 2003); Amira El Azhary Sonbol, ed., *Women, the Family, and Divorce Laws in Islamic History*. 1st edn, Contemporary Issues in the Middle East (Syracuse: Syracuse University Press, 1996); Judith E. Tucker, *In the House of the Law: Gender and Islamic Law in Ottoman Syria and Palestine* (Berkeley: University of California Press, 1998); Lynn Welchman, *Beyond the Code: Muslim Family Law and the Shariʿa Judiciary in the Palestinian West Bank* (The Hague: Kluwer Law International, 2000); Madeline C. Zilfi, ed., *Women in the Ottoman Empire: Middle Eastern Women in the Early Modern Era* (Leiden: Brill, 1997).

[49] See, for example, the ways in which eighteenth-century courts in Syria and Palestine sided with women in child support conflicts in Tucker, *In the House*, 131–35.

constraints of the established legal frameworks, of course, but their active defense of rights such as prompt payment of their dower, support for themselves and their children, and prescribed shares of inheritance ensured that these rights retained prominence in legal discourse. Their appearances in court were performative acts that helped shape and shift discourse to their advantage.

In thinking about female agency in law, Saba Mahmood's remarks on female agency in the context of the contemporary Egyptian mosque movement offer helpful cautions. We are tempted, she notes, to equate agency with resistance to domination, to the quest for individual freedom from external restraints, including the weight of custom and tradition. But we should interrogate our assumptions:

does the category of resistance impose a teleology of progressive politics on the analytics of power – a teleology that makes it hard for us to see and understand forms of being and action that are not necessarily encapsulated by the narrative of subversion and reinscription of norms?[50]

One of Mahmood's signal contributions is to invite us to think about agency not only or even primarily as the way in which women subvert (or consolidate) patriarchal norms, but also how they are "performed, inhabited, and experienced in a variety of ways."[51] This seems to me a very useful way to explore how most Muslim women have acted as agents within the legal tradition. They have not embraced, by and large, an adversarial form of agency but rather have participated in the legal system in a variety of ways, both asserting rights and accepting to fulfill duties and obligations. Our understanding of their actions is not advanced by assuming that this bespeaks a false consciousness that promotes collusion with patriarchy; rather, I want to proceed in this study of the law with female agency, and the ways in which women have apprehended the relation between the law and their own fulfillment in life, as open questions.

Few would dispute the notion, of course, that Islamic law has marked patriarchal features. We have ample evidence of the latter in the rules, for example, on guardianship and marriage. As mentioned above, except under the Hanafi school of law, all women regardless of their age were required to have a guardian give them in marriage, a guardian who could exercise the kind of judgment needed to make a good choice of mate. Among the Hanafis, a woman in her legal majority had the right to choose her own

---

[50] Saba Mahmood, *Politics of Piety: The Islamic Revival and the Feminist Subject* (Princeton: Princeton University Press, 2005), 9.
[51] *Ibid.*, 22.

marriage partner and arrange her own marriage, but her natural guardian retained the right to request an annulment of this marriage by the court if the groom did not have the qualities of "suitability" in the sense of a social and economic background as good as or better than that of the bride. The requirements of suitability or *kafāʾa*, which were developed in elaborate detail by jurists of the Hanafi school, established definite boundaries for a woman's choice. As Mona Siddiqui has pointed out:

> The objectives underlying the institution of *kafāʾa* go beyond the fear of "misalliance" whereby a woman may contract herself in marriage to someone who is not her equal ... choice of partners is socially important because both placement and choice link two kinship lines together. To permit, therefore, random mate choice could introduce radical changes in the existing social structure. Since individual selection of partners affects the social structure, *kafāʾa* may be interpreted as a legal argument carefully elaborated by a juristic desire to ensure control of social stratification.[52]

In Siddiqui's view, the jurists who developed the doctrine of *kafāʾa*, and the judges who enforced it, evinced more concern for the stability of class arrangements, from which we presume they personally benefited, than for a woman's unfettered exercise of her right to choose her husband. Women were active agents in the legal system, but this activity contended with doctrines and institutions that had qualms about some forms of female agency. Still, the openness of the courts to female litigants, and an ethos of justice for all, allowed women a significant role in the judicial process.

The ways in which women can act in the legal system is a topic of great current interest. As we shall see, many activists are concerned that "modern" judicial arrangements such as legal codes and centralized courts have actually diminished the possibilities for female agency in the legal system. How well do women know their rights under the new codes and what access do they have to the courts, which are often alien places with unfamiliar patterns of speech and practice? Activists want to encourage female agency through programs of legal education and campaigns to open positions in the Islamic legal system to women, as well as by inserting the female voice into doctrinal discussions.

I discuss these issues of agency, discrimination, male norming, and the pervasive gendering of the law in the following pages by taking a thematic approach to the subject of women and gender. I treat the topics

---

[52] Mona Siddiqui, "Law and the Desire for Social Control: An Insight into the Hanafi Concept of *Kafāʾa* with Reference to the Fatawa ʿAlamgiri (1664–1672)," in Yamani and Allen, *Feminism and Islam*, 65.

of: (1) marriage, (2) divorce, (3) the legal persona as guardian, witness, and property-holder, and (4) space and sexuality.

In each chapter I allude to relevant legal doctrine from the four major schools of Sunni jurisprudence as well as Shi'i law with attention to the ways in which doctrines developed in reference to textual sources on the one hand and historical contingencies on the other. I also attempt to pay attention to the many tensions in Islamic jurisprudence insofar as possible over the course of a long and varied history. My exploration of this doctrine is, necessarily, partial and somewhat idiosyncratic, based on my own sense of what seems most relevant or significant to the law and gender focus. The law is a vast textual arena and the processes involved in the development of the legal tradition were complex and varied, taking place in widely disparate times and places. I try my best to capture the flavor of this tradition and its methodologies, which were the products of some of the best minds of the time, by drawing primarily on a handful of legal texts produced by jurists from different legal schools from the classical and medieval periods. But I am very aware of the limitations and even arbitrary aspects of this approach. This is not a systematic study of the development of legal doctrine in the juridical literature (*fiqh*) on matters pertaining to women and gender. It is, rather, a modest attempt to suggest which issues occupied the minds of the jurists, to sketch however roughly the parameters of the intellectualized legal terrain when it came to gender issues. I cannot pretend that I supply a comprehensive survey of doctrinal positions and developments – that lies beyond the boundaries of my abilities and this study. I do want to stress, however, the importance of appreciating the many differences of opinion among the jurists, both within and among legal schools, and how those differences lent a certain flexibility and fluidity to the entire legal system. This system and the doctrines it produced are no longer intact, but I submit that there is an embedded approach and a texture to gender issues that remain relevant to the ways in which those issues are being confronted today.

I am interested not just in doctrine, but also in the lived experience of the law, the ways in which laywomen and men understood their rights and options, and the actions they took as a result. I am dependent here on scholars who have done research on the practice of Islamic law in various times and places, but the field still suffers from the paucity of such studies, especially in the pre-Ottoman period, so that the material is limited and somewhat disjointed. I also try to confront, in each chapter, the epistemological break in the law of the late nineteenth century and the entrance of the state as a central figure in modern legal systems: this was a watershed period that had far-reaching effects, for better and worse, on women and gender issues. Finally, I endeavor to outline some of the most significant recent developments in Islamic law, at the level both of practical reforms of legal practice and of challenges being mounted inside doctrinal discourse. I do not attempt, in the space provided, to write an encyclopedic account of the topic: there are many omissions of relevant facts, experiences, nuances, and approaches. But I have tried to cover most of what I think is critical to understanding the breadth and depth of at least a good number of the key issues that surround the question of women, gender, and Islamic law.

Woman as wife and man as husband: making the marital bargain

I begin with the topic of marriage because Islamic law privileges the marital bond. In the canonical legal treatises and collections of fatwas, in court proceedings, in the minds of reforming jurists, and in the priorities of today's female activists, marriage occupies a central and pivotal place. Jurists, reformers, and activists have studied and elaborated on the rules for contracting a marriage, and the rights and obligations of husbands and wives once married. Most jurists devoted considerable proportions of their general works to issues pertaining to marriage, and often gave the topic pride of place right after the discussions of religious ritual with which they open their treatises. The courts, at least in the eras for which we have evidence, registered many marriage contracts and provided a venue for litigation about marital rights. The reform-minded intellectuals of the modern period focused on abuses in marriage as a key target of criticism and revision. And, in recent times, activists have looked to the marriage contract itself and the definitions of male rights within marriage as particular targets for legal campaigns.

How can we understand the centrality of marriage in Islamic legal discourse and practice? The answer lies, in part, in the Qur'an and the hadith, the primary and revered sources of the law. Marriage is presented in the Qur'an as a major source of comfort and joy for both spouses, for men are told about their wives in lilting metaphor: "they are a vestment for you and you are a vestment for them" (2:187); and both men and women are informed that "He created for you, of yourselves, spouses, that you might repose in them, and he has set between you love and mercy" (30:21). A number of other verses deal with suitable marriage partners (2:220 and 4:22–23), proper marriage arrangements (2:235), and the rights and duties of husband and wife (4:34). Although these verses have been subject to various interpretations, particularly as to the amount of power they allocate to the husband in a marital relationship, there is little question that marriage is one of the most important human relationships and is recommended for almost everyone. The Qur'an gives moral guidance and rules for relationships between parents and children or between masters and slaves, for example, but the amount of space and level of detail accorded to marital relations stand apart. A number of scholars have remarked on the context of reform here: the Qur'an outlawed a number of abusive marriage practices that were current at the time, such as the son acquiring his deceased father's wife as part of his inheritance or secret marriages in which a woman had little power, in order to secure female rights within a marriage.[1] From this perspective, the Qur'an focused on marriage because it was such a major part of the progressive social reforms introduced by Islam. Others take a rather different view, arguing that the sixth- and seventh-century Arabian peninsula seems to have had a multiplicity of marriage customs, some of which allowed for matrilineal and matrilocal marriages in which women exercised much of the initiative in arranging and terminating marriages, and had permanent custody of their children.[2] In this latter scenario, the Qur'an consolidated a historic transition in the Arabian peninsula from matrilineal to patrilineal marriage practices in which women by and large lost out. Regardless of which view we embrace, the importance of marriage in substance and symbol to the new Islamic order cannot be denied, and Qur'anic verses supplied guidance to the jurists for the elaboration of marital regulations.

Hadith literature provided additional but more controversial material for the development of rules for Islamic marriage. These voluminous reports of the Prophet Muhammad's statements also had much to say about Islamic marriage: in part, they underscored the Qur'anic message as to the strong positive value of marriage, as in the report that the Prophet said: "O young men! Whoever among you has the ability should marry, for it restrains the eyes and protects chastity."[3] Many aspects of Muhammad's own life as well spoke to the comforts and blessings of marriage, from the early support of Khadija, his first wife, for his prophetic mission, to his decision to die in the arms of 'A'isha, one of several women he married after Khadija's death.[4] 'A'isha, in fact, became a major source of hadith material herself because of her intimacy with the Prophet and the way he consistently shared his

---

[1] See, for example, Fazlur Rahman, "Status of Women in the Qur'an," in *Women and Revolution in Iran*, ed. Guity Nashat (Boulder, CO: Westview Press, 1983), 37–54.

[2] For a summary of these arguments, see Ghada Karmi, "Women, Islam, and Patriarchalism," in Yamani and Allen, *Feminism and Islam*, 69–85.

[3] Ibn Hajar al-'Asqalani, *Fath al-Bari*, cited in Abou El Fadl, *Speaking in God's Name*, 206, n72.

[4] For details of Muhammad's marital relations, see the biography by Muhammad Husayn Haykal, *The Life of Muhammad*, trans. Ismail R. al-Faruqi (Plainfield, IN: North American Trust Publications, 1976).

thoughts with her. Not all hadith material, however, projects such an uplifting view of marriage. On the contrary, we have several versions of one notorious story: when asked about the act of prostrating before another human being (like himself), the Prophet reportedly told his followers: "It is not lawful for anyone to prostrate to anyone. But if I would have ordered any person to prostrate to another, I would have commanded wives to prostrate to their husbands because of the enormity of the rights of husbands over their wives." This particular hadith, and variations on it that dramatized these rights still further by adding a wife's obligation to be available for her husband's sexual desires even if she were on a camel at the time, or a wife's obligation to lick her husband's sores if requested, seemed to set marriage on a somewhat different footing. But, unlike Qur'anic material which is the word of God, the hadith can be examined more critically (although there are canonical collections with established reputations) in terms of their origins and modes of transmission. Khaled Abou El Fadl has made convincing arguments about both the structural and contextual peculiarities of these prostration reports as well as the credibility of one of the main transmitters of many of these different versions.[5] The possibility of critical selection or rejection of reports, and different choices made by different jurists, allowed for the development of many of the differences we find in the rules for marriage among various schools of law.

These rules can be divided into two broad categories: those that govern the drawing up of the marriage contract, and those that govern the rights and duties of husbands and wives after they are legally married. First, I want to consider the development of these rules prior to the modern era of reform with an eye to grasping the major outlines of legal thought and practice in the area of marriage as well as some of the key differences among Islamic legal traditions. I do not present here a comprehensive survey of all the positions and opinions, both majority and minority, of the various legal schools as they evolved over time, but rather attempt to outline what appear to have been some of the most significant aspects of legal doctrine as far as the position of women in marriage was concerned in some of the canonical texts. I also want to discuss not only this doctrine, but also some of the ways men, and women in particular, understood and activated their rights. Then I follow these doctrines and practices through the modern era of legal reform in the nineteenth and especially twentieth centuries as individual reformers and various state authorities grappled with the problem of

[5] Abou El Fadl, *Speaking in God's Name*, 210–18.

modernizing the law. Finally, I look briefly at a few of the issues of Islamic marriage that have invited the most attention in contemporary times.

ISLAMIC MARRIAGE: THE LEGAL TRADITION

The marriage contract

Marriage has a dual character under Islamic law: it is the fulfillment of a moral imperative to marry as an essential part of leading a good Muslim life, and it is a binding legal contract that must meet certain conditions in form and content. The jurists did not, in general, spend much time discussing the virtues of marriage: they assumed that almost all Muslims would marry (with the possible exception of a few with serious physical impediments that rendered sexual intercourse very dangerous or impossible) and they saw their task as one of providing guidance as to the proper procedures and conditions for arranging a marriage.

The contract of marriage or *nikāḥ* is a contract between a man and a woman with the specific purpose of legalizing sexual intercourse: the point of departure in most legal discussions of marriage is the fact that marriage renders sexual relations licit. A married couple may look at all parts of each other's bodies and they may engage in sexual intercourse. Within this basic definition, there was room for different emphases. Khalil ibn Ishaq, the fourteenth-century author of a standard work of Maliki *fiqh*, focuses on the husband's enjoyment of his wife's body.[6] Al-Marghinani, author of one of the most authoritative Hanafi works, states from the outset that "for us [the Hanafis] marriage is ownership by way of owning sexual pleasure in a person and this right is established by marriage."[7] Al-Hilli, in his fourteenth-century summary of the views of Shiʿi jurists, found complete consensus among the jurists that marriage was a commendable act (*mustaḥabb*) in the case of individuals who were capable (in a physical sense) and felt sexual desire; in the absence of such desire, there was no juristic consensus on the virtues of marriage.[8] The common thread in these initial discussions of marriage is that having licit sexual intercourse is both the primary motivation, and the most important effect, of the marriage contract. Jurists may vary somewhat in the emphasis they place on the couple's or the man's pure enjoyment of sex versus

---

[6] Khalil Ibn Ishaq, *Abrégé de la loi musulmane selon le rite de l'Imam Malek*, trans. G. H. Bousquet, vol. 2, *Le statut personnel* (Algiers: La Maison des Livres, 1958), 15.

[7] Al-Marghinani, *Al-Hidaya*, 2:460.

[8] Al-Hasan ibn Yusuf ibn al-Mutahhar al-Hilli, *Mukhtalaf al-Shiʿa fi Ahkam al-Shariʿa*, 10 vols. (Qom, Iran: Islamic Sciences Research Center, 1991), 7:107.

marital sex as the key to legal reproduction, but the marriage contract is first
and foremost for the establishment of licit sexual relations between a man and
a woman. At this level, the contract is one of equality between two consenting
adults enabling them to engage in sexual activity with each other.

The jurists took the notion of consent seriously: almost all jurists agreed
that the absence of consent from a woman in her legal majority, even if
married off by her natural guardian, invalidated a marriage contract. (See
chapter 4 for an expanded discussion of guardianship.) The exception here
are the Shafi'is, who required only "consent of the *thayyib* (non-virgin)
woman and the man, [presence of the] guardian who arranges the marriage
for the woman, and the witnesses" for a valid contract.[9] The implication is
that the virgin bride may indeed be married off without her consent and
against her will. Some Shi'i jurists as well empowered the *wali* (guardian), if
either the father or grandfather, to coerce their charge, if still a virgin, into a
marriage.[10]

If required, how was a woman's consent to a contract to be ascertained?
This was a serious question that occasioned reflection on the complexity of
human emotions and their expression. The reticence of the virgin, for
example, needed to be taken into consideration:

If the guardian consults her and she remains silent or smiles, this constitutes consent,
because the Prophet (upon him be peace and blessings) said, "The virgin
is consulted in [what pertains] to herself; if she remained silent, this was her
consent." And consent is likely the cause because she is embarrassed to demonstrate
desire by replying. And laughter is a stronger sign of consent than silence, as
opposed to if she cried because that is a sign of unhappiness and abhorrence.
And it is said: if she laughed in derision at what she heard, that is not consent, and if
she cried soundlessly, that is not refusal. And if this [proposal of marriage] is made
by someone other than her guardian, someone self-appointed or another delegated
to be her guardian, her consent cannot be ascertained until she voices it, because
her silence might stem from her not attending [carefully] to his words, and not be a
token of her acceptance.[11]

When it came to the non-virgin, such explicit assent was particularly
important, based on a saying of the Prophet that the non-virgin should be
consulted, and the assumption that "speech does not carry shame" for a
non-virgin.[12] A woman who was no longer a virgin could only assent to a
marriage by clearly voicing her agreement in terms that brooked no other
interpretation.

[9] Muhammad ibn Idris Shafi'i, *Islamic Jurisprudence: Shafi'i's Risala*, trans. Majid Khadduri
(Baltimore: Johns Hopkins University Press, 1961), 174.
[10] Al-Hilli, *Mukhtalaf*, 7:127–28.   [11] Al-Marghinani, *Al-Hidaya*, 2:477–78.   [12] *Ibid.*, 2:478.

The issue of consent was completely different in the case of a bride in her legal minority. All legal schools agreed that a girl's father had the right to marry her to whomever he chose without consulting her; the father enjoyed similar rights to marry off his minor sons. As minors, children lacked the legal capacity to give their permission for a marriage, much less arrange marriages for themselves. They could be married off without their consent and even against their stated wishes. Although boys and girls were equally under the thumb of their guardians, most of the jurists' discussion of the marriage of minors focused on girls, suggesting that this was the more common social practice. But while all the major legal schools gave fathers such overweening power in the case of a girl in her minority (with the age of minority variously defined as pre-puberty or less than nine years of age), they differed on some of the details. Most Malikis and Hanbalis held that only a father had this right while the Shafi'is extended this power to the grandfather as well in the absence of the father. Hanafis and Shi'a went even further and permitted any legal guardian to marry off a minor girl; in the case of a marriage arranged by anyone other than the father or grandfather, however, a girl could exercise her "option of puberty" (*khiyār al-bulūgh*) as soon as she came of age and request an annulment of the marriage from the court.[13] Jurists sometimes noted the possible tension between paternal rights and the welfare and happiness of a child: Ibn Hanbal, for one, noted his preference that even the minor be consulted by her guardian. Still, her father's decision to give her in marriage was valid, regardless of her wishes.[14]

I should stress here that agreement on a marriage contract did not imply immediate consummation of the marriage. In the case of a bride in her minority, her "delivery" to her husband awaited her legal majority (that is, the menses that signaled puberty) or, at a minimum, physical signs of her "readiness for intercourse" as discussed by the seventeenth-century Hanafi jurist Khayr al-Din al-Ramli, in his response to a husband's demand that his bride's father deliver her to him:

If she is plump and buxom and ready for men, and the stipulated *mahr* has been received promptly, the father is compelled to give her to her husband, according to the soundest teaching. The Qadi examines whether she is [ready] by [asking] whoever raised her and by her appearance; and if she is suitable for men, he orders her father to give her to her husband or not. And if there are none who raised her,

---

[13] *Ibid.*, 2:481; al-Hilli, *Mukhtalaf*, 7:141–42.
[14] Ahmad ibn Muhammad Ibn Hanbal, *Chapters on Marriage and Divorce: Responses of Ibn Hanbal and Ibn Rahwayh*, trans. Susan A. Spectorsky, 1st edn (Austin: University of Texas Press, 1993), 98.

then he requests a consultation from women. And if they say she is ready for men and can endure intercourse, he instructs the father to give her to her husband. If they say she is not ready, then he does not so instruct the father. And God knows best.[15]

Those "who raised her" would presumably be her mother and/or other women in the girl's family who would in this fashion have some input into the decision as to whether a girl was ready for a sexual relationship. A girl's father was fully empowered to agree to a marriage contract for his daughter, but he could not give her away physically until her readiness was in some way apparent.

It was not just a question of placing limits on the guardian's power to force his charge into marriage: in the case of a woman in her legal majority, the jurists were also concerned that a guardian not stand in the way of a "good" marriage. If a woman had an opportunity to marry a decent man who was suitable and offered an appropriate dower, her guardian should not restrain her. Al-Shafiʿi held that a guardian had no right to turn down such an acceptable proposal; if the guardian refused a woman permission for a good marriage, the matter should be turned over to the court, which could order the guardian to agree. If that did not work, the judge could appoint another guardian or even act as guardian himself.[16] The right of the guardian was also a duty to facilitate a good marriage in keeping with the pro-marital stance of the jurists.

The jurists defined a "good" marriage as one with a suitable groom and an appropriate *mahr*. What qualities made a groom suitable? Sunni jurists developed the concept of *kafāʾa* (suitability) to varying degrees. At one end of the spectrum stood the Hanafi jurists who constructed an elaborate set of criteria for ascertaining whether a man would make a suitable husband: his lineage, the length of time his family had been Muslim (an issue primarily in early Islamic times), his juridical status as free or slave, his piety, his wealth, and his occupation were the six areas in which he should be on an equal or higher level than his bride and his bride's guardian.[17] Maliki thought was initially minimalist on the issue, with Malik himself asserting that only piety should be considered relevant; measuring piety, essentially a state of mind and soul, was not easy but the jurists settled on a few outward manifestations of the lack of piety such as public drunkenness and

---

[15] Al-Ramli, *Kitab al-Fatawa*, 1:29–30.
[16] Dawoud S. El Alami, "Legal Capacity with Specific Reference to the Marriage Contract," *Arab Law Quarterly* 6, no. 2 (1991): 194.
[17] Al-Marghinani, *Al-Hidaya*, 2:484–86.

nakedness. Over time, some Maliki jurists expanded the concept of suitability to include the physical condition and wealth of the groom as well.[18] Shi'i thought, on the other hand, rejected the notion of *kafāʾa* except in the limited instance of a non-Muslim groom and a Muslim bride; all other considerations of "honor or wealth or lineage" were irrelevant.[19] *Kafāʾa* was a one-way street in the sense that the requirement of suitability could only be applied to a groom; the jurists assumed that a woman's marriage to a man of lower status would lead to her degradation but her marriage to a man of higher status would raise her to his level.

The evolution of the doctrine of *kafāʾa*, particularly as it applies to lineage, wealth, and occupation, offers some fascinating insights into shifts in social perceptions of status markers, and indeed, the jurists recognized the fact that the hierarchy of occupations, for example, might change over time.[20] What engages my attention in the context of the marriage contract, however, is the ways in which the doctrine was used variously to circumscribe the autonomy of the adult female or her male guardian. Although Hanafi jurists had defended the right of a woman to choose her own spouse, they subjected that choice to review by the woman's natural guardian: if a guardian thought the groom was not suitable in any way, he could ask a judge to annul the marriage. A woman only had a real choice within the parameters set by her family's social and economic status. Among other legal schools the doctrine of *kafāʾa* could operate quite differently to stay the hand of the guardian. If a guardian married his ward to an unsuitable man, other family members or the bride herself might object and ask the court to annul the marriage. Ibn Ishaq pointed out some disagreement in the Maliki school about whether a mother could go to court to prevent her daughter's father from marrying her off to a man poorer than she: he thought that the mother could obtain an annulment in such a case while others in the school held that the court should only intervene in the case of tangible harm arising from the absence of suitability.[21] The doctrine of *kafāʾa*, by targeting mésalliance, impinged on the marriage choices of both men and women alike, but it was activated primarily to control the choices made by a woman or her guardian to ensure that a woman did not marry beneath her. It was, in this sense, a symbol of the malleability of female identity: a woman took on her husband's status by association. It was also, by the same token, a

---

[18] Amalia Zomeño, "*Kafāʾa* in the Maliki School: A *Fatwa* from Fifteenth-Century Fez," in *Islamic Law: Theory and Practice*, ed. Robert Gleave and Eugena Kermeli (London: I. B. Tauris, 1997), 92.

[19] Al-Hilli, *Mukhtalaf*, 7:140.   [20] Siddiqui, "Law and the Desire for Social Control," 60.

[21] Ibn Ishaq, *Abrégé*, 28–29.

comment on the entwining of female status and family honor: any lowering of a woman's status would reflect badly on her family.

The other component of a "valid" marriage is a proper *mahr* (dower). The Qur'an enjoins believers to "give the women their dowries as a gift spontaneous" (4:4) and as one not to be returned: "And if you desire to exchange a wife in place of another, and you have given to one a hundred-weight, take of it nothing" (4:24). The jurists held that the payment of a dower to the bride from the groom or his family was an essential condition of the marriage contract and established a number of rules governing both amount and delivery. A marriage contract that failed to specify a dower was a valid contract, but by making such a contract the groom implicitly committed himself to the paying of a proper *mahr*, an absolute right of the bride.[22]

The amount of *mahr* could vary. Some jurists fixed a lower limit for the *mahr*: the equivalent of one quarter of a gold *dinar* or three silver *dirham*s (the exact value of these coins is not clear) according to most Malikis, and ten *dirham*s (or alternately five or even forty) for Hanafis as in the passage above. Shafi'is insisted on a *mahr* but most did not set a minimum requirement.[23] Although there was no absolute upper limit, legally speaking, many Shi'i jurists held that the *mahr* should not exceed 500 *dirham*s, an amount set on the basis of information about the *mahr*s paid by Muhammad to his wives.[24] There was clearly more concern that the *mahr* not be a derisory amount than worry about excessively high payments. The *mahr* could be paid in specie or in goods, although certain forbidden items, such as pigs and wine, were not legal tender. Shi'i jurists held that anything with a definite value, such as the husband engaging to teach his wife verses from the Qur'an (in keeping with a hadith narrative that the Prophet had approved such a *mahr*) or tailor her a garment, could be a component of a *mahr*, and the Shafi'is agreed that stipulated service was valid; the Hanafis, on the other hand, argued that only tangible property, money or goods, could be offered as *mahr*.[25] All the jurists agreed, however, that there should be a dower of some value, composed of legal specie or goods (and sometimes service), accessible to the bride (not located some distance away for example), which was to be paid in a timely and specified fashion (not in some

---

[22] Al-Marghinani, *Al-Hidaya*, 2:489–90; Abu al-Walid Muhammad ibn Ahmad ibn Muhammad ibn Ahmad Ibn Rushd, *Bidayat al-Mujtahid wa-Nihayat al-Muqtasid*, 4 vols. (Cairo: Dar al-Salam, 1995), 3:1270.

[23] Ibn Rushd, *Bidayat*, 3:1271–72; al-Marghinani, *Al-Hidaya*, 2:489.

[24] Al-Hilli, *Mukhtalaf*, 7:146–47.   [25] *Ibid.*, 7:149; al-Marghinani, *Al-Hidaya*, 2:496.

distant future or contingent upon a future event of unknown date such as the death of the husband).

Ordinarily, the bride should collect her *mahr* or at least a significant portion of it at the time of the signing of the marriage contract. Most of the earlier jurists appeared to assume that the entire *mahr* would be paid at that time and, failing the receipt of the full *mahr* as specified in the contract, a bride could refuse consummation of the marriage. Shi'i jurists "preferred" that the husband pay at least part of the *mahr* before consummation and, in any case, the full amount came due as a debt once he had sexual intercourse with his wife.[26] Most Malikis agreed that the consummation of the marriage entitled the wife to demand her full *mahr*.[27] By the twelfth century, Hanafi jurists were condoning a system whereby the husband pays the *mahr* in two installments: a prompt portion (the *mu'ajjal*) and a deferred portion (the *mu'ajjal*).[28] The prompt portion was ordinarily to be paid at the signing of the contract and a woman could refuse to consummate her marriage or travel with her husband until she had received it; the deferred portion was due to her at the time of her husband's death or upon repudiation. Although there is no mention of this practice in the Qur'an or canonical hadith, and at least some of the early jurists specifically rejected deferring any part of the dower, the division of the dower into these two portions came to be practiced in Egypt as early as the ninth century and eventually accepted by most legal thinkers.[29] By the eighteenth century, there is clearly nothing problematic about dividing the dower: among Hanafis, at least, it is part of the standard doctrine on *mahr*.[30] A bride's right to refuse consummation and all other marital rights to her husband until he paid her dower came to be restricted to payment of the prompt portion only.

The dower represented an important transfer of property and, as such, it could occasion disputes. A major area of contention was that of establishing whether consummation had actually occurred and thus the dower was due in full. Consummation was also a major issue after a divorce, because if a woman were divorced prior to consummation of the marriage, she was entitled to only half the specified *mahr*. In general, the jurists presumed that the marriage had been consummated if the couple were married, the bride had been delivered to her husband, and they had experienced privacy

---

[26] Al-Hilli, *Mukhtalaf,* 7:153–54.   [27] Ibn Rushd, *Bidayat,* 3:1279.

[28] Al-Marghinani, *Al-Hidaya,* 2:503.

[29] Yossef Rapoport, "Matrimonial Gifts in Early Islamic Egypt," *Islamic Law and Society* 7, no. 1 (2000): 1–36.

[30] Al-'Imadi as edited by Ibn 'Abidin, *Al-'Uqud al-Durriyya,* vols. 1–2 (Bulaq: n.p., 1300 H/1882–83 AD), 1:22–26.

(*khalwa*), legally defined as being alone together and "the door has been locked and the curtain let down."[31] A husband might protest that there were impediments to consummation despite having privacy together, such as the observation of a religious fast or menstruation, which had stood in the way of intercourse and thus released him from the payment of the full dower. The jurists differed as to how to establish the truth in the presence of conflicting testimony from the couple. Most Malikis thought that the bride's testimony should carry the day although a virgin bride might be examined by female experts to establish her claims; most Shafi'is held that the husband's testimony took precedence since he should be considered the defendant in the case (and the defendant's testimony ordinarily trumps that of the plaintiff in Islamic law).[32]

A final area of keen judicial interest was the establishment of guidelines for a "proper" *mahr*. While a legal *mahr* was anything the bride would accept as long as the requirements for minimum value were met, the proper *mahr*, the *mahr al-mithl*, was the dower held to be fair and appropriate for a particular bride. This was the dower which would be assigned to the bride if the contract failed to specify a dower, and this was the standard against which a dower could be measured if the court were called upon to establish the validity of a marriage arranged by a bride (in the case of Hanafi law) or a guardian (in the case of other schools). The proper dower derived from the background and qualities of the bride. A Maliki jurist called for consideration of her religion (whether Muslim or not), her beauty (both physical and spiritual), her wealth, the region where she lived, and her sister's dower and/or that of other women of her paternal line.[33] Al-Marghinani, a Hanafi, agreed that all these factors were relevant and added her age, her intelligence, the times in which she lived (whether a time of tranquillity or of troubles), and her virginity or absence of same.[34] Shi'i jurists agreed in the main with these factors, but also took into consideration the dowers of the women in the maternal line, not just the paternal line, the bride's refinement (*adab*), the purity of her lineage on both the paternal and maternal sides, and her reputation (*taḥsīn*), while subtracting for any defects or shortcomings.[35] The jurists did not attempt to weight these factors or attach absolute values to them with the exception of the factor of virginity: Shi'i jurists generally held that the absence of virginity reduced the dower by one-sixth.[36]

---

[31] Ibn Hanbal, *Chapters*, 66.   [32] Ibn Rushd, *Bidayat*, 3:1281.   [33] Ibn Ishaq, *Abrégé*, 52.
[34] Al-Marghinani, *Al-Hidaya*, 2:502.   [35] Al-Hilli, *Mukhtalaf*, 7:178–79.   [36] *Ibid.*, 7:168–69.

The discussions of proper or fair dowers allow us to reflect on how brides (or women in general for that matter) were valued and evaluated by male jurists. Although the doctrine of *kafā'a* implied that the bride's status was fluid, the doctrine of a proper *mahr* assigned a value to the bride based on her social background (lineage, the dowries of her relatives) and her personal qualities. It is the latter, particularly in comparison with the personal qualities that affected a groom's suitability, that hold our attention: age, beauty, virginity, and intelligence for a woman versus piety, health, and occupation for a man. There was some convergence of categories: personal wealth might be considered relevant for either party, appropriately enough in a legal system that gave women full rights to acquire and dispose of property. In general, however, these are contrasting categories. Youth, virginity, and beauty in women are the qualities of physical attraction that please men while piety, health and good occupations of men provide stability and comfort for women. While the marriage contract thus had a certain formal equality as a contract between two parties, the jurists' view of the complementary nature of the marital relationship was inscribed in the rules they developed about the special conditions of this kind of contract.

Witnessed agreement and *mahr* were essential conditions of the marriage contract without which a marriage was not valid. The jurists also held out the possibility of including voluntary conditions, or stipulations, in the marriage contract. Although a stipulation might not always work in the favor of the bride – the Hanbalis thought, for example, that the father of an under-age girl could stipulate in the contract that part payment of the *mahr* be reserved to him – most of the stipulations anticipated by the jurists expanded the rights of the wife. Other possible stipulations entertained by Hanbalis, who devoted the most attention to the subject, included prohibiting the husband from taking a second wife or a concubine, preventing him from removing his wife from her native city or even from her own house, and requiring him to accept to house and maintain his wife's children from a previous marriage.[37] Jurists of other Sunni schools agreed that stipulations as varied as not causing any harm to the wife, treating her with reverence, supplying her with quality clothing, and not subjecting her to hard labor could be inserted into a contract.[38] Shi'i thought diverged markedly from these Sunni positions. According to al-Hilli's compilation of diverse positions, Shi'i jurists rejected all stipulations that impinged upon a husband's marital rights, including his right to sexual intercourse after the

---

[37] Ibn Hanbal, *Chapters*, 154.　[38] Ibn Ishaq, *Abrégé*, 53; al-Marghinani, *Al-Hidaya*, 2:498.

conclusion of the contract, his right to marry a second wife or take a concubine, and his right to insist that his wife accompany him on journeys. Any stipulations that prevented the husband from realizing such marital rights were automatically invalidated. The one stipulation that Shi'a seemed to agree was acceptable was one whereby the husband pledged not to remove his wife from her home town after their marriage.[39]

How were stipulations to be made binding upon the husband? The Shi'a again took a minimalist position by tying stipulations to *mahr* payments. In their view, a bride could link the payment of a premium on her dower to her groom's failure to honor a stipulation: for example, a bride might agree to a dower of fifty *dinars* if her husband allowed her to remain in her hometown, but the dower would rise to a hundred *dinars* if he insisted that she move away.[40] Sunni jurists envisioned far more serious consequences for non-compliance by allowing the wife to seek a divorce in the wake of her husband's failure to honor stipulations. The original contract could give the bride a "right of option," that is, a right delegated by her husband to divorce him should he violate any stipulations. Alternately, she could go to court and request a judicial decree of divorce from the judge, who could then decide if the case warranted a divorce.[41] By allowing stipulations that could have a significant impact on a marriage by enforcing monogamy and otherwise limiting the husband's license to dictate terms within a marriage, and further providing for serious consequence in the event of violation, Sunni jurists introduced a wild card into the matrimonial regime. Without the addition of stipulations, however, the jurists interpreted marital rights and duties in such a way as to privilege the man.

The rights and duties of marriage

Once the contract has been signed and the marriage consummated, the rights and duties of a husband and wife within a marriage are contained, in large part, in the twin doctrines of *nafaqa* (maintenance) and *nushūz* (disobedience). *Nafaqa* is the maintenance that a Muslim husband must provide for his wife, regardless of her religion, as his chief legal obligation to her, a responsibility supported by verses in the Qur'an (2:233) and by several hadith; the Prophet Muhammad told husbands, for example, that in

---

[39] Al-Hilli, *Mukhtalaf*, 7:163–66.   [40] *Ibid.*, 7:166.
[41] Ibn Ishaq, *Abrégé*, 53; Ahmad ibn Abd al-Halim Ibn Taymiyya, *Fatawa al-Nisa'*, 1st edn (Cairo: Maktabat al-Qur'an, 1983), 228–29.

relation to their wives: "You are responsible for their subsistence and their clothing in fairness."[42]

The jurists agreed on the major components of this maintenance, namely food, clothing, and lodging. Many elaborated on what kinds of food were actually required: a man who was neither rich nor poor but of middling income, for instance, should provide his wife with meat every three days or at least "occasionally."[43] They also added other necessities of life, such as supplies of water, oil, wood, salt, the salary of a midwife (for her deliveries), cosmetics like kohl to line her eyes, and henna and creams for her skin and hair.[44] Lodging also entailed specific requirements: a wife was entitled to a separate room exclusively for her use (and that of her husband of course) with a door that she could lock with a key, and no one save her husband should enter without her permission.[45] There was some disagreement about whether she could insist upon having a servant. If the husband were rich, most Hanafis and Malikis thought he must provide her with one servant to help in the house while a minority opinion said two; if the husband were poor, there was still more divergence of opinion, with some jurists holding that the wife could do her own housework while others insisting that she should have at least one servant or slave to help her.[46] The calculation of these rights was a complex business, and some legal schools tended to fix standard maintenance rates by class. While the Malikis thought that there was too much variation in appropriate levels of support in relation to location, era, and class to assign absolute maintenance values, some Hanafis, Shafi'is and Shi'a quantified maintenance by assigning fixed sums for *nafaqa* according to the class backgrounds of the couple. Such quantification drove home the point that maintenance in specified legal amounts was the right of the wife.

A wife became eligible for such maintenance once she had been "delivered" to her husband. For Malikis, maintenance was tied to sexual intercourse: if both spouses were ready for intercourse and the wife was made available, then she must start to receive maintenance. Hanafis, Shafi'is and Shi'a thought that the wife should receive maintenance if she were ready for intercourse, regardless of whether her husband was: in the case of a woman in her majority married to a boy who was not yet ready for the consummation of the marriage, she should receive maintenance while she waited for

---

[42] Ibn Rushd, *Bidayat*, 3:1359.   [43] Al-Hilli, *Mukhtalaf,* 7:319.
[44] Ibn Ishaq, *Abrégé,* 132; al-Hilli, *Mukhtalaf,* 7:319.   [45] Al-Marghinani, *Al-Hidaya,* 2:649.
[46] Ibn Rushd, *Bidayat,* 3:1360–61; al-Marghinani, *Al-Hidaya,* 2:646.

him to mature.[47] The divergence of views is attributable, according to Ibn Rushd, to some fundamental differences in the understanding of *nafaqa*. The Malikis viewed maintenance as compensation for the enjoyment of a wife's body, while others saw it as provision for an individual in a state of "captivity"; in the latter case, maintenance should be paid if the wife had been delivered into her husband's keeping, whether he was capable of intercourse or not.[48]

When a man proved unable to meet his obligations to provide maintenance, legal schools varied as to the appropriate remedy. Hanafis held that the judge should step in and assign an appropriate level of maintenance to the wife, who would then be authorized to borrow this amount of money with eventual repayment to come from the husband. If the husband were absent, the judge might authorize the wife to use her husband's assets for maintenance, as long as they were appropriate for that purpose, i.e. food or clothing. A Hanafi judge would not, however, sell the property of an absentee to raise money for maintenance.[49] Hanbalis, Malikis, Shafi'is, and Shi'a, however, took a rather different view of the matter. If a husband were not able to meet his responsibility to provide at least basic maintenance (subsistence food, linen or cotton clothing) for his wife because of poverty or absence, then his wife could ask for divorce; should her husband refuse, the judge might counsel patience but then should impose the divorce if she wished it.[50]

It is abundantly clear in all these discussions of *nafaqa* that provision for a wife was not subject to the whim of the husband. Maintenance according to a certain standard of living in keeping with the economic situation of her husband was her right. Whatever her personal wealth or income might be, her husband was responsible for her food, clothing, shelter, and, in the opinion of many jurists, a host of other "necessities" of life. Failure to provide for her had serious consequences for her husband, from acquisition of debt to termination of the marriage. The Islamic judge was expected to act as an advocate for the wife by assigning her an appropriate amount of maintenance and helping her collect it from her husband. The jurists constructed the wife as her husband's dependent, but as a dependent with definite entitlements whose claims were to be treated with the utmost seriousness.

---

[47] Al-Hilli, *Mukhtalaf*, 7:320; Ibn Rushd, *Bidayat*, 3:1359.
[48] Ibn Rushd, *Bidayat*, 3:1360.   [49] Al-Marghinani, *Al-Hidaya*, 2:650.
[50] Al-Hilli, *Mukhtalaf*, 7:300; Ibn Ishaq, *Abrégé*, 135; Ibn Rushd, *Bidayat*, 3:1352.

The doctrine of *nafaqa* spelled out the wife's material claims on her husband, while the doctrine of *nushūz* fixed the price she was to pay. The concept of *nushūz*, disobedience or rebelliousness, might in theory be applied to behavior on the part of either husband or wife that violated the rights of the other spouse.[51] Most jurists discussed *nushūz*, however, exclusively in relation to a wife's responsibilities to her husband, what she must or must not do in order to retain her rights to maintenance. The husband's central right in marriage was his right to his wife's body: maintenance began when his wife became sexually available to him and could be terminated if she refused sexual intercourse or even his caresses, or left the marital domicile thereby making herself inaccessible to her husband. As al-Marghinani put it, "a husband's right to confine his wife at home is solely for the sake of securing to himself the enjoyment of her person"; and thus even if she refused intercourse, as long as she remained in her husband's house she should receive maintenance because he could force her to have sex.[52] Some jurists extended the husband's sexual rights to include the requirement that a wife obey her husband's orders to make herself attractive to him, for example by not eating offensive foods like garlic. If, on the other hand, a woman were to fall ill and not be physically able to sleep with her husband, this would not be *nushūz* as long as she remained in her husband's house where he could associate with her and she might be able to oversee domestic arrangements. The jurists differed as to whether she should receive maintenance if her absence were beyond her control: if she were imprisoned for debt, for example, some thought maintenance lapsed while others said it should be continued.[53]

The jurists tackled the tricky issue of the parameters of a husband's rights to wifely obedience versus his wife's religious and broader familial duties. A woman should not leave home to visit or travel without her husband's permission, but what if she wished to go on pilgrimage? Most differentiated between the annual hajj to Mecca, a ritual pilgrimage that all Muslims were enjoined to make at least once in their lifetimes if at all possible, and pilgrimages at other times and to other places. Shi'a and at least some Sunnis agreed that a woman could make the hajj without her husband's permission and, indeed, that he was required to continue her maintenance whether he traveled with her or not. In the case of other voluntary pilgrimages, however, most agreed that it was *nushūz* for a woman to go

---

[51] Vardit Rispler-Chaim, "Nushuz between Medieval and Contemporary Islamic Law: The Human Rights Aspect," *Arabica* 39, no. 3 (1992): 316.
[52] Al-Marghinani, *Al-Hidaya*, 2:644.   [53] Ibn Ishaq, *Abrégé*, 133–35; al-Marghinani, *Al-Hidaya*, 2:645.

without the permission of her husband.[54] Some of the discussions about personal religious devotion and *nushūz* veered into outright misogyny. Ibn Taymiyya, for example, in response to a question about a very devout woman who fasted during the day and prayed at night, refusing to come to her husband's bed, sided definitively with the husband:

> It is required for her to obey him if he calls her to bed, and that is the duty required of her. And as for praying at night and fasting during the day and thus disobeying him, how does a believing woman make such excessive religious observation her duty? And the Prophet said ... "A woman should not fast when her husband is present except with his permission, and she is not permitted [to do so] in his house without his permission."[55]

After citing this hadith, Ibn Taymiyya added a number of others to bolster his arguments that a woman should not engage in religious devotions that interfere with her husband's demands and pleasures, with the singular exception of fasting during Ramadan. Although Ibn Taymiyya's tone is by far the most strident, most jurists agreed that a wife could only defy her husband when it came to the fulfillment of required religious duties such as making the hajj or fasting during Ramadan. She could not extend or deepen her devotional practices if her husband felt that it interfered with his marital rights.

The jurists also agreed that it was *nushūz* for a wife to receive or make visits if forbidden to do so by her husband. The one exception to this rule lay in her right to visit with her parents and other relatives: her husband could not prevent her from seeing her parents at least once a week and her other relatives at least once a year. If her husband wished to have her company on his travels, however, there was disagreement: within the Hanafi tradition, for example, some say that a husband can take his wife wherever he wishes and others restrict this power to nearby destinations that would not cause undue hardships on the road. By the eighteenth century, the latter position appeared to be more widely embraced.[56]

Aside from obeying her husband's requests for sex and orders to remain at home or travel with him, were there other required duties the neglect of which constituted *nushūz*? Some jurists thought of marriage as a master–servant relationship: "the domestic service of a free husband is not permissible as a right of the wife by marriage contract because this would invert

---

[54] Al-Hilli, *Mukhtalaf*, 7:322; al-Marghinani, *Al-Hidaya*, 2:645.

[55] Ibn Taymiyya, *Fatawa al-Nisa'*, 232–33.

[56] Al-Marghinani, *Al-Hidaya*, 2:503; al-'Imadi, *Al-'Uqud*, 1:23, 32; al-Ramli, *Kitab al-Fatawa*, 1:27.

their relationship."[57] A wife's duties might include all kinds of housework, including cooking, cleaning, and laundry, according to some; others restricted the notion of required wifely service to sexual companionship.[58] One telling discussion involved whether a man could require his wife to nurse their child. Ibn Rushd noted that there were a number of opinions on the matter among Malikis: some jurists held that she was required to nurse the child without exception; some thought a poor or common woman could be so required but not a high-born woman; and still others held that no woman could be forced to nurse unless the baby rejected all other available breasts.[59] Shi'i jurists, in their typically egalitarian fashion that tended to eschew class differences and hierarchies, tended to concur that no wife could be forced to nurse, "whether she is high-born or low-bred, affluent or poverty-stricken, disreputable or noble."[60] If a mother did choose to nurse her baby, however, there was disagreement about whether or not she could collect a nursing "wage" from her husband, a wage always owed to a divorced wife who nursed the couple's child. Despite the great variety of opinions as to the extent of the husband's entitlements in the marriage, all jurists treated these entitlements as limited by law; the husband was the master of the house, without doubt, but his wife was not a mere slave or chattel. The jurists elaborated rules that outlined the rights and duties of husbands and wives in precise terms: there is little question about to whom the jurists gave the upper hand – this was a marital regime that legislated male dominance. But the husband had his responsibilities also that he might shirk only at the cost of losing his authority or even his wife.

The failure of either party to fulfill their gendered roles in marriage entailed consequences. A husband who did not provide maintenance for his wife had no right to her sexual services, and some legal schools also allowed her to seek divorce. A wife who did not obey her husband's legitimate demands, primarily to be available for a sexual relationship, forfeited her maintenance. Certain Qur'anic verses pointed to other possible sanctions:

> And those you fear may be rebellious
> admonish; banish them to their couches,
> and beat them. (4:34)

Ibn Taymiyya seized upon this verse as justification for beating disobedient wives, the only sanction he mentioned. Other jurists advocated an ascending scale of punishment for *nushūz*, first scolding, then suspending

[57] Al-Marghinani, *Al-Hidaya*, 2:496. [58] Rispler-Chaim, "Nushuz," 317. [59] Ibn Rushd, *Bidayat*, 3:1365. [60] Al-Hilli, *Mukhtalaf*, 7:304.

conjugal relations, and finally applying mild physical punishment. Yet others confined their discussion of consequences to the loss of maintenance.[61] No matter the sanction, however, *nushūz* could not but be a defining concept for marital relations, inscribing dominance and submission in the marital relationship.

The jurists further underscored a husband's right to sexual companionship by affirming the legality of polygyny. Qur'anic verses provided the basis for the rules:

> marry such women
> as seem good to you, two, three, four;
> but if you fear you will not be equitable,
> then only one, or what your right hands own
> so it is likelier you will not be partial.   (4:2)

There is little discussion of a man's right to marry up to four wives at a time; the jurists did not entertain questions about this right nor about the restriction of women to one husband at a time. What did draw their attention was the need to define "equitable" when it came to the treatment of wives. They focused on the allotment of a man's time (*qisma*) among his wives, elaborating on what it meant to treat wives equally. All wives, whether old or young, or married as virgins or non-virgins, had rights to equal time. The Malikis thought a nightly rotation was best, with the husband spending one day and one night with each wife in turn, although he might increase the time to two nights as long as he was consistent with all wives. The Hanafis held he could allot his time in larger chunks if he liked as long as he did it equally. There were some special exceptions: when he married a new wife, he could spend some extra time with her – seven consecutive nights in the case of a virgin bride and three nights for a non-virgin. He also might buy a wife's right to her time, with her agreement, so he could spend it with another wife, or a wife might donate her night to another. Should a wife refuse him on her night, he was free to spend the time with another wife of his choice. A man who went on a journey did not have to take all or none of his wives: he had the right to take one wife along if he chose and the time he spent with her would not count as part of his formal allotment. The Malikis and Hanafis thought he could choose whichever wife he preferred, but the Shafi'is thought he should select one by drawing lots.[62]

[61] Ibn Ishaq, *Abrégé*, 64; Ibn Taymiyya, *Fatawa al-Nisa'*, 233; al-Marghinani, *Al-Hidaya*, 2:644; Rispler-Chaim, "Nushuz," 319.
[62] Ibn Ishaq, *Abrégé*, 62–64; al-Marghinani, *Al-Hidaya*, 2:522.

The jurists agreed that although a man might be required to apportion his time equally, he could not be required to divide his sexual performance or his affections into equal parts. Whether he had intercourse with a given wife on her night was not the issue, rather "what is due is fairness, and fairness is in cohabitation, not in sexual performance for that depends on sexual vigor."[63] Still, wives had a right to "pleasure and companionship" which the husband should strive to meet. Among the Shi'a, there was some disagreement as a result over whether non-Muslim wives and/or slave wives had rights equal to those of free Muslim wives. Some thought that non-Muslims or slaves should only get half the time allotment of free wives, while others held that all wives had equal rights to the pleasures of marriage.[64] In all these discussions, the jurists took the position that the law should regulate what it could, namely the tangible division of time and the provision of maintenance in equal shares, and steer clear of lusts and affections that evade legislation. Yet, there is an undercurrent of tension here. They thought a wife had rights to sexual fulfillment and affection, but could a man in a polygynous marriage be required, somehow, to meet her needs? Although implicit here, it is not a question jurists will fully engage until the nineteenth century.

My discussion of the rights and duties of marriage as elaborated in the legal canon is not complete without some mention of temporary (*mut'a*) marriage, an alternate form of marriage in which rights and duties were defined very differently. Temporary marriage, in which the bride and groom agree to marry for a specified period of time at the end of which they are automatically divorced, was a form of marriage apparently well known at the time of the Prophet. The early jurists disagreed as to whether it continued to be sanctioned under Islam and, after a period of indecision, it was outlawed by all legal schools with the exception of the Ithna'ashari Shi'a.[65] Malik did not clearly forbid temporary marriage although he cited a hadith in which the Prophet Muhammad forbade it, and another report that the Caliph 'Umar had said that a couple who entered a temporary marriage should be stoned. Shafi'i took the position that a marriage contract with a specified time limit was invalid, but a couple might legitimately enter a marriage with the intention of making it temporary. Ibn Hanbal took a firm position against temporary marriage, finding even unexpressed

[63] Al-Marghinani, *Al-Hidaya*, 2:521.   [64] Al-Hilli, *Mukhtalaf*, 7:316–18.
[65] I. K. A. Howard, "Mut'a Marriage Reconsidered in the Context of the Formal Procedures for Islamic Marriage," *Journal of Semitic Studies* 20, no. 1 (spring 1975): 82–92.

intentions reprehensible and illegitimate.[66] By the twelfth century, Ibn Rushd could say with conviction (presumably not counting Shi'a as legitimate jurists) that "all of the jurists agree on its interdiction," disagreeing only as to the exact day on which the Prophet had pronounced this rule.[67]

Among the Shi'a, however, the Ithna' 'Asharis retained temporary marriage as a legitimate form, based on the Qur'anic verse:

> Such wives as you enjoy thereby,
> give them their wages apportionate; it is no
> fault in you in your agreeing together,
> after the due apportionate.   (4:24)

According to Shi'i jurists, a *mut'a* marriage contract needed to include a specified *mahr* and a definite period for the duration of the marriage which could range from hours to years. There was some disagreement as to whether a woman, particularly if she were a virgin, could arrange a temporary marriage for herself without the involvement of her family: some jurists required the permission of her father, while others held that she had the capacity to agree to a temporary marriage on her own as long as she did not disgrace her family. Temporary marriage relaxed many of the other rules of marriage. Many jurists viewed *mut'a* as a simple arrangement: the *mahr* was a rent paid for the groom's enjoyment of his bride for a specified period, after which there were no obligations. The wife could not claim maintenance nor did she have inheritance rights if her husband died during the term of marriage. Other jurists thought you could include stipulations in the contract that provided for inheritance and maintenance rights, while some even thought that the wife inherited from her temporary husband unless there was a stipulation to the contrary. There was also disagreement as to whether a man could marry more than four temporary wives at a time.[68] The extent to which a temporary marriage resembled a permanent marriage was thus a matter of considerable divergence: the Shi'i jurists acknowledged the legitimacy of *mut'a* marriage but they differed as to what rights and privileges it conferred. It definitely made sexual intercourse licit, but modified to various extents the marital regime of *nafaqa* and *nushūz*.

Marriage, as described in the legal canon, was a contractual relationship that conferred rights and duties in a highly gendered fashion. Husbands and wives, while subject to similar moral exhortations to support and cherish each other, were assigned very distinct responsibilities and privileges. The

---

[66] Ibn Hanbal, *Chapters*, 13, 115.   [67] Ibn Rushd, *Bidayat*, 3:1370.   [68] Al-Hilli, *Mukhtalaf*, 7:227–39.

jurists thus inscribed gender difference in the rules of marriage. This was not a regime of equality nor did it aspire to be one. Rather, the rules of Islamic marriage constructed the Male as breadwinner and patriarch of the household, and the Female as dependent and subservient. The legal canon, however, was not a monolith. As the jurists struggled with complex issues of fairness and human needs, they reached a range of different opinions about how the sacred texts should be given legal life. They were influenced by a number of factors, from the traditions of their sect and school to their own personal proclivities. The result was, as we have seen, a dizzying array of rules about marriage that varied from one sect or school to another, as well as within any given legal school, where multiple versions of doctrines might be developed simultaneously or over time. The continual growth, branching, and occasional pruning of legal thought produced a thick legal discourse that served as the touchstone for legal practice prior to the nineteenth century.

ISLAMIC MARRIAGE: PRE-TWENTIETH-CENTURY PRACTICES

How did ordinary women and men understand and live the law prior to the twentieth century? Was the legal discourse of the jurists indicative of legal practice? Were the Islamic courts and their clients cognizant of various interpretations of doctrinal points and did they draw on them to advantage? What kind of impact did the decisions of the courts and the activities of ordinary litigants in turn have on the development of Islamic rules for marriage? I am better able to pose than to answer many of these questions because of the limitations of our knowledge of legal practice prior to the twentieth century. Although reports of rulings according to Islamic law date back to the time of the Prophet and a formal system of judges and courts can be found as early as the Umayyad period in the eighth century, there are few extant records of legal practice for periods prior to the sixteenth century. We do have scattered legal documents – marriage contracts, for example – from earlier periods, but systematically preserved records of court actions that enable us to discuss in any detail patterns of legal practice when it came to marriage date only from the Ottoman period and cover Ottoman lands from the sixteenth through the nineteenth centuries. With few exceptions, then, the following discussion focuses on legal practices and developments during Ottoman times.

It seems to have been "customary," at least in many Ottoman cities, to register marriages in the court, a practice reinforced by a Sultanic decree in the sixteenth century that commanded the registration of all marriages.[69] This decree does not seem to have been consistently observed or enforced over the next few centuries, however, so that local religious authorities might oversee the signing of a contract that was not subsequently registered in court: in Rumelia, for example, it was common for the imam (religious ritual leader) of the quarter to conclude marriages without recourse to the judge and court.[70] In the cities of Syria and Palestine, practices of registration seemed to vary: the records of the Jerusalem court contain so many marriage contracts that most if not all marriages in that city must have been registered in court; in Damascus and Nablus, on the other hand, only a few marriage contracts appear to have been entered into the court records. We do not yet have enough information to understand these differences, but we can safely conclude that there was a range of practice when it came to registering a marriage contract. All the registered contracts adhere to the basic legal requirements of an offer and acceptance, a stated dower, and named witnesses to the agreement. This appears to have been the standard legal practice both inside and outside the courts.

The ability of women to arrange their own marriages in this period also varied. Most of the jurists of the official legal school of the Ottoman Islamic court system, the Hanafi school, had long held that a woman in her legal majority could arrange her own marriage without the participation of a guardian as we have seen above. In 1544, however, the Ottoman Sultan, exercising his prerogative as "Lord of the Caliphate" to interpret the shari'a, issued a decree forbidding women to marry without the express permission of their guardians, and instructing judges not to accept a marriage unless the bride's guardian had given his consent. Explaining that households will be "ruined" if women are allowed to act on their own, the Sultan assumed the stance of public patriarch and prescribed punishment for any who violated this order.[71] Despite the Sultan's intervention, many women, particularly if they had been previously married, continued to arrange their own marriages. In Dumyat (Egypt) in the sixteenth century, for instance, previously married women routinely handled their subsequent marriages.[72] In seventeenth- and eighteenth-century Syria and Palestine,

[69] Imber, *Ebu's-su'ud*, 165.
[70] Svetlana Ivanova, "The Divorce between Zubaida Hatun and Esseid Osman Aga," in *Women, the Family, and Divorce Laws in Islamic History*, ed. Amira El Azhary Sonbol (Syracuse: Syracuse University Press, 1996), 117.
[71] Imber, *Ebu's-su'ud*, 168–71.
[72] Amira El Azhary Sonbol, "Adults and Minors in Ottoman Shari'a Courts and Modern Law," in Sonbol, *Women, the Family, and Divorce*, 247.

jurists invariably took the dominant Hanafi position that an adult woman could not to be compelled to rely on, or even consult, her guardian. Regardless of their Sultan's decree to the contrary, the jurists of the Arab lands repeatedly affirmed a woman's right to enter a suitable marriage without interference.[73] It is impossible to say how many mature women actually exercised the right to arrange their marriages: it was fairly common for women to be represented in the court by an agent (*wakil*) who would convey their acceptance of a contract, but we have no way of knowing if this agent was a guardian with authority over them or merely a person they delegated to do their bidding. The fact that the jurists revisited this matter upon occasion, always affirming this right, does suggest that women were continuing to press the issue and that their actions helped preserve the Hanafi doctrine of the legal capacity of the mature woman to arrange a marriage in the face of inroads by the state power.

Females in their legal minority could be married off without their consent, of course, and it appears that it was not uncommon for families to make such arrangements in Ottoman times. We have many examples of marriage contracts drawn up for children, especially girls, in the court records, as well as evidence for the custom of making oral agreements to marry young children which would be binding once the children came of age. The jurists of the time agreed that a child marriage should not be consummated until the girl was physically ready for sexual relations, as discussed in the doctrine above. Still, a review of cases in nineteenth-century Palestinian courts reflects many of the different abuses no doubt inherent in this practice: marriages were consummated before the girl was "ready"; guardians pocketed the girl's dower; persons without proper authority, like a stepfather, made marriage arrangements for their own ends. Many of these girls who had been married off as minors did prove able to exercise their divorce option (*khiyār al-bulūgh*) once they came of age.[74] Still, the difficulties of protecting vulnerable girls despite the many rules governing their marriage arrangements are all too apparent. That people brought these issues to court attests to the prevalence of child marriage but also to the belief that child brides should not be victimized and that the courts could be expected to provide redress.

Adult women could better protect themselves by taking advantage of the right to insert stipulations into the marriage contract, with the agreement of

---

[73] Al-'Imadi, *Al-'Uqud*, 1:18–19, 31; al-Ramli, *Kitab al-Fatawa*, 1:24.
[74] Mahmoud Yazbak, "Minor Marriages and *Khiyar al-Bulugh* in Ottoman Palestine: A Note on Women's Strategies in a Patriarchal Society," *Islamic Law and Society* 9, no. 3 (2002): 386–409.

the groom to be sure. We have the most consistent information on this practice in the case of Egypt, where a marriage contract drawn up as early as the ninth century conferred upon the bride the power to effect the divorce of any second wife her husband might acquire and sell or manumit any slave woman he took as a concubine. In addition, the contract stipulated that the bride could make and receive visits with her family members whenever she wished.[75] By Mamluk times (thirteenth to fifteenth centuries), a variety of stipulations had become commonplace, such as allowing a wife to opt for divorce should her husband drink wine or fail to house and support her children from a previous marriage.[76] In the Ottoman era, the technique of expanding a bride's rights through contractual stipulation continued apace: a woman might insert clauses into her contract that gave her the right of divorce if the husband did any number of things, including taking a second wife, changing their residence against her will, traveling more than once a year, moving permanently to a distant location, or beating her with enough force to leave marks. The Islamic courts of sixteenth-century Egypt registered contracts with such stipulations for both Muslim and Christian (Coptic) couples, the latter of which were not required to register their marriages in the Islamic court but often chose to do so for reasons we do not fully understand.[77] Many of these stipulations underscored the rights to fair treatment that many jurists thought women enjoyed in any case; their inclusion in the contract seemed to serve the purpose of reminding the husband of his obligation to treat his wife decently as well as giving the wife clear means of redress. Other stipulations, such as those concerning a second wife or concubine, meant that the husband effectively suspended his legal right to polygyny in the context of this particular marriage.

One study of seventeenth-century marriage contracts registered in Cairo estimates that a third of them included stipulations, the most detailed of which were often found in the contracts of previously married women of comfortable artisanal or merchant-class backgrounds. These women spelled out the rules for their marital relationships with careful attention to their personal freedoms. A woman might stipulate that her husband should not prevent her from going to the public baths, visiting her lady friends when she wished, receiving visits from her children, other relatives, and friends whenever she wanted, and making the pilgrimage to Mecca. Others might

---

[75] Rapoport, "Matrimonial Gifts," 14–15.
[76] Yossef Rapoport, *Marriage, Money and Divorce in Medieval Islamic Society* (Cambridge: Cambridge University Press, 2005), 74–75.
[77] Mohamed Afifi, "The Personal Laws of Egyptian Copts," in Sonbol, *Women, the Family, and Divorce*, 204.

specify precisely what kinds of clothing (silk garments) or housing (living with her family) she expected her husband to provide or agree to.[78] It is abundantly clear in such contracts that the brides were shifting the terms of the marital relationship by restricting their husbands' authority over them: they were negotiating the terms of *nushūz* that would govern these marriages. Wives were still expected to obey their husbands, but stipulations put certain demands for obedience off limits while they also raised the bar for the amount of maintenance (*nafaqa*) a woman could expect to receive. The development of stipulations in the marriage contract was a way of altering the *nushūz–nafaqa* balance that shaped the marital relationship.

Not all women were in a position to insert stipulations into their marriage contracts. In the case of Egypt, it was older and more affluent women who seemed to have the assurance and clout needed to insist on stipulations. In eighteenth-century Syria and Palestine, it was rare for any marriage contract to contain stipulations. I cannot say with any certainty what accounts for this difference. In both areas, as provinces of the Ottoman Empire, Hanafi law was the official school of the court system but other schools continued to have a presence: the Shafiʿi and Maliki schools had many adherents in Egypt, as did the Shafiʿi and to a lesser extent the Hanbali schools in Syria and Palestine. This legal pluralism promoted by mutual recognition among the Sunni schools of law meant that the richness and diversity of doctrine on stipulations and other issues were preserved in both regions. It appears likely, therefore, that local customs rather than doctrinal difference lay at the root of the divergence in the use of stipulations in marriage contracts.

Although stipulations might upon occasion modify the gendered regime of female maintenance in return for male authority, there is no evidence of any real legal challenge to this definition of marriage. Women were very active, however, in the defense of their rights to maintenance. Yossef Rapoport notes that, by the fifteenth century, marital *nafaqa* in Mamluk Egypt and Syria was routinely assigned and paid in cash, not in kind, and women pressed their husbands for payment of daily allowances and annual clothing costs to such an extent that marriage could produce serious legal indebtedness for husbands.[79] In eighteenth-century Syria and Palestine women frequently came to court to ask the judge to assign them a fixed amount of maintenance from their husbands who, whether from absence or inability, were failing to support them properly. The judge imposed an

[78] Nelly Hanna, "Marriage among Merchant Families in Seventeenth-Century Cairo," in Sonbol, *Women, the Family, and Divorce*, 152–53.
[79] Rapoport, *Marriage, Money and Divorce*, 59–63.

appropriate level of maintenance payments, calculated to supply the necessary provisions for a woman of her status, on the husband, authorized the wife to borrow the money she needed if her husband was not forthcoming, and held the husband responsible for any debts his wife so incurred.[80] This was clearly a standard practice of the courts, one that women could rely upon to coerce their husbands into holding up their end of the marriage bargain, a bargain that could place heavy and unremitting burdens on men.

The legal mechanisms for ensuring wifely obedience were not so clear. A husband could, of course, divorce his wife at will, as we shall see in the following chapter. He was also authorized, at least in theory, to suspend maintenance payments to a disobedient wife. In my own surveys of court cases in Ottoman Syria and Palestine, I did not find much evidence for the withholding of maintenance as a punitive measure; rather, almost all litigation surrounding maintenance focused on the husband's inability to pay. Nor was there anything in the court records to suggest that husbands could forcibly return their wives to the marital home. The jurists of the time did agree that a wife owed her husband obedience, particularly in regard to her presence in the marital home, and that her failure to remain or return home at his request rendered her disobedient (*nāshiza*) and led to the forfeiture of maintenance payments. In the fatwa literature, however, it was rather dramatic defiance that qualified as "disobedience." In one example, a woman left her husband to attend her sister's wedding in another town with the understanding she would return in a month; when she had not returned in a year's time, she was found to be disobedient.[81] We need more research on other times and places in order to learn if the legal requirement of obedience was or was not a commonly used tool of marital discipline.

I do not want to leave the impression that all pre-twentieth-century Muslims adhered faithfully to the rules of Islamic marriage. Certainly the inhabitants of the cities and towns of the Ottoman Empire knew what an Islamic marriage contract should contain and how a marriage should be arranged: all extant marriage contracts adhere to the legal guidelines. The sheer volume of cases brought to the Islamic courts confirms the fact that people also knew their rights under the law and were reasonably sure the court would protect them. This was certainly the case when it came to dower and maintenance, matters for which women in particular often called upon the court to secure their rights in marriage. Not all marriages were registered in court, however, despite orders from Istanbul. And the courts

---

[80] Tucker, *In the House*, 74–75.   [81] *Ibid.*, 64.

and jurists were no doubt much more in control of the situation in urban areas where dense networks of Islamic institutions (mosques, schools, etc.) helped extend and deepen the hold of the law. The rural hinterland was a different matter, and some of the jurists were known to complain about extra-legal and un-Islamic marriage practices among the peasants. Still, the overall impression is one of pre-twentieth-century communities where people practiced various forms of Islamic marriage, with its assignment of gendered rights and duties. Legal doctrines as elaborated by jurists were being actualized in the court setting as women and men sought to secure their rights and force others to meet their obligations. There was no fundamental alteration in the laws on marriage, but there were discernible accommodations of local custom and, more significantly for our present concerns, support of the kind of women's rights, such as the rights to make stipulations or collect maintenance, that blunted the sharp patriarchal edges of Islamic marriage.

REFORM AND MARRIAGE

A process of reforming and codifying Islamic law began as early as the mid-nineteenth century, when Ottoman reformers working in an official capacity, and their counterparts in British-controlled India, introduced commercial and penal codes and courts of largely European inspiration, effectively removing these matters from the jurisdiction of Islamic law. The laws governing most family relationships, including marriage, were not initially part of this state-sponsored reform project. The official elites, whether indigenous or colonial, focused their attention on the laws most directly affecting the economic and political interests of modernizing states. Family matters were more conveniently left to "traditional" Islamic law and Islamic courts, which served as symbols of the Islamic identity and cultural continuity of the new political order. Prior to World War I, there was little interest on the part of state officials in the rethinking and reform of Islamic laws governing the marital relationship.

Rather, it was Islamic thinkers like Muhammad 'Abduh, Muhammad Rashid Rida, and, a bit later, al-Tahir al-Haddad, men who might upon occasion hold official position but identified primarily with the traditional religious intellectual elite, who raised questions about the need to reform the Islamic laws governing marriage in the late nineteenth and early twentieth centuries as part of a more general discussion of the ways in which Islam should and could adapt to the demands of the modern world and the challenges of western encroachments. They called for a return to the sources, the Qur'an and prophetic traditions, in order to capture and rekindle the essence of the Islamic message and reinterpret the law accordingly. They wanted to modernize Islamic law, to ensure its continued relevance to the lives of contemporary Muslim communities; they were interested not necessarily in codifying the law, but rather in interpreting its rules in ways that would allow Muslims to live in accord with their religion in the modern world. They tended to distance themselves from *fiqh* literature in favor of focusing on the original Islamic message and exploring how that message was to be realized in their times. Obviously, they were feeling the pressures of change: much of the shari'a was already sidelined by the new codes of European design. Furthermore, by the late nineteenth century, many members of indigenous elites, women in particular, were beginning to criticize the Islamic rules for marriage and divorce as inimical to the development of strong and healthy families central to the building of national life. And European colonialists were apt to point to laws that discriminated against women in the family as evidence for the inferiority of Islamic culture and the need for European tutelage.

Faced with these challenges to the continuity and integrity of the shari'a, reform-minded 'ulama' returned to the texts in order to face the future. In the case of marriage, they examined key sources, especially the Qur'an, to uncover the Islamic bedrock of the marital relationship. Al-Tahir al-Haddad, a reformist Tunisian *'ālim* of the early twentieth century, came to the conclusion that Islamic marriage should be based on "feelings of love and sympathy," on the mutual affection of two souls at peace with each other.[82] He further explored the Islamic view of marriage by surveying six of the most prominent Tunisian 'ulama', both Malikis and Hanafis, as to their views on a dozen related issues, including one directly focused on companionate marriage: "Is the woman at home an equal companion of her husband and do they participate together in undertakings, or is she a minor under his control, like a tool in the household [intended] to implement his decisions …?" The responses suggest a range of opinion in 1920s Tunisia among the most influential jurists. Drawing on material from the Qur'an and hadith, some objected vigorously to thinking of a wife as a tool to be used to carry out her husband's orders, but rather stressed the partnership of spouses in household projects and their reciprocal companionship. Others supported the idea of a hierarchical household in which male leadership was ordained by Islam because of the greater physical strength and worldliness

---

[82] Al-Tahir al-Haddad, *Imra'atuna fi al-Shari'a wa-l-Mujtama'* (Cairo: al-Majlis al-A'la li-l-Thaqafa, 1999), 43.

of the man, but noted that his power over his wife had definite limits.[83] The very posing of such a question, of course, suggests that companionate marriage was on the agenda for discussion, that the "essence" of marriage was a topic of considerable interest, and that reform-minded 'ulama' were ready and willing to tackle the details of marriage with such guiding principles in mind.[84]

On the issue of a woman's right to participate in the arrangement of her marriage, for example, Muhammad Rashid Rida (Syrian-Egyptian, 1865–1935) pointed out that the forced marriage of women by despotic relatives belonged to the pre-Islamic dark ages; Islam gave women rights to accept or refuse a marriage. Although a *wali* plays a role in marriage arrangements, primarily by assuring that his charge marries a suitable man, Rida cited two separate hadith narratives that document the Prophet's insistence on the full consent of a woman to any marriage.[85] When al-Tahir al-Haddad polled the Tunisian 'ulama' in the 1920s on the same question, we find predictable differences between the Hanafis among them who upheld the woman's right to choose her husband, and Malikis who traditionally gave the father the right of coercion (*jabr*) over his daughter. Even among the Malikis, however, there is clearly some rethinking of the issue. One Maliki mufti cited with approval the hadith establishing the Prophet's opposition to any forced marriage: in this narrative, a young woman whose father had married her off to her cousin asked the Prophet if the arrangement needed her permission, and he responded that indeed it did. In citing this narrative, al-Najjar, the Maliki mufti, is revising the Maliki doctrine that a father can marry off his daughter as he pleases by insisting on her permission for any valid marriage arrangement.[86]

Discussions of *nushuz* followed similar paths as jurists interrogated the sources. Rida acknowledged that the Qur'an (4:34) criticized women who defied their husbands' authority and called for graduated punishment, including beating, to discipline them. He was quick to note, however, that a number of hadith actively discouraged wife-beating, finding it a repugnant act under all circumstances. Nor should one jump to the

[83] *Ibid.*, 67–85.
[84] This is not to suggest that his ideas immediately carried the day. Tahir al-Haddad was vilified and his career ruined after his book was condemned by Tunisian 'ulama' and subsequently banned in his homeland. See Mounira Charrad, *States and Women's Rights: The Making of Postcolonial Tunisia, Algeria, and Morocco* (Berkeley: University of California Press, 2001), 216–17.
[85] Muhammad Rashid Rida, *Huquq al-Nisa' fi al-Islam wa-Hazzihina min al-Islah al-Muhammadi al-'Amm: Nida' ila al-Jins al-Latif* (Cairo: Maktabat al-Turath al-Islami, 1984), 19–20.
[86] Al-Haddad, *Imra'atuna*, 81.

conclusion that marital conflict was necessarily the fault of the wife; Rida thought that a man could be guilty of *nushūz* as well and that only careful exploration of the problems with help from both the spouses' families could clarify the situation.[87] Some of the Tunisian 'ulama', while recognizing the concept of *nushūz*, also limited the husband's right to demand obedience from his wife to his commands to come to bed or not leave the house – in all other matters she could do as she pleased. Others left it to the wife to judge whether her husband's commands were within reason according to the customs of her class or locality.[88] Throughout these discussions of *nushūz*, jurists reminded their readers that marriage was a moral regime, a partnership in which husband and wife cooperate for the good of their family and community, and that the problem of *nushūz* should not arise in a marriage founded on love and companionship.

This solicitude for healthy marriages also translated into reformist opposition to the practice of polygyny. Muhammad 'Abduh raised the issue in 1898, characterizing polygyny as an act permitted by the Qur'an only upon the condition of equal treatment of co-wives, a virtual impossibility. Rida followed up with a lengthy discussion of the topic based on material from the Qur'an and Prophetic sayings and practices. The Prophet's own experience of polygyny was set aside as exceptional, the product of special circumstances, in favor of a close reading of the Qur'anic injunction (4:2) that a man should only practice polygyny if he could be just and fair. Rida pointed out that feelings are never equal or fair, and the challenge is then one of making sure that differences in feelings do not produce unequal treatment. Given the difficulty inherent in this undertaking, Rida thought a responsible Muslim might conclude that he should marry only one wife. Equally central to his argument was his belief that monogamy was the best form of marriage, most likely to result in the kind of happy and stable union that was best for the nation, although national priorities might at times allow for polygyny – if, for example, there were a temporary surplus of unmarried women.[89]

Malak Hifni Nasif, an Egyptian woman who wrote in an Islamic reformist mode during the first decade of the twentieth century, also embraced the idea of companionate marriage as an aspiration of the "modern" woman:

they [modern women] are not satisfied with just clothing and food like a domestic servant, but they prize marital happiness more than before and they know that if

---

[87] Rida, *Huquq*, 38–42.   [88] Al-Haddad, *Imra'atuna*, 70, 77.   [89] Rida, *Huquq*, 45–52.

love is not at the foundation of the marital relationship and there is no devoted companionship, the couple will be incompatible and quarrelsome.[90]

Nasif was particularly concerned about marriage age, and identified the practice of marrying off young girls to older men as anathema to companionate marriage and a major obstacle to the formation of a modern household, as injurious to under-age brides and their husbands alike. How could a young girl possibly know how to satisfy her husband, manage his household, his money, and his servants, and raise his children? Early marriage increased the incidence of infant mortality and the likelihood of producing ailing offspring, and posed real dangers to the psychological and physical health of young mothers. She therefore argued that age sixteen should be the minimum marriage age for girls. Differences in age also placed insurmountable barriers between husband and wife, and "turned the natural order upside down."[91] Nasif did not object to arranged marriage and the close participation of families in the marriage contract, but she did think that prospective spouses should be able to meet under supervision in order for them to ascertain their compatibility. Nasif was more focused on the female experience of marriage than were most of the male reformers, but she fully concurred with their position that a "modern" companionate marriage could and should be lived under Islamic laws and principles.

The theme of modern marriage and the good of the nation reveals some of the reformers' foremost concerns. Reforming Islamic marriage was a demand of religion, an attempt to realize God's justice in the modern world, but it was also a political project that aimed at strengthening the social fabric of the Muslim community so that Islam as a religion and the various Muslim nations could resist European control and fashion their own futures. Islamic reformers argued that a monogamous, companionate marriage (although one in which there was a complementarity rather than an equality of roles) best met the criteria of a true Islamic marriage as developed in the sources, and also could serve as the foundation for a strong modern nation. The Muslim jurists who developed these ideas, however, were not primarily responsible for the subsequent construction of reformed legal codes that came to regulate marriage in most Islamic countries. Indeed, they were engaged not in a systematic review of the rules of Islamic marriage for bias or discrimination, but rather in an exploration of the sources and principles upon which "modern" notions of Islamic marriage could be

---

[90] Malak Hifni Nasif, *Al-Nisaʾiyat: Majmuʿat Maqalat Nushirat fi al-Jarida fi Mawduʿ al-Marʾah al-Misriya* (Cairo: Multaqa al-Marʾa wa-l-Dhakira, 1998), 57.
[91] *Ibid.*, 79–82.

based. The actual reform of laws governing marriage was a project that drew on their ideas, but was largely the work of state-sponsored officials taking a piecemeal approach to the problem of reform as they worked to extend the power of modern nation-states.

I do not mean to imply that the state had not previously been in the business of regulating marriage: as I noted above, the Ottoman state over-saw the system of Islamic courts that registered marriage contracts and adjudicated marital conflicts, and even attempted, at times, to require that all marriages be registered in court. Still, the Islamic judicial system, with its diversity of schools, doctrines, courts, and jurists of both official position and unofficial standing, eluded comprehensive state control. With the Ottoman Law of Family Rights (OLFR) of 1917, however, the state stepped up its regulation of the marital institution and self-consciously sought to bring the marriage practices of its citizens into sync with its vision of modernity. For example, articles 4–6 of the OLFR forbid guardians to marry off girls younger than nine and boys younger than twelve, and further allowed the marriage of girls between the ages of nine and seventeen and boys between the ages of twelve and eighteen only with the permission of the court. According to Norman Anderson, the legal basis for these articles was the position of three early jurists, Ibn Shubruma, 'Uthman al-Batti, and Abu Bakr al-Asamm, who argued that there was no legal justification for marrying off a ward before she or he had reached puberty. In the Explanatory Memorandum accompanying the OLFR, the framers validated these articles not only on the basis of these minority opinions, but also by citing the evils of child marriage and the responsibility of the Ruler to impose rules for the good of the community. In subsequent reform codes, promulgated in most Middle East countries over the course of the twentieth century, the framers continued to expand the principle of *takhayyur* to

any opinion put forward in one of the Sunni schools; or even to doctrines advocated by early jurists at a time before the schools became crystallized, by one of the Sunni schools which previously existed, but have now become extinct, or by a later jurist of highly independent views ... on some occasions they ventured to adopt a doctrine which was really of Shi'i origin, although they seldom, if ever, acknowledged this in regard to legislation promulgated in a predominantly Sunni country.[92]

In selecting a particular doctrine in response to each legal question, the framers of these codes were, of course, engaged in the fundamental trans-formation of Islamic law from a shari'a of vast textual complexity and

---

[92] Anderson, *Law Reform*, 50.

interpretive possibilities to a modern legal code of fixed rules and penalties. In the process, they changed and standardized many of the practices and understandings of Islamic marriage.

First, from the promulgation of the OLFR in 1917 to subsequent personal status codes issued in Algeria, Egypt, Indonesia, Iraq, Jordan, Kuwait, Lebanon, Libya, Morocco, Pakistan, Syria, Tunisia, and Yemen, it was clear that the various states intended to take full control of the marriage process.[93] Almost all reformed codes insist that a marriage, to be legally recognized, must be registered by a judge or other designated state official. Most codes required that the court collect certain kinds of information about the bride and groom: in the OLFR, prospective couples must furnish their names, religions, occupations, parents, and marriage eligibility, and the court should then verify the information.[94] Registration procedures served as the primary mechanism for enforcing other aspects of the reformed codes, because a marriage that did not conform to the new rules on child marriage or polygyny, for example, could not be registered. In some cases, such as the Indonesia Marriage Act of 1974, a marriage without valid registration had no validity whatsoever.[95] In other cases, such as in Egypt, an unregistered marriage is still a valid marriage under Islamic law, but it has no standing in court and therefore neither spouse could resort to the court to assert marital rights or call in obligations. Often, there were prescribed penalties as well for participating in marriages that violated certain rules of the code.

The authors of these codes worked within a framework of piecemeal correction of marriage practices that appeared to be blatantly discriminatory or perhaps out of date. The codes addressed many of the aspects of marriage most closely associated with problems of the gendering of rights and duties, including child marriage, guardianship, contract stipulations, *nafaqa/ nushūz*, and polygyny. Following the precedent of the OLFR, most fixed a minimum age for marriage, at anywhere from nine to sixteen for girls, and twelve to nineteen for boys. Anyone facilitating the marriage of children

---

[93] The following discussion of twentieth-century legal codes is based on: the text of the codes of the Arab World in Dawoud Sudqi El Alami and Doreen Hinchcliffe, *Islamic Marriage and Divorce Laws of the Arab World* (London: Kluwer Law International, 1996); those of India and Pakistan in David Pearl, *A Textbook on Muslim Personal Law*, 2nd edn (London: Croom Helm, 1987); and those of Indonesia and Malaysia in M. B. Hooker, *Islamic Law in South-East Asia* (Singapore and Oxford: Oxford University Press, 1984).

[94] This, and all subsequent discussion of the Ottoman Law of Family Rights of 1917, is based on the version published in "Ottoman Law of Family Rights (Qanun Huquq al-ʿAʾila)," in Yusuf Ibrahim Sadr, ed., *Majmuʿat al-Qawanin*, trans. ʿArif Afandi Ramadan (Beirut: Matbaʿat Sadr, 1937).

[95] Hooker, *Islamic Law in South-East Asia*, 272.

below the minimum age was usually subject to criminal penalties, and such marriages, although they might or might not have legal validity, could not serve as the basis for legal actions in court. Alongside a minimum marriage age, most codes also set ages for full competence in marriage, generally in the range of fifteen to twenty for a female, and seventeen to twenty-one for a male; to marry at a younger age required the consent of the court, and often the girl's guardian as well, both of whom should consider whether the benefits outweighed the harms of early marriage. This was something of an innovation. Islamic jurists had been concerned about the consummation of marriages with minors who were not physically ready for sexual intercourse, but they had never discussed the imposition of a minimum age post-puberty for signing a marriage contract, so that countries which do not have a reformed code, like Saudi Arabia, Bahrain, Qatar, and the Arab Emirates, also do not have a minimum marriage age.[96] Implicit in a minimum marriage age is the distinctly modern notion that marriage could be harmful to physically mature teenagers, could limit their options and their development, considerations that are being inserted into the Islamic legal structure. Whether such rules had the impact intended is another question: one study of the effect of minimum marriage ages on actual marriage practices in Indonesia found that age at marriage was steadily rising in the second half of the twentieth century, but not in a way that correlated with the passage of the National Marriage Act in 1974.[97]

The reformed codes have had rather less to say about the ways in which women could bolster their position with the strategic insertion of stipulations into the marriage contract. The Syrian code (1953), for example, did follow the Hanbali lead in allowing women to insert stipulations that could reinforce some benefit to the wife, such as level of maintenance or place of residence, or even restrict one of the husband's rights, such as the right to take a second wife. In the latter instance, however, a husband could not be absolutely prevented from doing what the law permits in marriage, i.e. taking a second wife, so a husband's violation of that sort of stipulation could enable the wife to dissolve *her* marriage but not that of the new wife. In general, in the OLFR as well as the codes of Jordan, Iraq, Lebanon, and Morocco, the wife was permitted, with her husband's agreement, to insert stipulations that did not violate the law or trespass on the essence of marriage (a stipulation restricting a husband's sexual access to his wife

---

[96] Munira Fakhro, "Gulf Women and Islamic Law," in Yamani and Allen, *Feminism and Islam*, 258.

[97] Mark Cammack, Lawrence A. Young, and Tim Heaton, "Legislating Social Change in an Islamic Society – Indonesia's Marriage Law," *American Journal of Comparative Law* 44, no. 1 (1996): 45–73.

would therefore not be acceptable), and any violation of such stipulations could trigger her right to insist on divorce. Although the subject of stipulations was thus broached in many of the modern reformed codes, discussion of the matter was terse: the codes do not generally give examples of stipulations nor do they provide for procedures that would encourage the use of stipulations, such as making room for them in a standardized marriage contract. Overall, what we have is a passive approach to stipulations; unspecified "reasonable" stipulations are allowable, but there is no suggestion of the possibilities they offer for the individualized reform of marriage.

The reformed codes dealt in a similarly minimalist fashion with the subject of maintenance. In most twentieth-century codes, the husband is required to provide for his wife: in the words of the 1992 Yemeni law, the husband provides a "lawful domicile, maintenance, and clothing that befits them both" (art. 41). A wife has a right to these basics of food, clothing, and shelter in most codes, and a few, like that of Iraq, add the costs of medical care and domestic help if appropriate to the woman's status. The level of support required is variously calibrated to her status (Syria), his ability (Algeria), or both their circumstances (Tunisia). Thus most codes have retained the basic notion that the husband is the provider in a marriage, although some assign the responsibility of maintenance to the wife, if wealthy, in the case of a destitute husband (Libya), a provision with some basis in the legal tradition. The only dramatic departures from a marital regime in which the husband is the family's assigned breadwinner came in the form of family laws promulgated by socialist governments in the People's Democratic Republic of Yemen (1974) and the Republic of Somalia (1975) which made husbands and wives equally responsible for maintaining themselves and their households depending on their abilities.[98] Subsequent revisions and replacements of these laws have since reinstituted the sole responsibility of the husband for maintenance. The codes do not, in any case, treat the issue of maintenance in any significant detail: the jurists' elaborate discussions of the standards of material support, privacy, and conviviality in maintenance arrangements have receded, to be replaced by a rather bare-bones enumeration of basic needs.

The topic of *nushūz* (disobedience) receives somewhat more detailed treatment in many of the reformed codes, although, contrary to at least some indications in the legal canon and the positions of Islamic reformers, only wives, not husbands, seem to be responsible for avoiding *nushūz* in a

---

[98] See Anderson, *Law Reform*, 74.

marriage. The codes vary as to what kinds of obedience a husband can demand from his wife. At one end of the spectrum, it is sexual companionship alone, and therefore disobedience is defined as a wife's refusal to be available to her husband, by leaving the house without his permission and ignoring his demands that she return. Jordan, Kuwait, and Syria, for example, define the disobedient wife as simply one who refuses to cohabit with her husband without justification – one possible such justification is her fear that she might suffer harm at his hands. At the other end of the spectrum, the wife's legal duties expand to obeying her husband generally and according him the respect he deserves as head of the household (Algeria), supervising the matrimonial home and all its affairs (Libya), working in the house in a manner appropriate to her station (Yemen), and showing respect towards her husband's parents and other relatives (Morocco); her failure to perform any of these myriad marital duties could be labeled *nushūz*. Although the core formula for marital relations of *nafaqa/nushūz* was thus preserved in most of the codes, they vary enormously in their definitions of what a husband can demand in the way of obedience, from the minimum of providing sexual companionship to a rather full array of domestic services in keeping with the range of possibilities present in canonical *fiqh*. The sanctions for *nushūz* are similar in most current codes, however: the disobedient wife loses her right to marital maintenance.

The "modernization" of Islamic law had taken a curious turn initially with the institution of the *bayt al-ṭāʿa* or "house of obedience." In Egyptian laws of 1897 and 1931 (The Regulation of Shariʿa Procedure), a husband who had secured a decree of his wife's *nushūz* from the court could then ask the local police to assist him in forcibly returning his wife to the marital home, the house of obedience.[99] Although there is no textual support for this practice in the Qurʾan or hadith, or among the canonical jurists, the institution had legal life in Egypt up to 1967, when it was cancelled by ministerial order.[100] The Jordanian Law of Family Rights (1951), article 33, similarly empowered a husband to seek the help of police to escort his *nāshiza* wife to the conjugal home "by force," but article 37 of the 1976 Jordanian Law of Personal Status subsequently limited the penalty for disobedience to forfeiture of maintenance only.[101] Forcible return to the conjugal household has largely disappeared in law and practice, but its

---

[99] Dawoud S. El Alami, "Law no. 100 of 1985 Amending Certain Provisions of Egypt's Personal Status Laws," *Islamic Law and Society* 1, no. 1 (1994): 120, n. 4.

[100] Ron Shaham, *Family and the Courts in Modern Egypt: A Study Based on Decisions by the Shariʿa Courts, 1900–1955* (Leiden: Brill, 1997), 73.

[101] Welchman, *Beyond the Code*, 231.

history is an interesting instance in which a modern innovation, calling upon the repressive apparatus of the state to enforce wifely obedience, took on the aura of tradition without, in fact, enjoying backing or precedent in Islamic legal theory or practice.

A final issue the reformed codes tackled was that of polygyny, one of the most central and troubling problems in the minds of Islamic modernists. Despite their arguments that polygyny was an inferior form of marriage, and one that threatened the health and future of the nation as a whole, many of the reformed codes treated the matter gingerly. The Explanatory Memorandum that accompanied the Ottoman Law of Family Rights echoed many of the criticisms of polygyny, but the Law itself left the man's right to marry up to four wives fully intact.[102] Codes in Jordan and Egypt hardly touched on the subject, so that a man could legally marry a second wife without even informing the first. Other codes, drawing on the Qur'anic exhortation to marry more than one wife only if they could be treated equally and fairly, gave the courts responsibility for determining the likelihood of equal treatment. In the Syrian code, for example, a man must have the permission of the court for a polygynous marriage and the court may withhold permission if it deems the man unable to support more than one wife properly. In Pakistan, under the Muslim Family Laws Ordinance (1961), an arbitration council composed of representatives of the husband, the first wife, and the judge investigates a husband's request to take a second wife; the council must conclude that a second marriage is "necessary and just" based on evidence of the first wife's infertility, ill health, etc. before the second marriage can be registered. In Iraq and Morocco as well, the permission of the judge, who screens the request for any possible injustice, is required for a second marriage. And in Tunisia, the code took the radical step of prohibiting polygyny altogether, and subjecting the parties to a second marriage contract to criminal sanctions.[103] The codes have varied, then, from complete toleration to outright prohibition of polygyny.

How can we understand the striking absence of uniformity in the reformed codes when it comes to issues so clearly central to marriage and marital relations, like guardianship, wifely duties, or the practice of polygyny? In part, it is a product of the nature of Islamic law, the availability of a number of different schools, doctrines, and opinions on which reformers drew as they searched for rules that seemed, to them, to fit present circumstances and concerns. Employing the methodology of *takhayyur*, they could pick and choose from among many possibilities. None of the reformed codes, as far as

---

[102] Anderson, *Law Reform*, 62.   [103] See *ibid.*, 110; Pearl, *A Textbook on Muslim Law*, 72.

I can determine, slavishly follows one jurist or the majority opinions of one school; rather, they are patchwork quilts made out of legal doctrines from a variety of sources. Furthermore, reformers could avail themselves, when necessary, of the practice of *ijtihād*, or interpretation of the sources, as openly advocated and pursued by Islamic modernists. The restrictions or outright prohibitions that some placed on polygyny, for example, were justified by a reexamination of the relevant Qur'anic verses and conclusions reached about how best to realize their full intent in the modern period. Those who framed the reform codes were not necessarily steeped in traditional Islamic legal sources or methods, but they were able to draw on the discussions of a generation of 'ulama', like Muhammad 'Abduh or Muhammad Rashid Rida, who were both knowledgeable and creative. Finally, the reformers had the power of their respective states behind them. Theirs was not simply an intellectual exercise in reviewing the law, but also a state project geared to specific agendas: in every case legal reform entailed the assertion of state power over religious courts and personnel as well as basic questions of identity implicit in marriage practices. The appropriate age for marriage, or role for a father, or responsibility of a husband were all matters of import for the fashioning of social practices and institutions that could contribute to the development of the nation just as they symbolized the "modernization" and unity of the population. I am not suggesting that the state through legal reform sought to eliminate the power of the family in favor of state control of all social relationships; on the contrary, some aspects of the new codes actually expanded family involvement in the lives of a married couple. But family control of marriage was now to operate under the watchful eye of the state, whose courts and jurists had ultimate authority over marriage practices. That each nation-state approached these issues somewhat differently was a product of variations in the concrete context of the reform process.

To what extent did these legal reforms intersect with some key aspects of feminist theory: the liberal issue of discrimination, the woman-centered concern to capture female experience, or the deconstructive project of confronting basic gendering practices? Certainly some of the reforms were geared to the amelioration of what seemed to be discriminatory rules for marriage: the increased regulation and even prohibition of polygyny is one such example and the insistence on female consent to all marriage arrangements is another. I would argue, however, that despite some attempts to improve women's situation the law continued to discriminate rather openly between men and women: in the whole matter of marital duties, there is little pretense of male–female equality. Nor is there much trace of a concern with the particular female experience of marriage. Indeed, the reformed codes are virtually silent on many of the "private" aspects of marriage that occupied the attention of the jurists. A wife's rights to sexual satisfaction in marriage or her need of companionship in the domestic setting, issues which the jurists had discussed in minute detail, have disappeared in the reformed codes, replaced by a series of brief regulations that speak only to her rights to food, housing, and medical care. The reformed law has narrowed the scope of intervention into conjugal relations. And finally, many of the basic gendering strategies appear to be intact. The husband as breadwinner, household head, and ultimate authority versus the wife as dependent and subservient are inscribed in the reformed codes in almost all cases, with the fleeting exception of the codes promulgated as part of radical socialist programs. Still, the law has continued to be a focus of ongoing discussions and reform projects, an arena of significant contest over what Islamic marriage means. We need to look at a few currently controversial issues to get a sense of how ordinary women and men are joining the discussion.

RECENT DEVELOPMENTS

There are a number of lively legal issues surrounding Islamic marriage law that have engaged the attention of jurists and laypeople alike in recent years. I cannot hope to cover all the hot issues here, but rather will focus on two: campaigns against polygyny, and the reservations concerning marriage that many Islamic states entered when signing CEDAW (The Convention for the Elimination of Discrimination against Women).

The practice of polygyny has occasioned considerable debate in recent times. In Malaysia, for example, women's groups have organized to conduct a "Campaign for Monogamy," launched on March 16, 2003.[104] The campaign followed on years of discussion and memoranda sent to state authorities, primarily under the leadership of the Malaysian organization Sisters in Islam, expressing concern about the practice of polygyny. Under the Malaysian Islamic Family Law Act of 1984, polygamous marriage was possible within limits set by a number of other reformed codes: a man who wished to marry a second wife could only do so by applying to the shari'a court. The court was to scrutinize his application to ensure that the proposed marriage would satisfy a number of conditions, including: (1) the proposed marriage was just and necessary; (2) the man had the financial ability to support present

---

[104] For information on this and other activities of Sisters in Islam, see their website: www.muslimtents.com/sistersinislam.

and future dependents; (3) he had the ability to accord his wives equal treatment; (4) the proposed marriage would not cause harm to the first wife; and (5) the first wife would not experience a drop in her standard of living. Malaysian women's groups had long expressed concern, however, that these controls on polygyny were being steadily eroded. Various state jurisdictions implemented the process of scrutiny randomly, if at all, and some key amendments, including the removal of the condition concerning the first wife's standard of living, had been passed. Men would engage in polygamous marriages abroad or in states with lax processes, and then, after paying a token fine, register the marriage after the fact. In addition, the women's groups pointed to several missing elements in the legislation, including a requirement that the first wife be informed of her husband's application for a second marriage and that she have easy recourse to divorce if she wished.

The campaign did not confine itself to a critique of the details or lax enforcement of the law. Sisters in Islam and their allies engaged basic questions about Islamic marriage. Was polygyny a right of Muslim men? Did Muslim wives have a say as to whether they would have a co-wife? Their "Memorandum on Reform of the Islamic Family Laws on Polygamy" (December 11, 1996) explored the textual basis for polygyny, including the Qur'anic verse 4:3 that talks of marrying two, three, or four only if you can deal with them justly, and verse 4:129 that comments on how difficult (impossible) it is to deal justly between women.[105] Drawing on the translation and commentary of Abdullah Yusuf Ali, an Islamic modernist, they reach the conclusion that the Qur'an actually recommends monogamy. The Memorandum also cited a Prophetic tradition in which the Prophet Muhammad forbade his son-in-law 'Ali to marry another woman until he divorced his wife Fatima, Muhammad's daughter, because such an act would trouble and harm her. And, according to their reasoning, the requirement to deal justly and without harm would surely entail the first wife's consent to a second marriage. In light of such textual guidance and recent experience with polygyny provisions, the memorandum called for a number of reforms and revisions, including: strict enforcement of the four conditions a polygamous marriage must meet, and reinstatement of the fifth condition about the first wife's standard of living; the increase in penalties, both fines and prison terms, for practicing polygyny without permission; institution of a new application form for permission that would require detailed information and supporting documents to prove that all legal

---

[105] Sisters in Islam and Association of Women Lawyers, "Memorandum on Reform of the Islamic Family Laws on Polygamy" (December 11, 1996), www.sistersinislam.org.my/memo/040197.htm.

conditions were being met and that the wife's consent had been obtained; and inclusion of polygamous marriage as grounds for divorce in the standard *ta'liq* certificate. The last refers to a standard list of conditions that, if agreed upon in advance, activate the wife's right to a divorce; polygamous marriage would be added to the current grounds of desertion, non-maintenance, and cruelty. The Memorandum thus combined doctrinal discussion, the Islamic case for restricting polygyny, with a set of recommendations as to how to put some teeth and consistency into current legislation as well as institute new provisions, particularly in regard to the first wife's consent.

The Malaysian women's groups thus built their case with care, situating their concerns and conclusions squarely within the framework of Islamic doctrine and the Islamic reform tradition. There was not, however, much response from the state. One high-profile case of enforcement came in the spring of 2002 when the Kelantan State Assembly Speaker was found guilty of committing polygyny without consent of the shari'a court and local authorities. Sisters in Islam applauded the verdict but decried the penalty, a light fine, submitting that an onerous fine and a jail sentence would have been more appropriate. After another year of little remedial action, they led the Coalition on Women's Rights in Islam in the opening salvos of the Campaign for Monogamy, announcing four aims: (1) to educate people that polygyny is not the norm in Islamic marriage; (2) to promote a commitment to monogamy; (3) to enable a first wife to get a *ta'liq* divorce if she did not want to remain in a polygamous marriage; (4) to help women make informed decisions by securing their right to know the marital status of the man they are marrying, their right to be informed if their husbands are contemplating another marriage, and their right to choose to stay in or leave a polygamous marriage and not suffer hardship. The third and fourth aims could only be realized, of course, with the full cooperation of the state, which was charged with the administrative and judicial oversight of the practice of polygyny: it was up to state authorities, according to the Coalition on Women's Rights, to institute the necessary procedures for the registration of existing marriages, the application for polygamous marriages, and the arrangements for divorce, property, and maintenance settlements that would safeguard the rights of women and children.

In response to vocal opposition to the Campaign from muftis and other religious figures in Malaysia, the Coalition was quick to point out that it had not called for an outright ban on polygyny; it was not anti-Islamic. Rather, the Coalition was united in its desire to further the Islamic demand of justice in marriage. The Campaign for Monogamy thus took the religious high ground by carefully basing its program on Islamic text and Islamic ethics, and by eschewing any reference to non-Islamic marriage practices. I cannot speculate as to how successful this campaign is likely to be in terms of the eventual elimination of polygyny in Malaysia, but the strategies it has used to confront common problems of achieving legitimacy and efficacy for legal reform have been impressive.

Engagement with the UN-sponsored Convention on the Elimination of All Forms of Discrimination against Women (CEDAW) has been a very different approach to the reform of marriage laws, using the strategy of conforming to international standards rather than indigenous traditions. CEDAW, which first entered into force in 1981, requires all States parties to eliminate discrimination on the basis of gender in public and private spheres. The Convention has been ratified or acceded to over the years by upwards of 169 countries, including a number of countries with predominantly Muslim populations such as Egypt, Indonesia, Iraq, Jordan, Kuwait, Libya, Morocco, Pakistan, Saudi Arabia, Tunisia, and Yemen. Although they are parties to the Convention, all of these countries have availed themselves of the opportunity to enter reservations to certain articles of the Convention on the grounds of incompatibility with religion or a "higher law." Many of the reservations focus on the articles most relevant to marriage matters: article 15 which gives women full equality with men in all civil matters, including rights of freedom of movement and choice of residence; and article 16 which accords to women the same rights as men in the matters of choice of marriage and spouse, as well as equality of rights and responsibilities within marriage.

Egypt's explanation of reservations to these two articles invoked the Islamic shariʿa and its provision for *mahr* and maintenance for the wife as instituting an "equivalency of rights and duties so as to ensure the complementarity which guarantees true equality between spouses, not a quasi-equality that renders the marriage a burden on the wife." Morocco made similar reservations, referring to the "framework of equilibrium and complementarity" of Islamic law. Jordan noted that the wife's domicile was legally that of her husband, and Morocco and Tunisia both made article 15 subject to its compatibility with their Personal Status codes as they pertained to marital residence. All these reservations weigh the provisions of CEDAW against an "Islamic" legal standard that stresses complementarity in the marital relationship rather than the equality mandated by the convention. Ann Meyer has declared herself "very skeptical" about the claims that the current Personal Status codes of these countries are sacrosanct and that, in any case, there is a "single, settled, and definitive model of family law that was obviously binding on all Muslims." She argues, rather persuasively, that the codes vary greatly and, in any event, they have been continuously subject to reform in the twentieth century – there is no insurmountable barrier to changing the codes in ways which would accommodate the provisions of CEDAW. As it stands, the reservations amount to a rejection of the substance of the Convention. She also notes that the Islamic countries are not alone in holding up a "higher" law or tradition that precludes compliance with CEDAW: the United States in fact has yet to ratify CEDAW in part on the (shaky) grounds that such action would entail amending rights provisions in the US Constitution, and the Vatican has been openly hostile to CEDAW and women's equality in general on the basis of Church Tradition.[106]

Has this engagement with an international rights framework had an impact on Islamic law and marriage practices? Meyer asserts that Moroccan feminists, for example, have been enthusiastic in their embrace of international human rights norms, seeing the clear endorsement of women's equality as providing a platform from which to push for the reform of discriminatory laws in their country. Certainly the CEDAW requirement that all States parties report every four years on progress made on the goal of bringing domestic laws into compliance with CEDAW, and receive comments and recommendations in response, has helped to keep issues of legal equality in public view, at least when states have followed the reporting process.[107] Whether this has worked to speed the pace of reform is another matter. Certain practices repeatedly singled out for comment by the CEDAW Committee that reviews the progress reports, like the continued legality of polygyny, have yet to undergo serious review in most states. In an era of heightened sensitivity to the imposition of western models, and the renewal of allegiance to principles and practices held to be Islamic, the invocation of international standards may not always have a positive effect. Some of the more promising campaigns for legal reform, as in the case of the Campaign for Monogamy in Malaysia or the "woman's divorce" campaign in Egypt, which I discuss in the next chapter, are careful to situate themselves within a fully indigenous Islamic framework. Still, the clarity and consistency of CEDAW in articulating women's rights as an essential and incontrovertible

---

[106] See Jane Connors, "The Women's Convention in the Muslim World," in Yamani and Allen, *Feminism and Islam*, 351–71; and Ann Elizabeth Meyer, "Rhetorical Strategies and Official Policies on Women's Rights: The Merits and Drawbacks of the New World Hypocrisy," in *Faith and Freedom: Women's Human Rights in the Muslim World*, ed. Mahnaz Afkhami (Syracuse: Syracuse University Press, 1995), 104–32.

[107] See the various progress reports submitted to the Committee on the Elimination of the Discrimination against Women, available through the International Women's Rights Action Watch, www.iwraw-ap.org.

aspect of the international human rights regime continue to facilitate important discussions about the relationship between local practices and international norms.

CONCLUSION

What has Islamic law had to say about marriage? I have not found it easy to provide a neat summary of the rules because of the diversity of legal opinion among the classical jurists, the reforming thinkers and officials, and contemporary activists. The bedrock of the law is the sacred texts, the Qur'an and Prophetic Traditions, which have much to say about marriage, but a great deal of this material is open to variations in interpretation and, indeed, can even have some apparently contradictory indications. The growth of different legal schools, and a spectrum of legal doctrines even within these schools, illustrates the possible breadth of legal opinions among thinkers working with essentially the same methods and sources. Many of their differences revolve around what we might consider relatively minor issues, such as the proper phrasing of a marriage proposal or whether a husband must supply his wife with one or two servants, but other matters go more to the heart of the institution. The Shiʿi acceptance of temporary (*mutʿa*) marriage, anathema to the Sunnis, is one such extreme divergence, but even within Sunni circles we find very significant differences about whether, for example, a husband can physically coerce his wife into obedience. It was in keeping with the nature of Islamic law, an uncodified law based on a sustained process of jurisprudential activity, to develop a range of opinions and possibilities, most of which were based on firm judicial ground.

But I think there is still a core collection of doctrines that set the tone for the marital relationship: the issues of guardianship in one form or another and the marital bargain of *nafaqa* for absence of *nushūz* have been constants in Islamic marriage. This does not mean that these doctrines cannot, and have never been, challenged on the basis of the sources, but they do represent central elements in most legal expositions of marriage arrangements and relationships. There can be little argument, I think, about the discriminatory character of these doctrines, at least in terms of liberal notions of equality. Men and women do not always have an equal say in the making of the marriage contract, or in the running of the marital household. Many legal reforms (reducing the power of the guardian, controlling polygyny) have been oriented towards the incremental increase of a wife's rights vis-à-vis her husband, with the goal of achieving eventual equality. This piecemeal approach to attacking discrimination in marriage has so far proceeded slowly and most of the basic elements of discrimination are still intact in contemporary laws and practices.

From the woman-centered perspective, of course, not all difference is discriminatory. Muslim women can lay legal claim to maintenance for themselves and for the care of their children, a right to wages for the work of nurturing that has long eluded their counterparts in the West. Islamic law recognizes the fact that most women will bear and raise children, and provides for rights that are not simply hollow echoes of male rights, but rather institute serious claims to respect and recompense for women's contributions to their families and their communities. The law also places heavy burdens on the husband by making him responsible for the material support of his wife, his children, and all the expenses of the household, burdens that belie the image of a life of carefree patriarchal privilege. As the law usually now stands, however, there has been a rather heavy trade-off for the recognition of women's special needs: women have been subjected to restrictions on their freedom of movement in return for their entitlements in the household. The few reform codes that have tackled the issue of a husband's authority straight on, like that of the short-lived PDRY, have done so by eliminating the husband's special responsibility for maintenance as well. Is it possible to retain legal recognition of a woman's life-cycle and the related needs without confirming legal inequalities? Islamic activists are struggling to answer this question.

Finally, Islamic laws governing marriage certainly draw on ideas about gender in the various societies in which they are developed and applied. They did not arrive full-blown, but rather are the result, in their various forms, of a long historical process of juristic elaboration in particular social contexts. In marriage law, there are discursive constructs of Woman (dependent, vulnerable, weak) and Man (authoritative, worldly, strong) that are both pervasive and persuasive. There is a complex set of rules, many of which relate, in an unspoken fashion, to notions of basic gender difference and gender hierarchy. Insofar as I can tell, most of these constructs have survived in present-day marriage law with little fundamental alteration, and reinforce, and are reinforced by, the prevailing gendering practices in the societies they inhabit.

3

Woman and man as divorced: asserting rights

Marriage, while an institution of critical and central importance in the Islamic legal landscape of social relations, was not required or necessarily expected to be a permanent one. Rather, Islamic legal discourses and practices recognized that, upon occasion, marital relations might be better terminated; there is no moral dictum of "till death do us part" and no legal insistence on the indissolubility of the marital tie as in much of the Christian tradition. A number of verses in the Qur'an address the question of divorce in a tone that suggests that ending a marriage, while not to be taken lightly, may be preferable to continuing in a relationship that does not fulfill its purposes. Men are enjoined, insofar as their wives are concerned, to "retain them honorably or set them free honorably" (2:231), but cautioned against taking overly hasty decisions to divorce their wives: "if you are averse to them, it is possible you may be averse to a thing and God set in it much good" (4:19). Clearly marriages can fail and relationships can sour, and a man may ultimately decide, as verse 4:19 continues, to "exchange a wife in place of another." Before such a serious decision is reached, however, the Qur'an counsels reconciliation if possible:

> And if you fear a breach between the two,
> Bring forth an arbiter from his people
> and from her people an arbiter, if they
> desire to set things right; God will
> compose their differences ... (4:35)

When such differences cannot be reconciled, however, divorce lends legitimate recourse for a marriage that no longer brings the promised joy and mutual support. Certain Qur'an verses, as we shall see below, also lay the foundations for the elaborate rules developed by the jurists for the different forms of divorce and attendant obligations.

Divorce was also very much a part of the life of the early Muslim community, and a number of hadith record the Prophet Muhammad's attitudes and intercessions, including his cautionary statement that "Of all the permitted things divorce is the most abominable with God." But there was no question about the legality of divorce: other hadith narratives empower all men of age, unless insane or in various states of mental incapacity, to divorce their wives without grounds or the intervention of the court or judge.[1] The Prophet Muhammad married at least one previously divorced woman, Zaynab bint Jahsh, and according to some reports seriously considered divorcing another of his wives (Hafsa) but changed his mind at her request. So although Muslim men might be encouraged to think carefully about divorce, they were clearly given the right to divorce their wives at will and divorce carried no discernible stigma. Women, as we shall see below, had far more limited rights of divorce as the law developed so that divorce became an area for substantial discrimination on the basis of gender. Whether such strong gendering of the rules of divorce reflects the spirit of the Qur'an and the hadith remains a matter of much debate among today's scholars and legal activists.

I begin with some discussion of the ways in which Muslim jurists developed the doctrines on divorce. As with the doctrines on marriage, the rules of divorce came to vary across and within legal schools as the jurists differed in their interpretations of the sacred texts. I want to point out some of these differences, especially those with ongoing relevance to divorce today. There is also a varied history of legal practice prior to the twentieth century that helps us understand how both male and female members of past Muslim communities thought about, and pursued, their rights and opportunities under divorce laws, and contributed in some measure to the modification of doctrine. Again, much of what we know about pre-twentieth-century legal practices dates to the Ottoman era so I necessarily focus on divorce in that period. The legal reform efforts of the later nineteenth and twentieth centuries sometimes targeted divorce as an area of discrimination and opened up discussion on the aspects of divorce that appeared to be most prejudicial to women and, as we shall see, many of the revised legal codes made modest attempts to expand women's rights in divorce as a result. Finally, a number of present-day legal campaigns have focused on divorce, which has proven to be a hotly contested area; I will discuss a couple of the more recent efforts that engage issues of gendered rights in Islamic laws of divorce.

---

[1] Al-Marghinani, *Al-Hidaya*, 2:536.

ISLAMIC DIVORCE: THE LEGAL TRADITION

The jurists developed rules for a number of different types of divorce. I will confine my discussion here to the most common forms of divorce, *ṭalāq*, *tafrīq*, and *khulʿ*, although the jurists also addressed the rules for several other types of divorce including *īlāʾ* (a form of oath, to abstain from sexual relations with his wife), and *liʿān* (a denial of paternity by a husband). Since the modern jurists discuss the latter two forms of divorce in rather abstract and archaic terms, if at all, and we have little evidence that they were much practiced in any Islamic period, I have chosen to focus on the types of divorce that we know were practiced on a significant scale. As the jurists developed the doctrines for these divorce procedures, they paid considerable attention to the differences in male and female capacities: men had far more leeway when it came to divorce, empowered as they were to divorce their wives at will, while women could initiate divorce only on limited grounds and generally under the auspices of the court.

Ṭalāq

The standard "man's divorce," *ṭalāq*, is a unilateral repudiation of a wife by her husband; in its baldest form, a man could end his marriage simply by pronouncing a formula of divorce, after which his wife must wait a statutory period (*ʿidda*) before the divorce was automatically finalized. There was no role for the court, no possibility of contest by the wife, and only limited obligations imposed on the husband for payment of any dower he owed and temporary support of his wife while she waited for the divorce to be finalized.

The jurists discussed three primary types of *ṭalāq*. The "better" (*aḥsan*) kind of divorce was one entered into slowly and cautiously, but one that did not unduly prolong the process for the woman. A husband should pronounce the formula of divorce only when his wife was between menstrual periods, and then he should not have relations with her for three menstrual cycles, after which time they would be formally divorced. He could change his mind about the divorce at any point during the three cycles and resume the marriage, because this kind of divorce was revocable; also, once the divorce was final, the couple could remarry if they wished. The jurists discussed a variation on this divorce, the "good" (*ḥasan*) divorce, in which a husband utters three separate pronunciations of divorce in three consecutive periods between menstruations. The divorce is effected only by the final pronunciation, and the woman must then wait an additional three menstrual cycles (an *'idda* or waiting period) before she is completely free of her marital bonds and can remarry. This type of divorce is irrevocable in the sense that the husband cannot change his mind after the third iteration of the divorce and the couple may not remarry unless the woman has married another man in the interim and has been divorced or widowed. In a third type of *ṭalāq al-bid'a* (the divorce of innovation or the "triple *ṭalāq*"), the husband simply pronounces three divorces at once while his wife is not menstruating and she immediately enters her waiting period. This divorce is also irrevocable.

Many of the jurists were not altogether comfortable with the prospect of divorce, noting that moral and ethical considerations also applied: "Divorce is fundamentally prohibited because it ends marriage which has both spiritual and material benefits."[2] And from early on, they had mixed feelings about these types of *ṭalāq*. Malik, for example, thought that only the *aḥsan* type of divorce was valid, while Shafi'i accepted all three types of *ṭalāq* on the grounds that divorce itself is a legal act and the Prophet had not objected when a man, in his presence, had divorced his wife three times with one iteration. Most jurists favored the more gradual revocable divorce, not least because it held open the possibility of reconciliation. They openly encouraged women to employ their charms to win back their husbands:

A woman who has been reversibly divorced may adorn herself and ornament herself because she is permitted to her husband if marriage exists between them. The return [to marriage] is desirable and the adornment may encourage him, and therefore it is permitted.[3]

Hanafis held that the act of intercourse alone, or even lustful kissing and caressing, nullified the divorce and reestablished the marriage, a position accepted although not preferred by Malikis as well, but Shafi'is insisted on a formal statement by the husband of his intention of resuming the marriage and forbade him to consort with his wife until he had made one. As long as the three-cycle period had not expired, all agreed that, in a revocable divorce, a husband could choose to return to his wife regardless of her wishes. If she were to claim that she had experienced three menstrual flows since the pronouncement of divorce, however, her word must be accepted and her husband could no longer take her back. She was the "authority" for the end of her *'idda* and in that way retained some small veto power over her husband's otherwise unilateral field of action in *ṭalāq*.[4]

---

[2] *Ibid.*, 2:532.   [3] *Ibid.*, 2:587.

[4] Ibn Ishaq, *Abrégé*, 73–75; Ibn Rushd, *Bidayat*, 3:1392–94, 1447; al-Marghinani, *Al-Hidaya*, 2:583–84.

In the case of the irrevocable forms of *ṭalāq* (the three pronouncements whether made sequentially or all in one iteration), once all three pronouncements were uttered a husband lost the option of taking his wife back. Indeed, he could not even remarry his former wife with a new marriage contract until she had contracted and consummated a marriage with another man, and then been divorced and passed a waiting period, in keeping with a hadith narrative that held that the Prophet had said she must "taste the sweetness of another" before she could be lawful again to her first husband.[5] The jurists differed in some of the details. The Malikis held that the interim husband must be a fully adult man, while Hanafis held that an adolescent would do as long as he were capable of sexual intercourse. The question of whether such an enabling marriage could be entered into solely for the purposes of legalizing remarriage was also debated. Most Hanafis, for example, thought that such a marriage and divorce, while abominable, did fulfill the legal requirements and render a woman permissible to her first husband. A woman's testimony to the fact was sufficient evidence:

If he divorced her three times and she then said; "I completed my *'idda* and married [another husband], and he consummated the marriage, and then divorced me, and then I completed my *'idda*," and the passage of time is sufficient for that, then it is legal for her husband to believe her if the preponderance of his belief credits [her story].[6]

A Hanafi minority opinion, from Abu Yusif, took the opposite position: any marriage arranged solely with an eye to divorce and remarriage to a first husband was invalid and could not have the desired effect.

The jurists also tackled the question of intention: the emphasis on *ṭalāq* as the outcome of an oral pronouncement inevitably raised issues. The Hanbalis were, as usual, most concerned with questions of intention: did a slip of the tongue, for example, whereby a man said "you are divorced thrice" instead of "you are divorced once" result in an irrevocable divorce? The Hanbali Ibn Taymiyya thought not, because the intention trumped the actual pronouncement; Malikis agreed that a divorce formula pronounced without intention, as in the case of a phrase repeated without understanding, would have no effect, and most Shi'a concurred. The Hanafis, on the other hand, came to take the position that the pronouncement of the triple divorce formula, even as a joke, was binding on a husband and he could not retract it no matter what his true intention.[7] The issue of coercion further

---

[5] Al-Marghinani, *Al-Hidaya*, 2:589.   [6] *Ibid.*, 2:581.
[7] Ibn Ishaq, *Abrégé*, 75; Ibn Taymiyya, *Fatawa al-Nisa'*, 247; al-Marghinani, *Al-Hidaya*, 2:536.

sharpened the differences. Hanafis generally held that divorce pronounced under compulsion was valid on the grounds that a man could choose whether to yield to threats or actual violence against his person. Ibn Hanbal opined, however, that if a man were tortured or beaten in order to get him to pronounce a divorce, if for example his leg was squeezed or he was exposed to the heat of the sun, the resulting divorce was not valid. Ibn Ishaq outlined the more expansive Maliki position that a man who pronounced the divorce formula under even a threat of violence, including threats of death, beatings, imprisonment, burning, or the murder of his child, had not made a valid *ṭalāq*, but Malikis maintained some doubt as to whether the same was true in the case of threats of damage to a man's material possessions.[8]

In addition to the matter of intention, the jurists also discussed a man's capacity to pronounce a *ṭalāq*. Despite the fact that the drinking of alcohol was prohibited under Islamic law, the jurists devoted considerable thought as to whether a divorce pronounced by an intoxicated man was effective. Most Hanafis thought that a drunk who was in a refractory state but still "rational" could pronounce a valid divorce, but if he had drunk enough to produce a headache and affect his reason, the divorce was not effective. Many Hanbalis took a similar position, distinguishing between the "irrationally" intoxicated man who later has no memory of his actions while drunk and the man who could recall that he had pronounced a divorce: in the latter case, but not the former, the divorce was valid. Most Malikis and Shafiʿis, on the other hand, held the drunk responsible for his actions no matter what his condition, although minority opinions hesitated if he had lost all powers of discernment.[9]

The jurists were less apt to credit the actions of a man suffering from mental illness. In general they agreed with Ibn Hanbal's view of the mentally disturbed: "Since he does not conduct his life rationally, his divorce pronouncement is not valid. The same is true of a man delirious with fever and of the sleeping man."[10] Some Hanbalis, along with Shiʿi jurists, also held that extreme anger was a form of temporary insanity, so that divorces pronounced in a state of irrational anger were discounted as well. But could an insane man prevail upon his guardian to pronounce a divorce? Shiʿi jurists, while disallowing any divorce pronounced by the insane man himself unless he had returned to his senses, thought his guardian was

---

[8] Ibn Hanbal, *Chapters*, 130; Ibn Ishaq, *Abrégé*, 75–76; al-Marghinani, *Al-Hidaya*, 2:536.

[9] Ibn Hanbal, *Chapters*, 127, 165; Ibn Ishaq, *Abrégé*, 75; Ibn Rushd, *Bidayat*, 3:1438–39; al-Marghinani, *Al-Hidaya*, 2:536–37.

[10] Ibn Hanbal, *Chapters*, 127.

empowered to manage his affairs for his benefit and, to that end, could separate him from his wife.[11]

A final topic of interest to the jurists in their discussions of *ṭalāq* and capacity concerned the efficacy of a divorce pronounced by a man in his terminal illness. All the jurists held such a divorce to be valid, but they differed in their assessments of the critical issue for a woman, namely whether she would then inherit from her former husband. Ordinarily, a divorced woman loses all rights to the inheritance she receives by law from her husband. In the case of a woman divorced during her husband's terminal illness, however, some jurists applied special rules. While the Shafiʿis thought such a woman had no right to inherit from her husband, Hanafis preserved her inheritance shares as long as she had not completed her *ʿidda*, Shiʿi jurists extended the period of inheritance to one year after the end of her *ʿidda*, and Hanbalis allowed her to inherit as long as she had not remarried. Malikis took the most liberal view of the matter by allowing her to inherit from her husband's estate for an indefinite time no matter what her marital status.[12] With the exception of the Shafiʿi jurists, most interpreters of the law clearly intended to mitigate the effects on a woman of a divorce pronounced by her husband at a time when he was possibly impaired and at any event would not have the luxury of reconsidering his decision.

The power a husband enjoyed to divorce his wife at will was underscored by the jurists' acceptance of the divorce by oath or the suspended divorce, that is, of the practice of a husband taking an oath that made *ṭalāq* conditional on a future event or action. A man could swear to divorce his wife if she behaved in a certain way (if she left the house, spoke to another man, gave birth to a girl, etc.). He could also condition such a divorce on his own actions by swearing divorce should he fail to repay a debt or honor other specified obligations to his wife or others within a certain timeframe. Once the act in question had been committed (or omitted), the divorce was automatically effected regardless of any change of heart on the part of the husband. While such oaths could be sworn for an almost infinite number of reasons, there were some problematic conditions. The jurists held that the husband could set neither any absurd or impossible conditions ("if I touch the sky" or "if this rock is not a rock"), nor unknowable ones ("if God wills it"). But he was well within his rights to take such an oath on what we might consider very trivial matters indeed, including his wife's refusal to cook his favorite meal or his neighbor's failure to return

[11] Al-Hilli, *Mukhtalaf,* 7:331–32, 362; Ibn Taymiyya, *Fatawa al-Nisaʾ,* 244.

[12] Al-Hilli, *Mukhtalaf,* 7:333–37; Ibn Rushd, *Bidayat,* 3:1440; al-Marghinani, *Al-Hidaya,* 2:577.

borrowed property.[13] For Hanafis, the act of oath-taking itself, regardless of the substance of the oath, constituted serious business and could lock a man into a divorce that he might otherwise wish to reconsider. Men did have almost unlimited powers to divorce their wives, and further could employ the oath of divorce to secure compliant behavior from their wives or even add emphasis to promises they made to their wives or to other people. But the law was clear about the consequences: a man was bound by the terms of his oath as he pronounced it, and could not sidestep the resulting divorce once the conditions of the oath were fulfilled. Hanbalis, on the other hand, who also discussed such oath-taking, were more skeptical about the practice and focused on the intention of the husband when he took such an oath: he could avoid activation of the divorce by arguing that he had not truly intended to divorce his wife in these circumstances.[14] Ibn Taymiyya took yet another stance in the fourteenth century when he asserted that the oath of divorce was analogous to the swearing of oaths by the name of God, which could be cancelled by acts of atonement. The strong reaction to his position, namely his arrest and trial, as well as his failure to gain any kind of following for this notion, suggests the level of commitment to the binding nature of the oath of divorce.[15]

Ṭalāq was thus conceived as a man's divorce, available to the husband at any time and in any place. A woman did not have a reciprocal right of unilateral divorce, but she could acquire the ability to choose divorce if her husband delegated his power of *ṭalāq* to her. Jurists from the main Sunni schools of law recognized the right of the husband to delegate such power, although they differed in their understandings of the conditions related to such delegation (*tafwīḍ*). Hanafis thought that when a husband told his wife she could "choose" or that "the matter is in your hands," she acquired the right to divorce her husband only in the immediate time and place; should she arise and go elsewhere, the delegation lapsed unless her husband had specifically told her she could divorce herself whenever she wanted or had tied the choice of divorce to a definite condition such as his acquisition of a second wife. Some Hanbalis agreed that the wife's option of divorce did not last beyond the sitting in which it was granted although others thought it was valid until the husband reconciled with his wife by having sexual intercourse with her. Malikis held that such a delegation remained in force

---

[13] Ibn Ishaq, *Abrégé*, 84–89; al-'Imadi, *Al-'Uqud*, 1:36, 40, 43; al-Marghinani, *Al-Hidaya*, 2:569–574.

[14] Ibn Hanbal, *Chapters*, 198; Ibn Taymiyya, *Fatawa al-Nisa'*, 248–254.

[15] See Rapoport, *Marriage, Money and Divorce*, 96–110, for a discussion of this issue in the context of loyalty oaths in Mamluk society.

until the husband cancelled it, although he was not allowed to cancel a delegation that was tied to a condition such as the taking of a second wife. The import of such delegation was diluted, at least by some Hanbali and Shi'i jurists, by the notion that a wife so delegated was only empowered to pronounce a single, revocable divorce, which would result in final divorce if her husband chose to honor it by abstaining from intercourse with her for three menstrual cycles.[16] While the effectiveness of any blanket delegation of divorce to a wife was thus limited by most jurists, conditional delegation conferred some real powers on a woman. A man who delegated his power of *ṭalāq* to his wife, should he, for instance, take a second wife or fail to provide proper maintenance, gave his wife a real option to leave the marriage if he violated the terms they had presumably agreed upon. Some jurists even thought that a husband who could not provide proper maintenance was obligated to let his wife choose divorce.[17] *Ṭalāq* was a man's divorce, but one which, as far as the jurists were concerned and a husband was willing, could amplify and lend accountability to the marriage contract.

Tafrīq

Although women did not have reciprocal rights of divorce, a judge might step in to annul a marriage at the request of a woman or her family under certain circumstances. This annulment (*tafrīq* or *faskh*) was a court procedure whereby a wife, her family or, according to some schools, a husband could request that a defective marriage be annulled.

The jurists differed as to what precisely constituted defects in a marriage severe enough to warrant annulment. A husband's impotence (*'unna*) was the one condition that all jurists seemed to accept as grounds for annulment. An impotent husband could not satisfy his wife's right to sexual intercourse and thus the primary purpose of marriage, legitimating sexual intercourse, could not be fulfilled. But how was the judge to establish that a husband had not and could not have intercourse with his wife? Absent the husband's accession to his wife's claim that he had not had intercourse with her, the judge could have the wife examined by women experts; a finding of virginity established the credibility of her claim. In the case of a woman found to be deflowered (*thayyib*) who claimed that her husband had not consummated the marriage and requested an annulment, Hanafi jurists

---

[16] Al-Hilli, *Mukhtalaf,* 7:338, 378–80; Ibn Hanbal, *Chapters,* 126, 167; Ibn Ishaq, *Abrégé,* 89–92; al-Marghinani, *Al-Hidaya,* 2:558.
[17] Ibn Hanbal, *Chapters,* 80.

acquiesced only if the husband concurred; should he take an oath that their marriage had indeed been consummated, his oath took precedence in keeping with the standard rules for evidence.[18] Hanbali jurists, on the other hand, when faced with the problem of a deflowered woman asking for an annulment on the grounds of impotence, placed the burden of proof on the husband. The man should be sequestered in a room alone with his wife and asked to produce a sample of his semen in a cloth which he could then display to the judge. And how would the judge be able to ascertain that this was truly semen and not egg white? Ibn Hanbal remarked that the specimen could be thrown on the fire: if it solidified it was egg white, but if it burned up it was semen.[19] In all cases, whether the woman was a virgin or not, a husband was given one year from the day his wife appeared before the judge to demonstrate his potency; at the end of a year, the woman should be granted an annulment and released from the marriage without penalty.

While impotence figured as an absolute defect in a marriage, the jurists were less unified in their position on other deficiencies in a husband. Hanafi jurists were divided as to whether a wife could demand an annulment if her husband suffered from insanity, leprosy, or scrofula (tuberculosis of the neck): majority positions did not allow for annulment in these instances because the purpose of marriage (sexual intercourse) could still be fulfilled, but there were minority positions to the contrary on the basis that a wife should be empowered to escape from the harm of having such a husband. Shi'i jurists tended to allow an annulment only if a wife had not known about these conditions when she agreed to the marriage or if they had worsened substantially after marriage. Malikis and Shafi'is generally allowed annulments when these conditions were present regardless of when they arose.[20]

The jurists were also of different minds in the case of a husband who had gone missing and neither his whereabouts nor whether he was dead or alive was known (a *mafqūd*). The Malikis established a clear procedure for a wife who wished to be released from her marriage to a missing person. As long as there was no news of her husband, she could go to the qadi or other local authority and ask for the initiation of a waiting period of four years; if her husband did not reappear or send news within this period, she would be given a divorce and could then remarry. If her husband returned before she remarried, however, she would be sent back to her husband. Once she had remarried, her first husband could not reclaim her unless it could be shown

---

[18] Al-Marghinani, *Al-Hidaya*, 2:620. [19] Ibn Hanbal, *Chapters*, 79–80.
[20] Al-Hilli, *Mukhtalaf*, 7:362; al-Marghinani, *Al-Hidaya*, 2:621.

that people had falsely testified to the death of the first husband.[21] Shi'i and Hanbali law were similar in some respects: both of these schools assigned a waiting period of four years, four months, and ten days, after which the deserted wife received a divorce and could remarry. According to at least one Hanbali opinion, this waiting period could be as short as one year if the husband had failed to leave her any means of support. Shi'i doctrine held that her first husband, should he return, could reclaim her during the waiting period but all his marital rights were terminated once it finished. The Hanbalis, on the other hand, gave the missing husband full marital rights if he returned, regardless of how long he had been gone or whether his wife were remarried. He might choose to restore the marriage or, if he wished, he could opt to recoup the dower he had paid and allow the divorce to stand.[22]

The Hanafis took a critical view of the other schools' accommodation of such requests for divorce. Al-Marghinani reviewed the Maliki arguments and found them wanting. He noted that they usually cited a decision of the Caliph 'Umar to release a woman from marriage to a missing person, but added that 'Umar had later changed his mind. He also faulted the notion that a husband's absence was comparable to a husband's impotence in the sense that it deprived a wife of her basic rights in marriage: "It [the absence] is not analogous to impotence because the missing person may succeed in returning but impotence rarely is resolved if it has endured for a year."[23] As far as the Hanafi school was concerned, a woman remained the wife of her husband until she received reliable notice of his death or until he could be presumed dead under Hanafi rules, that is some period of time defined variously as 99 years, 120 years, or until all members of his peer group were dead, none of which was likely to be of much use to a grass widow.

The differences among schools are particularly striking because they seem to be underpinned by rather diverse views of a wife's rights in marriage. For most jurists, the wife's right to petition for a divorce from a missing husband was connected to her right to enjoy intimacy in marriage – the recurring reference to impotence is more than a simple analogy because it evokes a woman's right to sexual companionship. The jurists did not dwell on the issue of material support: whether a missing husband left his wife with sufficient property to support herself was not at issue in their discussions. Where they diverged was on the issue of gendered sexual rights in marriage.

[21] Ibn Ishaq, *Abrégé*, 118.
[22] Al-Hilli, *Mukhtalaf*, 7:374; Ibn Hanbal, *Chapters*, 77–78, 114; Ibn Taymiyya, *Fatawa al-Nisa'*, 278.
[23] Al-Marghinani, *Al-Hidaya*, 2:905.

The Hanafis asserted that a husband's right to the enjoyment of his wife's person, similarly to his rights to his other property, persisted even when he was absent, while most other jurists held that a woman's right to sexual companionship in marriage set some time limits: a wife could be asked to be "patient" for a limited period of time, after which she should be released from the marriage bond so that she could remarry. These were not minor differences of emphasis, it seems to me, but rather signaled a fundamental disagreement about how to weigh the rights of husbands and wives in a marriage: did the right of a husband to property in his wife override her right to sexual satisfaction? We find a wide variety of answers to this question.

Tafrīq was usually depicted as a woman's divorce, but some jurists thought it was available to the husband as well in certain circumstances. Al-Shafiʿi and his followers held that a husband could seek an annulment of the marriage if his wife suffered from leprosy, scrofula, insanity, or physical defects of her genitalia which prevented intercourse. Most Hanafis demurred on the basis that a husband could always escape from a harmful marriage by pronouncing a *ṭalāq* and therefore effectively reserved *tafrīq* to the petitions of women. And for a woman who could meet the criteria, this was certainly the most favorable type of divorce because a *tafrīq*, even though initiated by the wife, preserved all her rights to post-divorce property settlements (such as the balance of her dower and the costs of a waiting period, etc., to be discussed below) just as in a *ṭalāq*.

Khulʿ

Khulʿ was another type of "woman's divorce" of arguably lesser benefit to women. The basic meaning of *khulʿ* upon which most jurists agreed is that of a divorce desired by the wife in return for compensation paid to her husband. But this definition leaves many of the important details in question. How much compensation? Must the husband consent and/or participate in the process? What are the roles of the court and the judge? These are clearly no small matters and could make an enormous difference in whether *khulʿ* was or could be a true "woman's divorce" that could lend women the kind of choices that men enjoyed by virtue of their untrammeled right to *ṭalāq*.

As they developed the doctrine of *khulʿ*, the jurists often made explicit reference to the texts. The Qurʾanic verses most frequently cited to provide the basis for *khulʿ* were the following:

> It is not lawful of you to take what you have given them
> unless the couple fear they may not maintain

God's bounds; if you fear they may not maintain
God's bounds, it is no fault in them for her to redeem herself.   (2:229)

If a woman fear rebelliousness or aversion
in her husband, there is no fault in them
if the couple set things right between them;
right settlement is better; and souls are very
prone to avarice. If you do good
and are godfearing, surely God is aware of the things you do.   (4:128)

Although these verses do seem to establish the principle that an aversion on
the part of the wife for her husband, or perhaps the development of a
mutual dislike that may lead one or both of the spouses to stray outside the
marriage, is sufficient reason for negotiating a divorce, crucial matters of
compensation, consent, and the role of the court are not explicitly
addressed. In their elaboration of rules for *khul*, the jurists could also rely
upon hadith literature, most importantly the narrations of an instance of
khul in the time of the Prophet Muhammad. The wife of Thabit ibn Qays,
Jamilah bint 'Abd Allah, came to the Prophet and told of how she did not
dislike her husband for any moral or religious failings on his part, but that
she feared for her own transgression if she remained married to him,
presumably because she was not attracted to her husband and therefore
might stray. The Prophet then asked her if she were willing to return the
garden she had been given by Thabit, and she said yes. Then he had Thabit
accept the garden and divorce his wife. In one version the Prophet told
Thabit to accept the garden and divorce her, while in another standard
version he "ordered" him to separate from her.[24]

This was the basic material that the jurists worked with to develop the
doctrine of *khul* and, as with most Islamic legal sources, it left open to
interpretation a number of questions about principles and procedure so that
we subsequently encounter considerable diversity in the doctrine, both
among legal schools, and even within the same school. First, the matter of
compensation, how much a woman could be required to sacrifice to leave a
marriage, was critical to the feasibility of the divorce: a woman would not be
able to avail herself of a *khul* divorce if the price were too high. Second,
whether *khul* required the willing participation of the husband and, in

---

[24] Muhammad ibn Isma'il Bukhari, *Sahih al-Bukhari*, trans. Muhammad Muhsin Khan, 9 vols. (Medina:
Islamic University, 1974), 7:150–51; Jalal al-din 'Abd al-Rahman al-Suyuti, *Al-Tawshih Sharh al-Jami'
al-Sahih*, 9 vols. (Riyadh: Maktabat al-Rushd, 1998), 7:3320–3321.

particular, whether the husband's agreement was absolutely required, thus giving him veto power over the process, was a central and contested issue. Third, ideas about the role of the court and the judge in the evaluation of a case of *khul'* reflected significant differences in the characterization of *khul'*: was it a type of judicial divorce or was it an extra-judicial agreement? All three aspects of *khul'* speak to how the jurists thought of gender relations. Could women be empowered to decide upon a divorce without jeopardizing power relations within the family? Did women have special vulnerabilities that made the exercise of such power a virtual impossibility? Did the law and legal institutions bear responsibility for protecting women, perhaps against themselves, in matters of conjugal relations? The debates over *khul'* crystallized many of these issues.

First, the jurists tackled the appropriate amount of compensation owed to a husband if a woman wanted a divorce. I could not identify a single or even dominant position on this issue, but rather a broad range of possibilities. The most common opinion across schools was that a husband should not take more than either the amount of the *mahr* (dower) or "what he gave her," which might include the *mahr* and any presents of jewelry, clothing, etc. The dominant Hanafi opinion was that while it was "abominable" for a husband to take more than the amount of the dower, he could negotiate for more: any amount he could extract was, strictly speaking, legal although amounts in excess of the dower were morally reprehensible.[25] Ibn Hanbal also did "not like" a man to take more than the dower in a case of *khul'*.[26] Ibn Rushd, summarizing the range of opinion among Malikis, noted that there was a difference of views as to whether a husband can take anything at all back from his wife on the basis of Qur'an 4:20: "And if you desire to exchange a wife/ in place of another, and you have given/ to one a hundred-weight, take of it nothing."[27] Prevailing Shi'i opinion among the majority Ithna' 'Asharis was that the husband should take only the amount of the *mahr*, not more,[28] while the (Shi'a) Zaydis held that the husband does not in fact have a right to receive any compensation at all.[29] Later Hanafi jurists added that the wife could also waive rights to maintenance during her *'idda* (waiting period) if this were made a clear condition of *khul'* as well as her rights to receive maintenance for her children by her divorced husband for a specified period of time.[30] Hanafis found it legal to waive this right as part

[25] Al-Marghinani, *Al-Hidaya*, 2:597–98. [26] Ibn Hanbal, *Chapters*, 80.
[27] Ibn Rushd, *Bidayat*, 3:1400. [28] Al-Hilli, *Mukhtalaf*, 7:391–92.
[29] Y. Linant de Bellefonds, "Le 'Hul' sans compensation en droit hanafite," *Studia Islamica* 31 (1970): 185–95.
[30] Al-Ramli, *Kitab al-Fatawa*, 1:54–55; al-'Imadi, *Al-'Uqud*, 1:51–55.

of *khul'* for the entire period of a mother's custody (*ḥiḍāna*); Malikis
thought the wife could agree to bear the costs of child support during her
pregnancy and nursing period, but there were mixed opinions as to whether
her responsibility for support could be prolonged beyond the weaning of
the child.[31]

The whole matter of compensation often hinged, in various discussions,
on an assessment of the feelings of husband and wife: if the husband also
wanted to end the marriage and felt antipathy toward his wife, then he
should not take anything from her.[32] Indeed, if both parties want divorce,
then it is not *khul'*, but rather *mubārā'a*, divorce by mutual agreement, and
some thought both parties should waive all claims.[33] The Hanafi school
agreed that this kind of divorce is a divorce by mutual discharge, and Abu
Hanifa thought all claims from marriage dropped, including any unpaid
mahr and *'idda* maintenance, while his disciple Muhammad said that these
rights were still active and a woman could collect her unpaid *mahr* and other
marital rights.[34] Shi'i opinion, according to al-Hilli, varied in case of
mubārā'a between allowing a husband to retain the unpaid balance of the
mahr and assigning him the total *mahr*.[35] All schools seemed to agree that if
the husband were really the instigator of divorce against the wishes of the
wife, then it was not *khul'* at all, but rather *ṭalāq* and the wife retained her
rights to her entire *mahr* and maintenance.

So we find a rather wide range of opinion on the matter of legal compensation in the case of *khul'*, from nothing at all to whatever the husband can
extract. There was considerable tension in these discussions between the
task of divining the appropriate rules for this procedure and that of laying
out the moral issues. What was permissible in terms of compensation was
not always what was moral or just, and the entire matter of fixing compensation was further complicated by problems of determining intentionality.
The wide variety of opinions among and within legal schools makes it
difficult to assess shifts in interpretation over time: there was such a range of
possibilities that jurists of any given era could differ considerably. Among
the Hanafis, at least, we do see some movement toward acceptance of
compensation well beyond the *mahr*, including child support, as a standard
form of compensation.

The jurists differed less in their discussions of the second critical aspect of
khul', that of the husband's agreement. Most often, the husband's agreement

---

[31] Ibn Ishaq, *Abrégé*, 70–71.   [32] Ibn Hanbal, *Chapters*, 272.
[33] Ibn Rushd, *Bidayat*, 3:1399.   [34] Al-Marghinani, *Al-Hidaya*, 2:601–02.
[35] Al-Hilli, *Mukhtalaf*, 7:391.

to the procedure formed part of the basic definition of *khul*ᶜ. This agreement was an exchange of property on the part of the wife in return for her husband's right in her person. The wife was in effect buying her husband's marital right to her so that her husband was an essential (and necessarily willing) party to the sale. The basic procedure of offer and acceptance reflected this understanding. Either the husband or the wife could make an offer of *khul*ᶜ and an acceptance by the other party gave it effect.[36] I did not find much deviation from this position, with the exception of some Shiᶜi jurists who concurred that the husband's agreement to a *khul*ᶜ was essential but thought that there were circumstances in which the husband's agreement might be legally required (*wājib*). If, for example, a wife says to her husband, "I will not obey you, and I will not serve you, and I will not wash myself for you, and I will go to your bed in something you despise if you do not divorce me," or if a husband actually experiences such acts of aversion on the part of his wife, then he is required to agree to a *khul*ᶜ.[37] Thus, while the jurists always assumed that the husband's agreement was a basic part of the *khul*ᶜ process, in the context of a total breakdown of the marriage that agreement might be made obligatory.

The third major feature of *khul*ᶜ, the role of the court and the judge, depended in large part on whether jurists characterized *khul*ᶜ as a type of *ṭalāq* (unilateral repudiation on the part of the husband in which the court plays no role) or *faskh/tafrīq* (a judicial decree of annulment). Maliki jurists held *khul*ᶜ to be a *ṭalāq* for compensation, and therefore neither judge nor court was necessary.[38] The Hanbalis agreed that no judge was necessary to the procedure even though they characterized *khul*ᶜ as a form of judicial separation: Ibn Rahwayh thought that *khul*ᶜ should include a process of arbitration in which each party had an arbitrator and the arbitrators could suggest that the couple agree on separation.[39] Within the ranks of Hanafis, Shafiᶜis and Shiᶜa we find diversity of opinion on the issue, with some jurists characterizing *khul*ᶜ as a type of *ṭalāq* and some as *faskh*.[40] The jurists did not usually speak explicitly to the role of the court, but it is possible to argue that there were implications: *faskh* was a judicial procedure that requires a judicial ruling, and even though some jurists said *khul*ᶜ was a special type of *faskh* that did not require a judge, others left the question of the court open.

And certainly, many jurists were well aware of the possibilities for abuse of *khul*ᶜ, and they often stressed the important role of the courts in correcting

---

[36] Al-Marghinani, *Al-Hidaya*, 2:598. [37] Al-Hilli, *Mukhtalaf*, 7:383.
[38] Ibn Ishaq, *Abrégé*, 66. [39] Ibn Hanbal, *Chapters*, 250–51.
[40] Al-Hilli, *Mukhtalaf*, 7:387.

any injustices. Ibn Ishaq (a Maliki) called upon judges to be alert to false *khulʿ* divorces, which could take place under a number of circumstances: (1) if the wife had been compelled in any way according to witnesses; (2) if the husband had a defect that might be grounds for an annulment without penalty to the woman; (3) if the husband had already repudiated her and he was trying to change it into a *khulʿ*; and (4) if the husband had pronounced the formula for *ṭalāq*, not for *khulʿ*. In all these cases, the divorce was still valid, but the husband was required to return any compensation he had received from his wife.[41] Jurists were also concerned that a wife might agree to a *khulʿ* inadvertently, and therefore some set stringent proofs for proving her desire to leave the marriage. According to some Shiʿi jurists, it was not enough for a woman to say *"khalaʿa* me and I will give you what I took from you"; she needed to make statements about her aversion such as "I will not honor your oaths, and I will not obey you, and I will entertain in your house without your permission, and I will have someone else sleep in your bed."[42] In discussions of improper *khulʿ*, the assumption was that the rights of the wife might be in jeopardy, and it was the role of the court and judge to police the procedure and rectify the situation, usually by restoring any past or future compensation to the wife.

The *ʿidda*

The divorcée, regardless of how she had been divorced, could not, legally speaking, make an entirely clean break from her marriage. The termination of marriage through divorce or widowhood thrust a woman into the liminal state of the *ʿidda*, a waiting period during which she was neither married nor unattached. During this period, she was not permitted to remarry and could be subject to considerable restraint on her freedom of movement.

The jurists were at some pains to explain that the *ʿidda* was required to ascertain if a woman were pregnant as a result of the marriage: it was the issue of paternity above all others that underpinned the timing and duration of the *ʿidda*. Once a divorce had been finalized by the pronouncement of a husband or court, a woman entered her waiting period. In the case of a menstruating woman, the jurists agreed that the *ʿidda* lasted for three full menstrual cycles; if a woman had passed through menopause and no longer menstruated, then the *ʿidda* was measured as three calendar months. As for women who had irregular periods because of illness or for no apparent reason, some jurists thought they should also observe the three month rule

---

[41] Ibn Ishaq, *Abrégé*, 70.　　[42] Al-Hilli, *Mukhtalaf*, 7:385.

while others held they should be placed under observation for nine months or the normal duration of a pregnancy, after which they could observe a three-month *idda*. Should a woman be pregnant or a pregnancy become apparent, then the period of the *idda* was extended until the birth (or miscarriage) of the child.[43] The thrust of these rules was clear: the child born during the *idda* was to be considered the legitimate issue of the marriage.

Some jurists confronted the issue of verification, particularly problematic in the context of measuring the *idda* in terms of a woman's bodily functions, about which she, more than any other person, could speak with true authority. As al-Marghinani noted: "If the woman in her *idda* said that her *idda* had ended, and her husband accused her of lying, her testimony under oath carries the day, because she is the custodian of that and she has been accused of lying, so she can take an oath like a plaintiff."[44] There were some limits placed on a woman's ability to define her *idda* based on physiological information. Al-Hilli, for instance, specified that the shortest possible *idda* was one of twenty-six days: a woman could testify that her period began right after the divorce and lasted for three days, after which there was a ten-day interval before another three-day menstrual period, ten-day interval, and final three-day period.[45] Still, if a woman's testimony about her periods did not overly strain credulity, it was within her power to determine how long her *idda* would last.

If establishing the paternity and therefore the legitimacy of a child conceived during the marriage were the only consideration in calculating the duration of the *idda*, then the rules for a widow should be identical to those for a divorcée. Most jurists seemed to agree, however, that a widow should pass an *idda* of a statutory period of four months and ten days. Al-Hilli discussed this difference in the context of the case of a missing person. If a husband had divorced his wife before or after he went missing, her waiting period could begin immediately with the divorce (even if she had yet to receive the news of it) and last for three menstrual cycles; subsequent news of his death would not alter the length of her *idda*. On the other hand, if a husband died while absent, the widow's *idda* of four months and ten days began only when she received the news of his death: she could not calculate the *idda* retroactively as could the divorcée because she needed to have a mourning period. Shafi'is agreed that a woman who was already in an *idda* after a divorce pronouncement should not have to extend it should her husband die: "because it [the *idda*] is required as a sign

---

[43] Al-Marghinani, *Al-Hidaya*, 2:622; Ibn Rushd, *Bidayat*, 3:1459–60; al-Hilli, *Mukhtalaf*, 7:485–86.
[44] Al-Marghinani, *Al-Hidaya*, 2:627.   [45] Al-Hilli, *Mukhtalaf*, 7:489.

of sadness for the loss of a husband and as an observance for his death, and
he had grieved her with his absence and she does not regret his loss." But
Hanafis required the period of four months and ten days even if the widow
had been divorced because "it [mourning] is required as a sign of grief for
the loss of the comforts of marriage."[46] Although the jurists were divided on
this issue, the extended *'idda* for the widow was clearly connected to notions
of wifely propriety, a need to mandate a public period of mourning and to
let the marriage bed cool a little longer for a widow than for a divorced
woman.

What could a woman expect and demand in terms of material support
during this enforced waiting period? Again the jurists disagreed. According
to Ibn Rushd, there was general consensus that a woman who had been
revocably divorced should be housed and given general support (*nafaqa*)
until her husband took her back or the *'idda* was completed. In the case of a
woman who had been irrevocably divorced and was not pregnant, there was
a spectrum of opinion as a result of adherence to different versions of hadith
concerning the *'idda* of Fatima bint Qays: Hanafis thought her entitled to
both housing and support (although widows received only housing),
Malikis and Shafi'is awarded her housing only, and Hanbalis thought she
had no rights at all to housing or maintenance.[47] Her right to housing, if
she were entitled to it, would normally be met through residence in her
husband's house, although some held that she should remain where she was
when the divorce occurred, whether that be her husband's house, her own
house, or her relatives' house. She could expect her housing to meet certain
standards: she should have quarters clearly separate from her husband and
she did not have to remain in a house in a ruinous state. Should her husband
behave in a licentious fashion with her (since she was no longer sexually
available to him), he could be required to leave the house. If her husband or
his creditors sold the house, or her husband lost his right to the house as a
result of the termination of an official position, she still had a right to stay
and finish her *'idda*.[48]

This right to housing was a privilege that could also shade into a form of
imprisonment. According to al-Marghinani, a divorcée who was receiving
maintenance was not allowed to leave the house where she was lodged at any
time during the *'idda*, but a widow could leave during the day in order to
make her living since she did not receive maintenance. A woman who had
received a *khul'* divorce, with the agreement that she surrender her rights to

---

[46] Al-Marghinani, *Al-Hidaya*, 2:629–30; al-Hilli, *Mukhtalaf*, 7:479–81.
[47] Ibn Rushd, *Bidayat*, 3:1470.   [48] Al-Marghinani, *Al-Hidaya*, 2:632; Ibn Ishaq, *Abrégé*, 122–23.

maintenance during the *'idda*, was also to be permitted into public space during the day to seek her livelihood. The jurists agreed that any woman who defied these rules and stayed out overnight or changed her lodging without permission forfeited all rights to her housing and any maintenance she was owed.[49] The benefits of the *'idda*, whether maintenance and housing or just housing alone, were contingent upon a woman's acquiescence to special restrictions on her movements, restrictions which highlighted the fundamental goal of authenticating the paternity of any child she might be bearing during the *'idda*.

The rules for the *'idda*, as elaborated by the jurists, bring the doctrines on divorce into sharper focus. It was only the wife, not the husband, who must pass a period in the limbo of neither marriage nor divorce, ostensibly to ensure the legitimacy of any child conceived before the divorce was pronounced. At one level, biology dictated this practice since only paternity, not maternity, can be at issue. At another level, the practices of the *'idda*, including various restrictions placed on women, problematized female sexuality: how could a man guarantee that he had sired his wife's child, particularly in the wake of a divorce? The rules devised for the *'idda*, while they attempted to minimize the potential for confusion over paternity, were obviously not foolproof given the difficulties of exercising absolute control over women, but did attempt to extend a husband's control of sexuality beyond the period of the marriage. Furthermore, the notion that a divorced woman should take some time to grieve for her change in status (if not for her mate), while her husband was free to marry immediately or, indeed, might already be married to several others, points to a fundamental asymmetry in doctrines on marriage and divorce. A wife needed a transitional time to absorb the change in her status and the "loss" of her man, while a husband was presumed ready to move on, literally at a moment's notice. Whether the rules for the *'idda* reflected the emotional states of actual spouses need not concern us here, but they do imply that, despite extensive judicial discourse on the gravity of the marriage tie, the jurists thought that men and women inhabited different emotional worlds in marriage.

We cannot help but be struck by the fact that the jurists took such a variety of positions on key issues of divorce such as the remedy for a missing husband or what constituted proper compensation in *khul'*. Working with roughly the same material, the jurists brought their own perspectives to bear on the development of legal doctrines of divorce. Although they were very much part of a context that privileged male power, they struggled with

[49] Al-Marghinani, *Al-Hidaya*, 2:631; Ibn Ishaq, *Abrégé*, 122; al-Hilli, *Mukhtalaf*, 7:472–73.

issues of fairness and decency. Still, equality between men and women was not part of their understanding of the world, nor of their aspirations for the future. Divorce law was discriminatory: they were not willing to give women the power, like that of men, to end a marriage unilaterally. They were alive, however, to the need to protect women from abuse at the hands of the unscrupulous and they offered paternalistic solutions to women in dire straits. These positions were fully consonant with a patriarchal view of women as less capable and dependent, a view the jurists inscribed in the law on divorce.

ISLAMIC DIVORCE: PRE-TWENTIETH-CENTURY PRACTICES

As in the case of marriage, we have little information on legal practices of divorce for much of the pre-twentieth-century period. The major exception, once again, is to be found in the Ottoman Empire from the sixteenth century forward because of the availability of Islamic court records, so it is primarily to the Ottoman period we turn to get some sense of how the law on divorce was understood and actualized by practicing jurists and laypeople prior to the reforms of the twentieth century.

We may assume that *ṭalāq*, as the easiest form of divorce, was also the most common, but because divorce by *ṭalāq* was not ordinarily registered in the court, we have no firm idea of its frequency. A couple might still resort to the court to resolve or record property settlements arising from a *ṭalāq*, giving us a glimpse into some of the possible dynamics and tensions in a unilateral repudiation. In one pre-Ottoman document from fourteenth-century Jerusalem, a woman acknowledged that she had received all that was due her in the wake of a *ṭalāq*:

> She acknowledged – Fatima ibna of ʿAbd-Allah ibn Muhammad al-Khaliliyya, who is present at al-Quds al-Sharif – in conformity with the shariʿa, while she was in a state of sound body and mind and legally capable of conducting her affairs, that she has no claim on her divorcer ... [she claims] no right or any remainder of a right, nor a bride price nor any remainder of a bride price, no [expense of] clothing or maintenance, and no alimony, and absolutely nothing from the matrimonial rights in the past and up to its [the document's] date.[50]

The Islamic court in eighteenth-century Damascus performed a similar notarial function, registering a number of such acknowledgments of the fact

[50] Huda Lutfi, "A Study of Six Fourteenth Century Iqrars from Al-Quds Relating to Muslim Women," *Journal of the Economic and Social History of the Orient* 26, no. 3 (1983): 259.

that a *ṭalāq* had occurred and that the divorced wife had received all of her due.[51] Why were such *ṭalāq* settlements recorded in the court? We can only surmise that men who had divorced their wives and paid what they owed by way of the balance of the dower and maintenance costs were anxious to avoid any future litigation that might come their way concerning the rights of their former wives.

Indeed, we have many examples of such litigation in which a divorced wife claims that her ex-husband failed to deliver what he owed, including the balance of her dower, the costs of her maintenance during the *ʿidda*, and perhaps the outstanding amount of a loan she made to him or personal property she had left behind. Women flooded into the Ottoman-period courts to sue for money and goods owed them by their former husbands, and they often seemed to meet with success, particularly in their claims for payment of the balance of the dower.[52] It is impossible to learn, in most cases, whether the judge's ruling subsequently resulted in a woman's actual recovery of her property. Furthermore, if the husband could point to a written acknowledgment that his wife had received all her rights, her case would falter. Such was the fate of a Damascene woman of considerable wealth who sued her ex-husband for recovery of her personal property, including household goods like pillows, bed and chair covers, plates, cups and boxes, as well as valuable items of dress such as kaftans, a silver belt, and a gold necklace. Despite the fact that her suit listed the standard personal property of an elite woman of the time, her ex-husband was able to carry the day (and keep the property) by referring to an earlier court document in which his wife had testified that she had received everything that belonged to her in the wake of a *ṭalāq*.[53] And there is little question that a husband could try to wiggle out of his obligations after a *ṭalāq* and the court might upon occasion collude: in one case from Ottoman Bulgaria concerning a man who had balked when it came time to pay the deferred dower, the court negotiated a deal whereby his ex-wife accepted one-half of what he owed as payment in full.[54]

Other kinds of legal disputes about *ṭalāq* found their way into court. Husbands and wives might disagree, for example, about whether a divorce had actually taken place, usually with the wife pressing for the court's validation of the divorce. One notable lady from eighteenth-century Jerusalem claimed in court that her husband had quarreled with her, insulted her, and then

[51] Tucker, *In the House*, 93.
[52] Peirce, *Morality Tales*, 230–31; Tucker, *In the House*, 93–95; Abdal-Rehim, "The Family," 104–05.
[53] Tucker, *In the House*, 94–95.   [54] Ivanova, "Divorce," 124.

pronounced a divorce which he subsequently disavowed; because she could produce witnesses, the judge ruled the divorce valid, in keeping with the Hanafi position that the actual words of *ṭalāq* always trumped intention.[55] In another case, in the Anatolian town of Aintab in the mid-sixteenth century, the court, helped along by an opinion from a local mufti, decided that a man who divorced his wife while in a state of illness-induced delirium was not bound by his words.[56] In these and other cases women were clearly eager to end the marriage on terms favorable to them and were trying to capitalize on pronouncements of divorce which their husbands later retracted or denied. They were usually successful if they could produce witnesses and there were no mitigating circumstances such as evidence of a husband's altered mental state.

Women also appealed to the court to recognize delegated and/or conditional *ṭalāq* when the stated conditions had been fulfilled. It was apparently not uncommon for husbands who were soon to embark on one of the Empire's annual military campaigns to delegate the power of divorce to their wives in the event that they failed to return in a timely fashion by making statements such as "If I do not come back within one year, let her be free."[57] This was a common practice in Mamluk times as well, when traveling husbands often left behind statements of divorce contingent upon their failure to return in a specified period of time.[58] Men might register such intentions in the court just prior to their departure, as did one soldier in 1541: "If I am unable to return and resume married life with my wife within three months, let her be divorced from me."[59] Sometimes, marriage contracts were drawn up which included the condition that a wife would be divorced if her husband disappeared for more than a stated period of time. In all such instances, the wife could activate the divorce by going to court with the evidence, either witnesses to her husband's statements on delegation or a court document in which her husband had recorded a conditional divorce, and requesting her full rights under *ṭalāq*.

We thus have ample evidence that the courts and the practicing jurists were alive to the nuances of the law on *ṭalāq*. It was a "man's divorce," but there were serious obligations incurred that the courts were bound to enforce. A woman who could reach the court was likely to meet with a sympathetic ear when it came to matters of dower and maintenance post-*ṭalāq*. She could be fairly certain that she could force her husband to honor the terms

---

[55] Mahkamat al-Quds (Jerusalem Islamic Court), s. 226, p. 156.   [56] Peirce, *Morality Tales*, 201–02.
[57] Ivanova, "Divorce," 120.   [58] Rapoport, *Marriage, Money and Divorce*, 77.
[59] Peirce, *Morality Tales*, 81.

of a *ṭalāq* he was trying to retract, or could convince the court to recognize a conditional *ṭalāq*. But this is not to say that women did not encounter obstacles in some instances, particularly when they lacked the critical evidence provided by legal documents or reliable witnesses. The law protected them when they worked carefully within its parameters and mobilized support from male relatives and other members of the community. Some of the hard edges of *ṭalāq* could thus be tempered, but this type of divorce remained the prerogative of men, and women exercised control only around the margins.

Tafrīq or *faskh*, as a female-initiated annulment which preserved a woman's rights, was surely preferable, but how common was it in the pre-twentieth-century period? As was noted above, the grounds for a *tafrīq* were few in Hanafi doctrine, limited to rare defects in the husband that constituted absolute impediments to the purpose of marriage, such as impotence or leprosy. We would expect, as a result, to find few if any annulments in the Ottoman records since the Ottoman courts followed these narrow interpretations of Hanafi law. Surprisingly enough, however, at least some of the Ottoman period jurists and courts were willing to entertain expanded grounds for *tafrīq*, most notably in the cases of a husband's blasphemy or desertion.

Blasphemy became accepted grounds for *tafrīq* because it was interpreted by Ottoman jurists to denote apostasy on the part of the husband, an act that automatically dissolves the marriage. Ebu's-su'ud, a foremost sixteenth-century Ottoman jurist, issued a fatwa to this effect:

Zeyd beats his wife, Hind, who is guilty of no offence. When 'Amr says: "It's against the shari'a. Why are you beating her?" Zeyd replies: "I don't recognize the shari'a." What should be done?

Answer: He becomes an infidel. Hind is irrevocably divorced (*bā'in*). She receives her dower and marries whichever Muslim she wishes.[60]

It is, in principle, the blasphemy of not recognizing Islamic law, by which the husband renders himself an apostate, which serves as the grounds for the dissolution of the marriage, not the abuse suffered by the wife. Still, there is other information in the fatwa, such as the fact that the wife is guiltless and another Muslim is questioning the husband's conduct, which invites us to think of blasphemy as part of a larger package of abusive behavior. We also have evidence that some women knew and took advantage of the fact that a husband who blasphemed provided them with the grounds they needed for

---

[60] Imber, *Ebu's-su'ud*, 196.

a *tafrīq*: in one case brought to the court in eighteenth-century Bulgaria, a mother requested and received a divorce for her daughter on the grounds that her husband had "cursed the faith and religion of my daughter."[61] Any verbal abuse that strayed into the territory of religion, and therefore might be interpreted as blasphemy, could be parlayed into grounds for *tafrīq* as long as there were reliable witnesses.

The other notable way by which women procured annulments in some of the Ottoman courts was by recourse to Shafi'i doctrine on the missing husband. Hanafi jurists of the period appeared to recognize the limitations of Hanafi doctrine in such situations, as the following fatwa from Khayr-al-Din al-Ramli, the renowned Hanafi jurist of the seventeenth century, suggests:

Question: There is a poor woman whose husband is absent in a remote region, and he left her without maintenance or a legal provider, and she has suffered proven harm from that. She has made a claim against him [for maintenance] but the absent one is very poor. Resources for her maintenance were left in his house and in his shop, but they are insufficient for her to avert poverty. She therefore asked the Shafi'i judge to annul the marriage, and he ordered her to bring proof. Two just men testified in conformity with what she had claimed, and so the judge annulled the marriage ... Then, following her waiting period, she married another man. Then the first husband returned and wanted to nullify the judgment. Can that be done for him when it was all necessary and had ample justification?

Answer: When the harm is demonstrated and the evidence for that is witnessed, the annulment of the absent one's marriage is sound ... It is not for the Hanafi or others to nullify this, as our 'ulama' have said in their fatwas.[62]

The thrust of Khayr al-Din's argument is clear: although Hanafi doctrine does not view a husband's absence and the consequent lack of support as grounds for an annulment, the Hanafi jurist stands ready to validate and accept the consequences of an annulment pronounced by a jurist of another school with a different doctrine. This position, in fact, opened the door to the widespread practice of women going to court to obtain annulments

[61] Svetlana Ivanova, "Marriage and Divorce in the Bulgarian Lands (XV–XIX c.)," *Bulgarian Historical Review* 21, no. 2–3 (1993): 58.
[62] Al-Ramli, *Kitab al-Fatawa*, 1:49.

when they had been deserted by their husbands, at least in the lands of Ottoman Syria and Palestine. In these cases, the courts neatly sidestepped the problem of Hanafi doctrine by allowing assistant judges from the Shafiʿi or Hanbali school to preside over these cases. In at least a few instances, this liberalization of the grounds for annulment even extended to cases where the husband was physically present, but failing in his duty to maintain his wife properly.[63]

Tafrīq thus emerged as an accepted and widely practiced form of divorce in some of the Arab lands of the Ottoman Empire, despite the fact that Hanafi law was so restrictive in its interpretation of the grounds required for an annulment. The leading Hanafi jurists of the time privileged the doctrines of other schools that facilitated these divorces, particularly in the context of blasphemy (often presented as part of a package of harmful abuse), and desertion and non-support. This position enabled some women in difficult marriages to initiate and obtain a divorce without their husbands' consent while retaining all their rights to dower and maintenance.

Khulʿ was even more commonplace. The majority of divorces in Mamluk society were apparently *khulʿ* divorces,[64] and this trend seems to continue during Ottoman times, at least among divorces that appear in the court records. The normal practice appears to have been to take *khulʿ* agreements to court for registration. For example, Madeline Zilfi found that ten to twelve women came to a court in eighteenth-century Istanbul every month seeking *khulʿ*, and this was in just one of several courts in the city.[65] In eighteenth-century courts in Bulgaria, *khulʿ* was the most common form of divorce.[66] In Cairo in the same period "many" wives stood before the judge to ask for *khulʿ*.[67] In Jerusalem, Nablus, and Damascus, *khulʿ* was the type of divorce most frequently encountered in court by far.[68] We cannot compare the incidence of *khulʿ* with that of *ṭalāq* because the practice was to register the former but not the latter in court. It is safe to say, however, that *khulʿ* divorces were a very ordinary occurrence. In Istanbul and Sofia, most *khulʿ* requests were preceded by "we don't have a good life together," "there was no understanding between us," or "there were quarrels and dissension between us."[69] In Syria and Palestine in the eighteenth century, *khulʿ* requests did not usually mention reasons or background;

---

[63] Tucker, *In the House*, 84–87.   [64] Rapoport, *Marriage, Money and Divorce*, 69.
[65] Madeline C. Zilfi, "'We Don't Get Along': Women and *Hul* Divorce in the Eighteenth Century," in *Women in the Ottoman Empire: Middle Eastern Women in the Early Modern Era*, ed. Madeline C. Zilfi (Leiden: Brill, 1997), 275.
[66] Ivanova, "Divorce," 118.   [67] Abdal-Rehim, "The Family," 105–06.
[68] Tucker, *In the House*, 97–100.   [69] Ivanova, "Divorce," 118; Zilfi, "We Don't," 279.

rather, a woman simply "asks" her husband to divorce her for a compensation.[70]

Compensation varied in this period, but typically entailed waiving the balance of the *mahr* and maintenance during the *'idda*; sometimes it included additional payments such as the return of goods that formed part of the initial (prompt) *mahr* and even an additional sum of money. For example, Kurduman Khatun, from a village outside Sofia, waived her rights to her deferred *mahr* of ten *kurus*, returned prompt dower goods including four kilos of wheat and two black calves, and paid an extra four *kurus*.[71] In one typical *khul'* agreement from early eighteenth-century Jerusalem, the wife waived rights to dower and maintenance, and agreed to forego maintenance for their child as well:

The woman 'Aysha bint Muhammad ? [whose identity is attested to by two witnesses] asked her husband, 'Amr al-Hamami ibn ? ibn 'Abd al-Qadus, to divorce (*khala'a*) her in exchange for his debts to her of the *mu'akhkhar* of her dower in the amount of fifty *ghurush* and the *nafaqa* of her *'idda* and the cost of her dwelling, and all other wifely rights before and after separation. He divorced her and she is responsible for the *nafaqa* of her son by him for a period of three years from this date. 19 Sha'ban 1152 H (1739 AD)[72]

I cannot know what might have preceded this couple's appearance in court, but it seems likely that they had already agreed on the *khul'* and compensation, and that the trip to court was for purposes of registration rather than litigation as such. Most of the cases of *khul'* in the records from Damascus, Jerusalem, and Nablus read in this way, as though they document prior arrangements. Standard practice on compensation varied somewhat, but was usually in excess of the balance of the dower, with the costs of the waiting period and child support as common additions. By the Ottoman period, then, generous compensation for *khul'* was the norm in both theory and practice.

The husband was almost always present in court to assent to the *khul'*. Could a woman obtain a *khul'* without her husband's consent? Material from Istanbul, Sofia, Damascus, Jerusalem, and Nablus always included the agreement of the husband as a part of the *khul'* procedure. At least one historian has seen cases in Cairo where the judge granted a *khul'* divorce over the husband's refusal,[73] but this does not seem to have been widely practiced. Nor is there evidence that the judge pressured the husband to agree, although we cannot rule out the possibility of behind-the-scenes persuasion.

---

[70] See Tucker, *In the House*, 97–98.   [71] Ivanova, "Divorce," 116.
[72] Mahkamat al-Quds, s. 230 (1738–1740 AD), p. 48.   [73] Abdal-Rehim, "The Family," 106.

The court, however, was not only a passive forum for registration of *khul*ʿ divorces. Abuses of *khul*ʿ also caught its attention. In eighteenth-century Istanbul, for example, a woman came to court to complain about forced *khul*ʿ: she claimed that her husband had coerced her into a *khul*ʿ agreement in order to take her *mahr*.[74] In eighteenth-century Damascus, a woman named Zaynab claimed that her ex-husband Muhammad had divorced (*ṭallaqa*) her five days ago and failed to pay her what he owed her: a deferred dower of fifty *ghurush*, maintenance during the *ʿidda*, and a long list of personal items which included gold earrings, a silver belt, a scarf, a loom, a rug, etc. The husband countered that the divorce was a *khul*ʿ in exchange for waiving all these items and produced two male witnesses to support his position. Zaynab in turn brought one man and two women to testify that the divorce had been a *ṭalāq*, and she carried the day.[75] The potential for litigation over the terms of a *khul*ʿ, or indeed over whether such an agreement had been made at all, no doubt helped encourage the standard practice of registering these divorce agreements in court.

While the practices of the Ottoman period certainly fell within broad doctrinal guidelines on *khul*ʿ, they restricted a woman's ability to use *khul*ʿ to her advantage: the husband was allowed to collect excessive compensation; his agreement was usually required; and the judge appeared to limit the role of the court to notarial functions unless there was an egregious violation of a woman's rights. As a result, it is unlikely that *khul*ʿ was a "woman's divorce" that effectively redressed the discriminatory operation of *ṭalāq* in this period. I cannot rule out the possibility that many women did willingly opt for *khul*ʿ and find it a good solution to their marital problems, but conservative interpretations of all three key elements did not make it easy for them to do so.

REFORM AND DIVORCE

As intellectuals of the late nineteenth and early twentieth centuries engaged in discussions about reforming Islamic law, in order, among other things, to move the law closer to the original intent of justice and fairness for both men and women alike, they focused a great deal of their attention on divorce and honed in on some of the abuses and injustices that had, according to their analysis of the situation, crept into divorce practices. Divorce was a

---

[74] Fariba Zarinebaf-Shahr, "Women, Law, and Imperial Justice in Ottoman Istanbul in the Late Seventeenth Century," in Sonbol, *Women, the Family, and Divorce*, 92.

[75] Tucker, *In the House*, 99.

topic that had received considerable unwanted attention from westerners, orientalist scholars and colonial administrators alike, who tended to present it as emblematic of the loose marital ties that characterized Islamic society, in contrast to their own societies where most legal systems rendered divorce either impossible or extremely difficult to obtain well into the second half of the twentieth century. It should come as no surprise, then, that a defensive tone crept into much of the reformers' discussion of divorce as they combated the image of *ṭalāq* as a male privilege that could be exercised on a whim.

Muhammad Rashid Rida, for example, approached the topic of divorce by reminding his readers of the sanctity of marriage and the high standards for marital happiness based on "love, closeness, cooperation, and tolerance."[76] Divorce honors the marital institution by acting as the remedy for a marriage that is not fulfilling this purpose of mutual dependence. Rida stresses the many ways in which the doctrine of *ṭalāq* also constituted an improvement upon the prevailing practices in the pre-Islamic period by limiting the number of times a man could pronounce divorce before it became irrevocable, and forbidding the material exploitation of women in the wake of divorce. Islam reformed preexisting practices so that men could no longer use divorce as a way to toy with their wives. But what about the fact that only men have the power to pronounce a *ṭalāq*? Rida explained away this male prerogative by noting that a man invests more in the marriage, in a material sense, through his payment of the dower and his responsibilities to his divorced wife and children, so he is less likely than a woman to rush into a divorce at the first sign of trouble. Women, whether as a result of the absence of material investment or natural disposition, are "quicker to anger and less forbearing," and might therefore leave a marriage for the least of reasons if they were given parallel powers.[77] The power of *ṭalāq* is safer in the hands of men, who are more patient, in keeping with the spirit of Islam that actually tries to avoid divorce through the use of arbitrators to reconcile the couple and by an overarching discourse that discourages recourse to divorce, as in the hadith "the most abominable of permitted things is *ṭalāq*."[78] The Tunisian 'ulama' surveyed by Tahir al-Haddad echoed the idea that although a man had the right of *ṭalāq*, he should only exercise it under circumstances that truly preclude a continuation of the marriage. A woman did not have reciprocal rights, of course, but at least one 'ālim thought it was in keeping with the "spirit" of the law that her husband should grant her a divorce if she were unhappy in her marriage. Another noted that a woman could acquire the power to divorce herself if she so

---

[76] Rida, *Huquq*, 160.   [77] Ibid., 162.   [78] Ibid., 165.

stipulated in her marriage contract (*ʿiṣmataha fi yadiha*).[79] None of the reformers questioned the male right to *ṭalāq*, and only a few were ready to extend that right to women under any circumstances, but most did call for honoring the spirit of the law by pronouncing *ṭalāq* only in the most extreme cases of incompatibility.

Tafrīq or *faskh*, a judicial decree of annulment, was the remedy open to women according to the reformers. In keeping with the classical *fiqh*, a woman could ask the judge to annul her marriage if her husband had a physical defect (impotence, castration) that precluded intercourse, or if he suffered from leprosy, tuberculosis, or any other disease judged to be both incurable and infectious by the doctors of the time. There was no debate on that score. Some reformers thought that the husband who was unwilling or unable to provide proper maintenance also opened the door to a decree of *faskh* at the request of the wife. At least one Hanafi *ʿālim* pointed out that Hanafi doctrine did not allow for such a solution, but Hanafis had long been willing to deputize a jurist of another school who could issue the annulment in such a case, and the modern Islamic court should follow this practice. In the case of a missing husband (*mafqūd*), we find a wide variety of opinions as to how soon an annulment can be issued in keeping with the divergences in doctrine, but the reformers abandoned the Hanafi position that such an annulment can only be issued after ninety-nine or more years in favor of the more flexible positions of other schools that call for a wait of anywhere from a few months to four years depending on the circumstances. The idea of granting an annulment in cases of incompatibility or abuse was more controversial: some reformers thought that spouses who did not get along should be eligible for *faskh*, while others ruled for reconciliation in all but the most extreme cases. Aggression and physical abuse on the part of the husband were sufficient grounds for most to grant a woman's request for an annulment, but a few held that a woman could only be free of an abusive marriage by choosing to ransom herself.[80] Overall, the reformers tended to expand the grounds and shorten the wait for an annulment in the case of a defective or abusive marriage.

Throughout much of the period of reform, *khulʿ* received relatively little attention compared to *ṭalāq* and *faskh*. Rida, for example, noted briefly that *khulʿ* could be a way for a woman to choose to leave a marriage, but his primary concern was that the compensation might be "defrauding or oppressive."[81] This construction of *khulʿ* as a procedure fraught with

---

[79] Al-Haddad, *Imraʾatuna*, 82, 94, 97, 103.
[80] Rida, *Huquq*, 169–70; al-Haddad, *Imraʾatuna*, 82–83, 93–94, 96–98, 101–03.
[81] Rida, *Huquq*, 125.

dangers of abuse persisted for decades: in 1959, Mahmud Shaltut included only a very short passage on *khul'* in his study of the shari'a, in which he noted that a woman could offer her husband a compensation to leave a marriage, but worried that a husband might oppress or harm his wife in order to coerce her to agree to a *khul'*.[82] The reformist discussion of *khul'* was relatively sparse as a result of these kinds of suspicions.

Nor did the reformers dwell long on the doctrines of the *'idda*. They agreed that the *'idda* was important in order to establish if a divorcée were pregnant, and had the additional function for the widow of allowing her a ritual period in which to demonstrate her attachment and loyalty to her husband. Rida added that the husband should maintain his wife in her *'idda* in the most generous manner he could manage and give other parting gifts as well, even though the classical jurists had differed on these issues. He held up Hasan b. 'Ali, the grandson of the Prophet, as an example of how to soften the blow of divorce for a woman: Hasan gave his divorced wives huge sums of money, and even apologized in a letter to one of them about this "small token from a departing beloved."[83] The arrangements of the *'idda* present the man with an opportunity to render divorce as palatable as possible for his wife, and, no doubt, can help belie the image of divorce as a heartless casting off of a wife who had outlived her attractiveness.

There were other voices speaking out for reform of divorce law, most notably those of local female activists and their male allies focused on women's issues in the early twentieth century. Social critics set their sights on both the ease of male repudiation and the difficulty of female-initiated divorce. In Egypt, women like Sa'diyya Sa'ad al-Din published articles in the women's press that addressed the toxic effects of unilateral repudiation: a woman's ever-present fear of divorce could not but sow feelings of mistrust and lay the foundation for a dishonest marriage, since a woman will use "deceit, lies, and cheating" if necessary to please a husband who has the power to divorce her whenever he pleases. Malak Hifni Nasif, another contributor to the Egyptian discourse on women's rights, presented a series of reform propositions to the Umma Party Congress in Egypt in 1911 which included the idea of prohibiting unjustified *talāq*.[84] In colonial Bengal in

---

[82] Mahmud Shaltut, *Al-Islam: 'Aqida wa-Shari'a* (Cairo: al-Idara al-'Amma li-l-Thaqafa al-Islamiyya bi-l-Azhar, 1959), 162.

[83] Rida, *Huquq*, 171.

[84] Beth Baron, *The Women's Awakening in Egypt: Culture, Society, and the Press* (New Haven: Yale University Press, 1994), 165, 184. See also Beth Baron, "The Making and Breaking of Marital Bonds in Modern Egypt," in *Women in Middle Eastern History: Shifting Boundaries in Sex and Gender*, ed. Nikki R. Keddie and Beth Baron (New Haven: Yale University Press, 1991), 275–91.

1919, a local periodical deplored the practice of casual divorce as exemplified by men who divorce their wives for "either too much or too little salt in the curry," and another ran a series of articles in 1917 and 1918 criticizing unbridled *ṭalāq* as a misinterpretation of the Qur'an.[85] And in Iran in the 1930s, the women's journal *Alam-e Nesvan* argued for the ideal of companionate marriage and legal reform so that men could no longer "throw their wives out of the house" whenever they wanted to.[86] Alongside the regulation and restriction of *ṭalāq*, many of these same activists discussed the need to enhance the ability of women to leave flawed or loveless marriages by expanding the grounds for *faskh* and ensuring the compliance of the court.

As in the case of laws governing marriage, various states took up these issues of divorce law in the context of the legal reform movements of the twentieth century. Mounira Charrad has argued, based on her study of women and legal reform in North Africa, that the impact of female activists or even reforming jurists was rather minimal when it came to the actual process of reform. By comparing the conservative outcome of reform in Algeria, where there was an active women's movement advocating legal change, with the liberal outcome in Tunisia, where there was no record of women's activity, she discounts the role of grassroots campaigns. She places the differences in the reformed legal codes squarely at the feet of the respective states and the character of their authority, specifically "the extent to which the newly formed national state built its authority in alliance with kin groupings or, on the contrary, on bases independent of them."[87] It is no doubt true that the various modern states sponsored the reform of Islamic law in relation, first and foremost, to national goals and alliances which varied from place to place. In the case of divorce law, at least, I think it is rather difficult to measure the impact of a variety of factors with any precision, including prior reformist discourse, women's activism, and the agenda of the national state in relation not just to kin groupings but also to a wide variety of strategies of power and control. Divorce laws, particularly the ease by which a man could secure a divorce and the difficulty of same faced by a woman, were very much a part of a wider discourse on issues of companionate marriage, the role of the family in relation to both the state and the individual, and women's rights. The states and courts addressed the subjects of *ṭalāq*, *faskh*, and *khul'* in the context of local discourses on

---

[85] Sonia Nishat Amin, *The World of Muslim Women in Colonial Bengal, 1876–1939* (Leiden: Brill, 1996), 125.

[86] Jasamin Rostam-Kolayi, "Expanding Agendas for the 'New' Iranian Woman: Family Law, Work, and Unveiling," in *The Making of Modern Iran: State and Society under Riza Shah, 1921–1941*, ed. Stephanie Cronin (London: RoutledgeCurzon, 2003), 157.

[87] Charrad, *States and Women's Rights*, 2.

Islamic legal reform and women's rights, as well as part of a broad program of codification by which states asserted novel control over family institutions and gender relations as key to the kind of social change needed for the strength and prosperity of the nation.

The doctrine and practice of *ṭalāq* had been pilloried by both Islamic reformers and women activists as degrading to wives, who could be easily cast off for any minor offense, and as detrimental to the very institution of marriage itself because it trivialized the marital bond by allowing it to be so casually severed. They subscribed, along with officials of the new nation-states, to the importance of sound marriages; they agreed that social progress rested on the healthy families produced by couples in stable and happy unions. The concept of divorce was deeply embedded in the Islamic tradition, however, so rather than calling for the prohibition of *ṭalāq*, reform efforts focused on its regulation and restriction. First, there were reforms that spoke to the issues of intention, since Hanafi doctrine had held that any pronouncement of divorce, regardless of the husband's intention, was in fact binding. The Ottoman Law of Family Rights (1917) invalidated divorces pronounced by men in a state of inebriation or under coercion, and a number of other codes followed suit, expanding the list of nullifying conditions to include insanity, disorientation, error, anger, senility, or even the pressures of disastrous times as in the codes of Jordan, Lebanon, Iraq, and Kuwait. In Libya, the issue of intention was confronted directly in article 32 of the 1984 law which held that a husband must intend *ṭalāq* and be fully aware of what he was saying in order for the divorce to take effect. Such reform was a simple adaptation of the Hanbali position on intentionality. Many, although not all, of the modern codes also prohibited the practice of taking an oath of divorce or suspending a divorce upon the fulfillment of some condition as in the codes of Iraq, Syria, Egypt, and Morocco.[88] A man's prerogative to pronounce a divorce was not in question, but a *ṭalāq* must be both intended and straightforward: incompetence, error, and manipulation were ruled out of order in the process.

Second, some reformers sought to bring *ṭalāq*, an extra-judicial procedure, under the jurisdiction of the court. A number of codes required that a husband register the *ṭalāq* in court as in Algeria, Iran, Lebanon, Pakistan, Jordan, Egypt, and Singapore, and the Iranian Special Civil Courts Act of 1979 required that he obtain either his wife's consent or the permission of the court. Libya instituted an arbitration process if the wife did not agree to

---

the *ṭalāq*, and the People's Democratic Republic of Yemen imposed mandatory divorce counseling in 1974, a requirement that was eliminated after unification with North Yemen in 1990 when extra-judicial *ṭalāq* was reinstated. Tunisia went the farthest by decreeing that no divorce could be pronounced outside the court, effectively abolishing the male prerogative of unilateral repudiation by allowing either husband or wife to file for divorce in court. A number of states, which continued to permit *ṭalāq*, including Algeria, Jordan, Kuwait, Syria, and Yemen after unification up to 1998, authorized the court to consider whether the husband had "abused" the right of *ṭalāq* or pronounced an arbitrary divorce without cause; in such a case, the court could award the injured wife benefits equivalent to one to three years of maintenance. Marriage contracts issued in Iran after 1982 included a standard stipulation that in the wake of a divorce that was not the fault of the wife, a husband must pay her half of what he had earned during the marriage.[89] The thrust of these reforms was to bring the court into the process of *ṭalāq*, as overseer, arbitrator, and authority for the resulting property settlement, all the while chipping away at the male prerogative of repudiation. The state strengthened its hand in divorce decisions, and the court increasingly became responsible for guarding against abuse.

How effectively the court performed as the guardian of women's interests post-*ṭalāq* may be open to some question, however: in one study of the court in Sanaʾa, Yemen from 1992 to 1995, not a single woman appeared in court to request expanded maintenance payments on the grounds that the divorce had not been her fault, despite the fact that the law clearly stated her right to do so.[90] On the other hand, a study of an Algerian court from 1984 to 1986 examined the application of a 1984 law requiring *ṭalāq* to take place in court and authorizing the judge to assign damages to the wife if the divorce were not her fault. Out of twenty-seven cases of *ṭalāq*, twenty-six were ruled to be the husband's fault and he was assigned damages, despite many attempts to argue that the wife had been disobedient by leaving the house or working without his permission.[91] In the Algerian case, the fact that *ṭalāq* must be pronounced in court ensured that both spouses went

[89] El Alami and Hinchcliffe, *Islamic Marriage*, 46, 100–01, 144–45, 191, 235, 245, 261–62; J. N. D. Anderson, "The Tunisian Law of Personal Status," *International and Comparative Law Quarterly* 7, no. 2 (1958): 271–72; Mir-Hosseini, *Marriage*, 57; Anna Würth, "Stalled Reform: Family Law in Post-Unification Yemen," *Islamic Law and Society* 10, no. 1 (2003): 20, 26.

[90] Würth, "Stalled Reform," 20–21.

[91] Ruth Mitchell, "Family Law in Algeria before and after the 1404/1984 Family Code," in *Islamic Law: Theory and Practice*, ed. Robert Gleave and Eugena Kermeli (London: I. B. Tauris, 1997), 199–202.

before the judge at the time of divorce, allowing for much greater judicial intervention in the property settlement.

A third approach to the reform of *ṭalāq* took the tack of leveling the ground by formalizing the delegation of *ṭalāq* to a wife at the time of the marriage. Lucy Carroll has traced how the courts of India, and later Pakistan and Bangladesh as well, usually upheld a woman's right to initiate a *ṭalāq* if she had a stipulation in her marriage contract that delegated the power of *ṭalāq* to her in the presence of a number of contingencies: in one such contract examined by a court in Calcutta in 1919, the husband had delegated his power of *ṭalāq* to his wife if he took a second wife without her consent, if he beat or mistreated her, or if he did not allow her to visit her parents. The court upheld her right to pronounce a *ṭalāq* and furthermore ruled that the delegation was irrevocable and the wife could exercise it whenever she wished after the contingency arose. Drawing on this legal tradition, some reformers on the subcontinent have promoted the use of the "Bombay Contract," a contract with standard contingencies for delegated divorce, including the failure to behave kindly and provide maintenance, the taking of a second wife, and general incompatibility, which obviously provides the wife with rather broad grounds for divorce. It is not clear, however, how widespread the use of this contract has actually become.[92]

The tactic of inserting the delegation of divorce in the marriage contract has also gained some popularity in postrevolution Iran. The Ayatollah Khomeini set the tone by noting in 1979:

If it is true that Islam accorded to men the right of divorce, it also gave this right to women. They can, at the time of marriage, ask for a delegation of divorce or place contingencies [in the contract]. Then they can insist on divorce when they wish or under certain contingencies, for example if the husband lacks respect [for his wife] or if he takes another wife.[93]

A 1980 law followed that authorized a number of such contingencies in the marriage contract, including maltreatment, the failure to pay maintenance, the taking up of a dishonorable occupation, etc. Both the husband and the wife must sign off on the contingencies, however, and it seems that contracts with an expansive list of contingencies are not very common. One of the major problems with the delegation of *ṭalāq* as a strategy for achieving

---

[92] Lucy Carroll, "*Talaq-i-Tafwid* and Stipulations in a Muslim Marriage Contract: Important Means of Protecting the Position of the South Asian Muslim Wife," *Modern Asian Studies* 16, no. 2 (1982): 284, 303–04.

[93] Quoted in Azadeh Kian-Thiébaut, *Les femmes iraniennes entre islam, état et famille* (Paris: Maisonneuve et Larose, 2002), 126.

gender equality is the same problem that dogs prenuptial agreements in general: couples are loath to anticipate and plan for troubling contingencies at the moment they are agreeing to marry, one of the more optimistic of human engagements.

A different approach to the facilitation of female-initiated divorce was to expand grounds and specify procedures for judicial annulment or *tafrīq/faskh*. The Ottoman Law of Family Rights (1917) initiated this method by drawing from a number of legal schools for guidelines on the grounds either spouse could use for *faskh*. In article 132, the OLFR listed a number of conditions or acts on the part of the spouse, including adultery, insanity lasting more than three years, imprisonment of more than five years, absence of more than five years, syphilis or epilepsy that was not revealed at the time of marriage, and endangerment of the other spouse's life as grounds for a person to seek an annulment in court.[94] Various reformed codes of the twentieth century incorporated these grounds but tended to reduce the required time periods, remove the gender neutral tone, and medicalize the evidence. In the Algerian code of 1984 a wife can petition for divorce if her husband is sentenced to a prison term or is otherwise absent for more than one year, while in Iraq, Jordan, Kuwait, and Egypt it is a prison term of three years and other absences of either one or two years. The codes of Jordan, Kuwait, and Morocco specifically call for the involvement of medical specialists in cases where physical defects are concerned, for "help shall be sought from Muslim doctors who are experts in defining the appropriate period and in determining the defects for which annulment may be sought."[95] Many of the reformed codes also added failure to maintain as grounds for a female request for *faskh*. A woman can petition for divorce if her husband fails to provide maintenance, and the judge is empowered to grant an immediate divorce unless the husband claims inability, in which case he is given a three-month grace period to come up with the costs of maintenance, as is the case in Egypt, Lebanon, Syria, Jordan, and Kuwait among other countries. The Libyan code has a similar article, but the wife will be granted a divorce in the context of her husband's inability to provide only if she was not aware of her husband's straitened circumstances at the time of their marriage.[96]

---

[94] "Ottoman Law of Family Rights (Qanun Huquq al-ʿAʾila)," in Sadr, ed., *Majmuʿat al-Qawanin*, arts. 132, 373–74.
[95] In the Kuwaiti code: El Alami and Hinchcliffe, *Islamic Marriage*, 140.
[96] *Ibid.*, 53, 57, 76, 105–06, 136, 139, 164, 192, 208, 233.

In many codes a wife can also sue for divorce on the grounds of injury (*darar*). Borrowing from the liberal Maliki version of injury, a wife can claim mistreatment or incompatibility that makes it impossible for her to continue in the marriage. The Egyptian code of 1929 had such a provision: if the mistreatment was proved, the judge was authorized to effect a divorce; if proof was scarce and the husband denied the charge, the judge should appoint two arbitrators, one from each spouse's family, to attempt a reconciliation. This is an interesting innovation, drawing on the Hanbali preference for arbitration, but placing it in the hands of the couple's relatives under the purview of the court. Should the reconciliation fail, then the codes differed in details. In Egypt the judge was to pronounce a divorce if the arbitrators found the husband responsible for the problems in the marriage, but if the wife were responsible the marriage would not be annulled. Other codes lay out a spectrum of fault and recompense: at one end, a husband who has mistreated his wife may be compelled to divorce her and pay compensation in addition to the usual divorce payments, and at the other a wife who is held responsible for the problems may have to pay compensation to her husband or even remain married against her will.[97]

In keeping with many other legal reforms of the modern period, the rules for *faskh* clearly strengthened the hand of the court: the judge interpreted the law on *faskh*, examined the evidence, appointed arbitrators as required, and usually ruled on whether a woman had sufficient grounds for a divorce. There was ample room for the exercise of judicial discretion. In one study of legal practice in Egypt in the first half of the twentieth century, half of the applications for *faskh* were rejected by the courts. The judges were not disposed to grant a divorce because of a husband's illness, and they considered beating and cursing to be injuries only in upper-class families, not for lower-class women.[98] After Law #44, which categorized the taking of a second wife as an ipso facto injury that constituted grounds for divorce, was passed in Egypt in 1979, most judges refused to apply the law on the basis that polygyny may produce injury (which must be proved), but is not an injury in and of itself.[99] In Yemen, between 1983 and 1995, it was virtually impossible for a woman to obtain a divorce on the basis of "violence" or "hatred" as the code envisioned unless she was a wealthy woman from an

---

[97] Shaham, *Family and the Courts*, 116–17; El Alami and Hinchcliffe, *Islamic Marriage*, 75, 108–09, 138, 191, 260.

[98] Shaham, *Family and the Courts*, 125, 131–32.

[99] Immanuel Naveh, "The Tort of Injury and Dissolution of Marriage at the Wife's Initiative in Egyptian Mahkamat al-Naqd Rulings," *Islamic Law and Society* 9, no. 1 (2002): 29–30.

elite family.[100] There is no mistaking the subjectivity of the judges in question: they are men who cling to a certain view of men, women, and the marital relationship, a view in which male dominance as expressed in the practice of polygyny and the disciplining of a wife is a right not easily legislated away.

Khul' was the last type of divorce to receive close attention from reformers. The Ottoman Law of Family Rights subsumed *khul'* under *faskh*. If a woman had requested a divorce, the judge was to select two arbitrators, ordinarily one from each spouse's family, who were to scrutinize the testimony and the evidence of marital problems in order to assign blame. After hearing the arbitrators out, the judge acts:

If the problems come from the husband's side, the judge separates (*faraqa*) them. If the problems come from the wife's side, there is a *khul'* for the *mahr* or a part of it. If there is no agreement between the two arbitrators, the judge appoints another legal body or a third arbitrator who is not related to either side, and the ruling of the arbitrators is final and not admitting of exception.[101]

Under this article, the decision that a *khul'* is the appropriate course lies in the hands of the judge, albeit with input from the families of the couple. The court also has the last word on compensation: the maximum amount is fixed at the amount of the *mahr*, but the judge may use his discretion to assign a lesser amount.

Egypt followed with a similar law in 1920. As amended in 1985, the law constructed the *khul'* type of divorce similarly as the result of a long process and invests the arbitrators with even more authority. The wife petitions the court, arbitrators are appointed, and reconciliation is attempted. If reconciliation fails, and the responsibility for the breakdown of the marriage rests with the wife, then compensation is decided upon by the arbitrators, who are not given any guidelines. In Tunisia, the role of the arbitrators in the process has been eliminated: all divorces, either at the will of the husband or at the request of wife go to the court for an automatic decree; the judge fixes compensation at his discretion either way.[102] The twentieth-century codification thus tended to vest control of *khul'* in the court, defining it in the process as a judicial decree of divorce rather than an instance of *ṭalāq*.

[100] Würth, "Stalled Reform," 23–24.
[101] "Ottoman Law of Family Rights (Qanun Huquq al-'A'ila)," in Sadr, ed., *Majmu'at al-Qawanin*, art. 130, p. 373.
[102] El Alami and Hinchcliffe, *Islamic Marriage*, 56–57, 245.

The court also engaged with the issue of proper compensation. If *khul'* is an agreement between husband and wife, then so is the compensation. But, with codification and the growth of the power of the court, we begin to see variations as to how proper compensation is to be determined. In Algeria, it is still the husband who decides on acceptable compensation. In Tunisia, Pakistan, Malaysia, and the Philippines, the court is empowered to set the amount in each case, while in Iraq, if the wife is at fault, compensation to her husband is fixed by statute at the amount of her dower.[103] Decisions on appropriate compensation can vary broadly even within one legal system. In Pakistan the court is instructed to fix compensation at not more than the "return of all marriage benefits." Within those guidelines, a husband might receive anything ranging from no compensation at all if he had been cruel (in the case of Munshi Abdul Aziz, 1985) to all the marriage benefits, including the full amount of the dower and maintenance, and the value of any presents the husband had given to his wife.[104] In Libya there is an interesting variation, with the wife often agreeing to compensate her husband in the amount of the balance of her dower once she has wed someone else; presumably the amount of her new (prompt) dower will be delivered to her former husband.[105] Most of these legal systems develop the idea that compensation should be commensurate with responsibility for the breakdown of the marriage, thereby lending still more weight to the court or court-supervised process that must now establish the dynamics of marital relations. While the canonical texts limited judicial investigation to establishing which party wanted the divorce, modern codes often expanded this investigation to include an assessment of the couple's behavior and assignment of fault. *Khul'*, viewed from the angle of compensation decisions, has come increasingly to look like *faskh*.

In the matter of the husband's agreement, some modern codes have retained the dominant classical doctrine that a husband's consent is essential to the process. The Yemeni law of 1992 made it clear that mutual consent must underlie *khul'*, and Kuwait (1984) defines *khul'* as a husband's *ṭalāq* in return for compensation to be mutually agreed upon.[106] Where elaborate judicial procedures of arbitration and court rulings have been put in place, as in Lebanon and Egypt before 2000, the issue of the consent of the

[103] Mohammed Altaf Hussain Ahangar, "Compensation in Khul': An Appraisal of Judicial Interpretation in Pakistan," *Islamic and Comparative Law Quarterly* 13 (1993): 133.

[104] *Ibid.*, 122–23.

[105] Aharon Layish, "Customary *Khul'* as Reflected in the *Sijill* of the Libyan *Shari'a* Courts," *Bulletin of the School of Oriental and African Studies, University of London* 51, no. 3 (1988): 429.

[106] El Alami and Hinchcliffe, *Islamic Marriage*, 134–35, 262.

husband may not be expressly addressed, but interpretation has generally held that the judge will seek the husband's agreement to a judicial separation and fix the amount of compensation after a somewhat unwieldy process is completed. The Pakistan courts first tackled this question directly. After some earlier decisions had tied *khul'* to the express consent of the husband, a landmark case, *Khurshid Bibi v. Muhammad Amin* (1967), explicitly empowered the court to decree judicial separation at the request of the wife and over the husband's objection. The Supreme Court in Pakistan gave an exhaustive opinion in the case, basing its ruling on materials from the Qur'an and hadith and concluding that the husband's consent was nowhere specified as an absolute requirement.[107] Under the Egyptian Law of Personal Status, Law #1 of 2000, signed on January 29, 2000, a wife may request and receive a divorce in court without grounds and without her husband's agreement as long as she returns the *mahr* and any gifts of jewelry she received from him at the time of marriage. There is an arbitration process built into the law, with one arbitrator to be chosen from each side; arbitration is supposed to last a maximum of three months if there are no children involved, and six months if children are present. If the arbitrators do not effect a reconciliation within that period, the court is supposed to grant the divorce regardless of the husband's wishes.[108] The Pakistani and Egyptian laws, while preserving a central supervisory role for the court, moved toward the institution of a true woman's divorce in the sense that the outcome of *khul'* was no longer to be held hostage to the agreement of the husband.

The reformers have also looked at the issue of support during the *'idda* and other payments post-divorce. Unless a woman had surrendered her right to support as a condition for obtaining a *khul'* divorce, or arbitrators in a *faskh* case had found her responsible for the failure of the marriage settlement and the judge ruled that she therefore forfeited her right to support, under most reformed codes a divorced woman was entitled to maintenance for at least the duration of her waiting period. Many codes (Egypt, Kuwait, Lebanon, Morocco) fixed the length of the *'idda* at not less than two or three months and not more than one year, in line, more or less, with current medical knowledge about typical menstrual and gestational cycles.[109] Women lost the ability to lay claim to waiting periods that were

---

[107] Pearl, *A Textbook on Muslim Law*, 104.
[108] See "Qanun al-Ahwal al-Shakhsiya al-Jadid," in Ahmad Ibrahim, *Ahkam al-Ahwal al-Shakhsiyya fi al-Shari'a al-Islamiya wa-l-Qanun*, 5th edn (Cairo: al-Maktaba al-Azhariyya li-l-Turath, 2005).
[109] El Alami and Hinchcliffe, *Islamic Marriage*, 143–44, 168–70, 212; Shaham, *Family and the Courts*, 142–46.

shorter or longer than these statutory limits. On the other hand, some states, such as Jordan and Syria, prescribed the payment of compensation equivalent to maintenance for as many as three years in the case of an arbitrary *ṭalāq*. The PDRY also awarded the marital domicile to the ex-wife as long as she had custody of her children. Post-divorce maintenance and compensation for women was a topic of key concern during the discussions of legal reform that took place in Palestine between 1994 and 2000 as the Palestinian National Authority prepared for statehood. Local women's groups proposed that maintenance be paid to divorced women for a period from five years to life, and that women receive one-half of the family property at the time of the divorce.[110] Although the process of devising a new legal code was shelved because of the political situation, we can expect these issues to be back on the agenda when planning for statehood begins again. At the behest, most often, of women activists and their allies, the issue of the *ʿidda* has evolved into a more general discussion of alimony and property settlements.

In the course of the twentieth century, the court asserted its authority over the intimate world of marital relations through reform of divorce law, while at the same time it has allied itself in many cases with the patriarchal family by institutionalizing familial control of marriage arrangements. In other words, the court gained new control over divorce while simultaneously formalizing the rights of the family. It was a balancing act similar to that performed in the sphere of marriage law: a modern family for a modern nation but yet one which retained distinct patriarchal features. The various actors in the history of modern divorce law, namely the State as legislator, the courts and judges as interpreters, the extended family as arbitrators, various medical personnel as experts, women activists as agitators, and the litigants themselves, all contributed to the trajectory of reform. The tensions among them help us understand the checkered history of divorce law, with its many starts and stops, in the modern period and inform ongoing efforts to change the law.

RECENT DEVELOPMENTS

On July 4, 2004, the All India Muslim Personal Law Board (AIMPLB) took up the question of *ṭalāq al-bidʿa*, or the "triple divorce," whereby a husband

---

[110] Lynn Welchman, "In the Interim: Civil Society, the Sharʿi Judiciary and Palestinian Personal Status Law in the Transitional Period," *Islamic Law and Society* 10, no. 1 (2003): 64–66; Würth, "Stalled Reform," 16; Dawoud El Alami, "*Mutʿat al-Talaq* under Egyptian and Jordanian Law," in *Yearbook of Islamic and Middle Eastern Law*, ed. Eugene Cotran and Chibli Mallat (London: Kluwer Law International, 1995), 2:54–60.

simply pronounces the divorce formula thrice and obtains an instantaneous and irrevocable divorce. The Board, set up in 1972 as an umbrella organization representing over forty different Muslim groups in India, was exercising its mandate to protect the personal laws of India's Muslim minority by acting as a consultant to the government when it came to the matter of any formal amendment to these laws. It was also responding, by all accounts, to a growing campaign that called for banning the triple divorce, a male prerogative that sowed insecurity and created hardship for Muslim women who could find themselves divorced and cast immediately out of their homes in an extra-judicial process against which they had no recourse. The major guiding piece of legislation on Muslim divorce in India, the Dissolution of Muslim Marriages Act of 1939, had expanded the grounds for *faskh* in line with other reformed codes.[111] The male right of *ṭalāq*, however, had not been addressed, so that Indian Muslim men entered the twenty-first century with their right to unilateral, extra-judicial, and instantaneous repudiation fully intact.

The problem of triple *ṭalāq* had been in popular consciousness for some time. *Nikaah*, a 1982 Indian musical directed by B.R. Chopra, told the story of a Muslim woman triply divorced by her beloved husband in a fit of anger. Although she manages to redeem her life through work, remarriage, and a climactic assertion of her independence, the injustice of the *ṭalāq* was crystal clear to the crowds who made this film into an Indian blockbuster.[112] At least one regional court subsequently took a position: the Allahabad High Court ruled in 1993 that triple *ṭalāq* was illegal and un-Islamic but the verdict was roundly decried by Muslim leaders. By the 1990s, women's groups had drawn up a number of model marriage contracts (*nikaahnamas*) which included provisions aimed at discouraging triple *ṭalāq* by, for example, specifying that the husband who divorces in this fashion must pay his wife double the *mahr* he owes her. And in April 2000, the National Commission for Women (NCW) called for a ban on triple *ṭalāq* as part of a report it issued on the minority community. According to its author, Sayeeda Hameed, NCW member and co-founder of the Muslim Women's Forum, India was lagging badly behind countries like Algeria, Iraq, Iran, and Indonesia, all of which have restricted or banned triple *ṭalāq*. Hameed and others had a chance, a year later, to present their case at a conference on

---

[111] See K. N. Ahmed, *The Muslim Law of Divorce* (New Delhi: Kitab Bhavan, 1978), Appendix IV, for the text of this act.

[112] Mahmood Farooqui, "Three Times Too Many," *Mid Day*, July 2, 2004, www.mid-day.com/columns/mahmood_farooqui/2004/july/86854.htm.

"Genuine Problems of Muslim Women and their Solutions" sponsored by the AIMPLB in New Delhi. Although the 'ulama' in attendance were not convinced to back a ban, they did hear out the arguments in favor.[113]

The proponents of a ban in the conference and elsewhere took a number of tacks as the debate heated up in the press in 2004. One was to argue that triple *ṭalāq* is, in fact, an un-Islamic practice, a holdover from pre-Islamic times that cannot be squared with the clear instructions of the Qur'an (4:35) that a process of arbitration and reconciliation is enjoined for every case of divorce. Another was to point out, as did Hameed, that many Islamic states had moved to eliminate triple *ṭalāq*, including their near neighbor Pakistan which had instituted the involvement of the court and required arbitration for every divorce in its Family Law Ordinance of 1961. A third was to document the ways in which triple *ṭalāq* had led to real injustices, such as that visited on Sameera, a young woman who was summarily divorced by her husband because he suspected she had contracted tuberculosis and did not want to foot her medical bills. Finally, a few reformers even took the position that the issue of triple *ṭalāq* pointed up the need to overhaul the system of Islamic law in India by legislating a codification of personal status law, thereby circumscribing the power of the qadis and the Islamic courts.[114]

When the AIMPLB met to consider the matter on July 4, 2004, the board fell short of instituting a ban but rather decided to launch a campaign to discourage triple *ṭalāq* by promoting the use of a model marriage contract that "suggests" that all marital disputes be handled by arbitrators or by a judge, and that triple *ṭalāq* be reserved for emergencies. Many of the advocates of reform were understandably disappointed. Some proponents of change, however, were pleased with the outcome, choosing to character-ize it as real progress and part of an ongoing campaign. Zeenat Shaukat Ali, a female AIMPLB member, saw it as an opening salvo:

Triple *ṭalāq* is not part of Koranic law. It has been distorted by patriarchal society. The time has never been so right to discuss what patriarchal Muslim society is doing to women. For me, the entire issue of the opposition to triple *ṭalāq* is that of the empowerment of women. It's a religious matter, which embodies itself in the fight for justice, a woman's dignity and human rights. It is unfortunate that it's

---

[113] Sayeeda Saiyidain Hameed, "Windows of Opportunity," *Communalism Combat* May 2001; Sakina Yusuf Khan, "Divorced from Reality – Amending the Triple Talaq Law," *The Times of India*, October 5, 2000.

[114] Asghar Ali Engineer, "Reflection on the Abolition of Triple Talaq – What Next?," *Asian Human Rights Commission* 6, no. 28 (July 12, 2004), www.rghr.net/mainfile.php/0618/749/; Manoj Nair, "Two Women Recall 'Triple Talaq' Trauma," *Mid Day*, July 4, 2004, www.mid-day.com/news/city/2004/july/87030.htm; A. G. Noorani, "The Big Idea: Reform, Reform, Reform," *Hindustan Times*, July 13, 2004, 10.

taken us over 50 years to understand this. This is largely because Muslims have been used as a vote bank and no one wants to take the right step to restore women's status.[115]

The decision to "discourage" rather than to ban the practice reflected in large part the opposition of many AIMPLB members to any move that might empower state intervention in Islamic legal matters. "A ban on triple *ṭalāq* would be interference in Shariat laws. Ideally *ṭalāq* should be pronounced once every month for three months, which doesn't mean that triple *ṭalāq* is invalid ... The board has no right to change what is written in the Shariat," according to one member.[116]

Despite the strong arguments against triple *ṭalāq* and the concerted efforts of reformers and women's groups, the campaign failed to achieve a ban, largely because of the history of relations between the state and the Muslim community in India. The issue was haunted from the beginning by memories of the Shah Bano case: in 1985 the Supreme Court in India had ruled that a Muslim man must pay alimony to his divorced wife despite the fact that she was not entitled to it under Islamic law. Muslim leaders protested what they perceived to be an infringement of their community rights and the state backed down, nullifying the decision of the Supreme Court through the passage of a bill reaffirming the applicability of the rules of Islamic law, the Muslim Women Protection of Rights on Divorce Act of 1986.[117] The inscribing of minority rights in the arrangements for legal autonomy has continued to exert a conservative drag on the process of reform in India. Activists cannot work through the legislature to obtain reformed codes, but rather must convince the 'ulama' and judges that different interpretations are in order. The specificities of the situation help us understand how a popular and well-organized campaign against triple *ṭalāq* could fall short of the mark.

Another campaign for the reform of divorce laws, aimed at reviving *khulʿ* as a true "women's divorce," met with somewhat more success. Activists in Egypt focused on *khulʿ* as the process most likely to address the problems many women faced when they tried to obtain release from a dysfunctional or abusive marriage. The reformers did not begin with a tabula rasa: the record shows that *khulʿ* had been fairly widely practiced in the late twentieth century. In the Nablus area in Palestine, where the Jordanian Law of

---

[115] Siddharth Srivastava, "Triple Talaq on Its Last Legs?," *The Day After*, July 2004, www.dayafterindia.com/july2004/societyhealth.html.

[116] Nair, "Two Women."

[117] Tahir Mahmood, "Islamic Family Law: Latest Developments in India," in *Islamic Family Law*, ed. Chibli Mallat and Jane Connors (London: Graham and Trotman, 1990), 297–99.

Family Rights (derived from the 1917 Ottoman law) was applied, a study of divorce by Annelise Moors, from the 1960s to the mid-1980s, found that *khulʿ* was common: there were 4.5 cases of *khulʿ* for every case of *tafrīq/faskh* recorded. Why were so many women getting this form of divorce, especially when it usually entailed the loss of the balance of their *mahr*, as opposed to a *tafrīq* divorce that preserved all their rights? Moors found that, in part, it was a commonly accepted solution for a divorce after the marriage contract had been signed but before the marriage was consummated, when a return of the *mahr* seemed a fair arrangement. In other cases, however, it was a way for a woman to get a divorce that could be arranged fairly quickly, and the husband's cooperation was purchased with the deferred dower. Such divorces required the husband's agreement to the procedure, including the amount of compensation, so that women often experienced hardship in the wake of *khulʿ*.[118]

Khulʿ was also very common in Iran in the 1980s, according to Ziba Mir-Hosseini. The Iranian Civil Code, following the lead of Shiʿi jurisprudence, distinguished *khulʿ*, a divorce at the wife's request entailing compensation to the husband, from *mubāraʾa*, a divorce sought by both husband and wife with no penalty for either. Still, Mir-Hosseini found that over 50 percent of all divorces registered in Teheran between 1980 and 1986 were *khulʿ* divorces in which women forfeited their *mahr*s. She argues that such high rates of *khulʿ* are only explicable as the result of a strategy on the part of husbands: they balked at divorce until they forced their wives to agree to a *khulʿ* so that they need not pay the *mahr* they owed.[119] Mir-Hosseini points to similar problems in Morocco, illustrated by the example of a woman who was abused by her husband and desperately wanted a divorce. Her father backed her, retained a lawyer, made a petition to the court, and negotiated a *khulʿ* divorce. Even with such strong support from her family, it took three years for her husband to agree to *khulʿ* and he drove a hard bargain which included her renunciation of maintenance for their son.[120]

Despite the rather modest record of *khulʿ* in respect to the strengthening of women's rights to divorce in the modern period (the exception here seems to be Pakistan), Egyptian reformers worked for almost ten years to draft and then shepherd a new *khulʿ* law through the Egyptian Parliament, meeting with final success in January 2000. The law was initially heralded as instituting a "woman's divorce" in order to provide a solution for Egyptian women who had long faced protracted delays in court after they initiated

---

[118] Moors, *Women, Property, and Islam*, 145.   [119] Mir-Hosseini, *Marriage*, 82.   [120] *Ibid.*, 105.

divorce proceedings. Ensuing discussions of the law, and the actual out-come of many of the suits filed under it, however, draw our attention to the complexity and difficulty of legal reform. Issues of interpretation of Islamic legal doctrines, constraints imposed by the broader social environment, and the role of laypeople in the development of the law have all played a part in the unfolding story of the new *khul* law.

The law itself was hotly debated from the first and there was disagree-ment among legal scholars as to its conformity with the shari'a. Shaykh Muhammad Tantawi, Grand Imam of al-Azhar, was present at the parlia-mentary debate and expressed the majority opinion of the forty scholars of the Islamic Research Academy that the law was fully in accordance with the shari'a. Although this view carried the day, thirty-one other scholars from al-Azhar had dissented and asked that the draft be withdrawn and revised in order to conform to the shari'a.[121] After the passage of the law, challenges of interpretation continued: in December 2002, the Supreme Constitutional Court heard a case contesting the constitutionality of the law because it contravened the shari'a by not requiring a husband's consent or giving the husband an opportunity to appeal the divorce. The court ruled that Qur'anic verses do indeed support the law as written.[122] The difficulty of achieving a consensus on what the shari'a actually "says" about *khul* had been made abundantly clear.

Nor can law and law-making be divorced from social context and cultural assumptions. For example, Egyptian parliamentarians added the provision for an arbitration process at the last minute; this was not part of the original draft of the law, which envisioned a quick and automatic decree of divorce at the woman's request. The addition of arbitrators and reconciliation sessions to the picture opened the door to complications and prolonged the process as husbands failed to show up for reconciliation; as a result, the recommended timetable for arbitration was seldom adhered to. In addition, the government did not issue an Executive Memorandum providing guid-ance on the implementation of the law so that the courts were left with considerable leeway on procedural questions, leading to routine delays.[123] Although the law passed through Parliament, these critical additions and oversights worked to perpetuate patriarchal patterns: women could sue for divorce but their requests would still be carefully scrutinized by family members and court officials who know best.

---

[121] Mariz Tadros, "Rooster's Wrath," *Al-Ahram Weekly*, January 20–26, 2000.
[122] Mariz Tadros, "Khul Law Passes Major Test," *Al-Ahram Weekly*, December 19–25, 2002.
[123] Mariz Tadros, "The Third Option," *Al-Ahram Weekly*, October 31–November 6, 2002.

The ultimate test, and eventual fate, of the *khulʿ* law lies in how it is understood and used by ordinary people. The initial expectation that women would rush to the court, once the law was passed, to get their long-delayed divorces quickly died out as the news of frequent delays spread. Of 2,695 suits filed in Cairo between March 1, 2000 and March 31, 2001, for example, only 122 had received a verdict as of the beginning of November 2002. As the courts dragged their feet when it came to the timetable for the arbitration process, fewer people were encouraged to file for *khulʿ*. Furthermore, local newspapers routinely portrayed women seeking *khulʿ* as immoral and their husbands as dishonored; women who filed for *khulʿ* divorce risked social opprobrium for themselves, their husbands, and their children. Finally, many women who did manage to get *khulʿ* divorces experienced problems in collecting child support: a government system set up to pay child support to the divorced woman and collect it from the ex-husbands was not working well.[124] The success of the *khulʿ* law as a "woman's divorce" is tied to how aggressively women press their rights to *khulʿ* in court and how much support they have from grassroots organizations like the Egyptian Women's Legal Assistance. Ongoing efforts by both individuals and organizations are clearly needed to convince the courts to expedite *khulʿ* procedures and to challenge public discourse on the respectability of *khulʿ*.

CONCLUSION

Islamic law on divorce, as outlined in the *fiqh*, was certainly discriminatory in the sense that men and women had very different options. As in the case of the laws on marital relations, I am struck by the great diversity of legal opinions over time and across space about how divorce should take place. From the outset, Muslim jurists were not particularly comfortable with divorce, the "most abominable of the permitted things," and this discomfort spawned a tide of regulation that spoke to divorce procedures, settlements, and residual rights. Men were privileged in the area of choosing divorce without recourse to judicial authorities, although the obligations they incurred as a result of *ṭalāq* were very much within the purview of the court. Women were much less free to choose divorce, and female-initiated divorce usually took place under the supervision of the judge. Within these broad constraints, the various legal schools could differ rather dramatically in how they interpreted the law. If we compare, for example, the majority Hanafi position on the grounds required for a female-initiated judicial

---

[124] Mariz Tadros, "What Price Freedom?," *Al-Ahram Weekly*, March 7–13, 2002.

divorce (only impotence or insanity) with the majority Maliki position (any injury inflicted by the husband) we get an immediate sense of just how divergent doctrines could be.

Still, there are areas in which legal thought is quite consistent and fully congruent with the central ideas of patrilineal and patrilocal marriage: in the wake of a divorce a woman leaves her house and is entitled only to temporary support. The underlying assumption is that the husband provides – the house, the food, the clothing – while the wife consumes, and once the marriage is over, she leaves with her own property intact but with minimal claims on his. The responsibility for her support devolves to another male, her father or brother at least temporarily, until, in the ideal case, she remarries after the completion of her waiting period. Discriminatory divorce laws make some sense if the woman is defined as a dependent consumer. The jurists were usually concerned with the specifically female experience of the process: they spent time elaborating on what women could expect after a divorce, and they held themselves and the courts responsible for insuring that women received their property and any support monies they were owed. The basic vision of male and female difference held true in divorce law, as the man was entrusted with the power to make a decision to end his marriage while the woman was placed under the guardianship of the court. How these laws worked out in practice was, of course, the business not just of doctrine and the jurists who interpreted and applied it, but also of the actions of the women and men who came to the muftis and the judges. We have seen ample evidence of their activity in the pre-twentieth-century period.

How do we evaluate the changes in divorce laws in the reform period in light of the engagement of feminist theory with issues of discrimination, the honoring of the female experience, and the confrontation of gendering practices in the law? Many of the reforms did address discriminatory rules for divorce, by limiting men's powers of *ṭalāq* on the one hand and expanding women's powers of divorce through *faskh* and *khul'* on the other. Outside of Tunisia, however, there is still little doubt about who has the upper hand when it comes to terminating a marriage: it is easier for a man to get the divorce he wants and it is harder for a woman to fight against the divorce she would like to avoid. Divorce law is still highly gendered and clearly discriminatory. One could argue that the female experience of marriage and divorce received even more of a hearing in the reform era: certainly many of the codes have addressed the issues of ill-treatment in the marriage and material support post-divorce that are so crucial to women's wellbeing. But the relief women have been offered is modest, limited in the main to the ability to sue for divorce on the grounds of abuse if they have family support and to receive limited extensions of the period of mainte-nance. The idea that a woman might be entitled to a significant portion of her husband's income or the marital domicile has surfaced at times, but has yet to be enacted into law in more than a couple of places. And finally, divorce law is still colored by a highly gendered vision of the power and place of male and female in a marriage. The male prerogative to divorce his wife without undue interference is a male birthright that has proven difficult to displace: when states have decreed reforms that restrict *ṭalāq* and expand women's access to divorce, the courts and the judges have often dragged their heels. And despite the fact that the (mythic) ideal of the provider/dependent relationship has been thoroughly undermined by the reality that most wives contribute to the income of the family alongside their husbands, the Family of Islamic law remains an institution in which the man is the putative provider and the woman is the designated dependent who is not required to contribute to the material support of her family and therefore cannot make claims to the fruits of her husband's labor once she is divorced. Divorce law reflects and abets this increasingly outmoded vision, one that is actively under attack in a number of campaigns of legal reform.

4

Woman and man as legal subjects: managing and testifying

The jurists who elaborated Islamic law and the courts which administered that law did not confine their attention, of course, to matters of marriage and divorce but rather ranged over many areas of human existence, from the ritual practices prescribed for devout Muslims to the punishments reserved for those who engaged in criminal activities. The lion's share of most works of *fiqh* and collections of fatwas, as well as cases in the court system, however, were devoted to subjects that pertain, in some fashion, to property: sales and purchases, rents, business partnerships, waqf endowments, pawns and securities, gifts, and inheritance were all discussed in precise detail. The law thus concerned itself in great measure with how property was to be managed, transferred, and made to yield benefits for its owners, preoccupations very much in keeping with the vital commercial environment of the time and place in which Islam arose.

The legal instrument most essential to property management, the contract, occupied a central place in the Islamic legal system. Undergirded by Qur'anic exhortations, "consume not your goods/ between you in vanity, except there be/ trading, by your agreeing together" (4:29) and "When you contract a debt/ one upon another for a stated term,/ write it down" (2:282), Islamic jurists developed a sophisticated law of contracts. The right of the individual to manage and dispose of his or her private property by contractual means was recognized and upheld by the law, although somewhat limited, at least in theory, by religious considerations including prohibitions on usury, trade in illicit objects (such as pork or wine), and the attachment of stipulations to a contract that violate ethical or ritual precepts.[1] But were there limitations placed as well on who, exactly, qualified as an empowered individual under the law?

[1] See Oussama Arabi, "Contract Stipulations (*Shurūṭ*) in Islamic Law: The Ottoman Majalla and Ibn Taymiyya," *International Journal of Middle East Studies* 30, no. 1 (1998): 29–50, for a discussion of the limitations on contractual freedom in Islamic law.

In his discussion of the person and the law, Dupret, following the lead of Ricœur, explored the issue of the individual as a legal subject:

the legal question of the subject of law (who is the subject of law?) also relates back to a moral question (who is the subject worthy of esteem and respect?) which, in turn, relates back to an anthropological question (what fundamental features make the self worthy of esteem and respect?) ... The question of "who" calls for identification, from whence comes the notion of "able subject". Posing this question is a matter of ascribing to someone an action or a part of an action. The attribution of the authorship of an act is fundamental to any imputation of rights and duties: it is the very heart of the notion of capacity.[2]

In this chapter I am concerned with the problem of the gendered subject of law. Was the capacity to enter into such contracts, to freely dispose of one's property within the limits set by religion, a gendered capacity? Did women have the right to control their property in the same ways as men? Did women suffer from certain legal disabilities as a result of being married, or not being married, or simply being women? In other words, was a woman's legal capacity when it came to her ability to manage property and be fully independent and effective in legal actions negatively affected by her gender, and was a man's legal capacity, by the same token, enhanced by his gender? The ability of women and men to participate in the economic activities of their society – to earn, to inherit, to save, and to dispose of property in the ways they wish – has a direct bearing on their position in the family and in the larger society. I will once more be asking about the issues of discrimination, of the extent to which the laws on property and legal capacity were gendered laws that distinguished male and female rights. Even when discrimination was not built into the rules governing property rights in an obvious fashion, we need to ask if the law was truly gender-neutral when it came to the ability to act as a fully empowered individual, as an equal legal subject.

In this chapter, I discuss women's and men's legal rights to acquire, manage, and alienate property, at the level of legal doctrine as well as in practice. In the course of exploring how people realized their property rights, I pay attention to inheritance practices that were key to cross-generational transfers of property, and to the institution of the waqf, which occupied a particularly important place in the history of women's management of their property. As we shall see below, however, certain aspects of legal doctrine and

---

[2] Baudouin Dupret, "The Person and the Law: Contingency, Individuation and the Subject of the Law," in *Standing Trial: Law and the Person in the Modern Middle East*, ed. Baudouin Dupret (London: I. B. Tauris, 2004), 23.

practice could work against full recognition of the adult woman as a legal person with capacities indistinguishable from those of a man. Rules governing the testimony of women in the court insinuated that women were not as credible as men, at least when it came to the presentation of particular kinds of legal evidence. Some legal schools also developed doctrines on guardianship that made women wards of their male relatives while at the same time limiting their ability to act as guardians for their own children. Islamic law, in theory and practice, struggled with some obvious contradictions when it came to the matter of female legal capacity.

I begin with a discussion of how the jurists approached the issue of gendered property rights and legal capacity, in an effort to explore some of these contradictions in doctrinal discourse. At the level of practice prior to the age of legal reform, I once more focus on the Ottoman period, the era for which we have the most abundant evidence. Thanks to the work of a number of scholars, we now know quite a bit about the extent and the limits of women's abilities to control their property in the Ottoman period, at least as far as elite women were concerned. When I turn to the nineteenth and twentieth centuries and the era of legal reform, I ask about the impact of reform on gender: did the shift in jurisdiction over most property matters from Islamic to civil courts affect women in differential ways? Did the reformers take up the issues of gendered inheritance rules, guardianship, and the roles women were permitted to play in the court? Finally, I turn to some of the hotly contested areas in Islamic law today, including discriminatory rules of inheritance and the residual rights of guardianship over adult women.

LEGAL CAPACITY AND THE ISLAMIC JURIDICAL TRADITION

In their copious discussions of the rules for handling property, whether buying, selling, pawning, lending, investing, endowing, or otherwise managing or disposing of property in land, goods, or money, the jurists made little distinction between males and females. An adult, as long as he or she were of legal age, was a legal subject fully empowered to enter into contracts and exercise sole control over the property that he or she owned, in Qur'anic exhortation: "if you perceive/ in them right judgment, deliver to them/ their property" (4:6). The jurists further elaborated on the topic of capacity in their discussions of interdiction (*ḥajr*), the narrow circumstances under which an individual of legal age could be retained or placed under another's legal tutelage.

Although adults, both male and female, were generally presumed to be competent to act independently on their own behalf, the jurists did raise at least one obstacle. Legal majority, as measured by the attainment of puberty, might not translate immediately into full legal capacity if an individual failed to demonstrate the required rationality, good sense, and mental maturity (*rushd*). The ninth-century Maliki jurist Sahnun addressed this issue:

> What if a boy or a girl attains puberty without showing responsible behavior (*rushd*)?
>
> Malik answered: Even if one is adorned with henna, he/she is not free to engage in buying, selling, donation, alms-giving, or manumission until he/she manifests responsible behavior.[3]

Such interdiction of a young person who had reached his or her legal majority and might even have been married (adorned with henna) was, at least in theory, gender-neutral. Male and female physical maturity/puberty, and thus legal majority, was, however, measured in distinct ways: according to al-Marghinani the evidence for male puberty was erection and ejaculation and the evidence for female puberty was menstruation. In both cases, if an individual were close to the normal age of maturity, his or her testimony to the presence of these phenomena was enough to establish legal majority.[4] When it came to mental maturity (*rushd*), on the other hand, males and females needed to possess the same traits: proper conduct, responsible behavior, and sound judgment. But how would these be ascertained by a judge? The Hanbali Ibn Taymiyya, who subscribed to very conservative views on female seclusion, held that female *rushd* need not be observed directly by the judge, but rather could be established through the testimony of close relatives or even, in the absence of same, by the circulation of news to that effect as had been the case with the women of the early Islamic community.[5] But while the maturity required for full legal competence might be established through different procedures, there was no question, even among the most conservative jurists, about the fact that, once having achieved that maturity, neither males nor females could be prevented from exercising their rights as subjects of the law.

It is worthy of note that, unlike in much of the western legal tradition, the marital status of a woman had no impact on her legal competence. European legal systems of the early modern period had placed most women

---

[3] As quoted in Oussama Arabi, "The Interdiction of the Spendthrift (*al-Safih*): A Human Rights Debate in Classical Fiqh," *Islamic Law and Society* 7, no. 3 (2000): 305.

[4] Al-Marghinani, *Al-Hidaya*, 3:1351–52.   [5] Ibn Taymiyya, *Fatawa al-Nisa'*, 166.

and their property under the legal authority of their husbands: in the extreme case of the English tradition of coverture, a husband exercised almost total control over his wife's property; on the continent, dowry systems protected the assets the wife brought to the marriage but usually gave the husband broad powers to manage this property; in Russia, where noblewomen were able to assert claims to separate property in the eighteenth century, "the elimination of gender-tutelage in marital property relations was a real innovation."[6] Although recent scholarship points to the many ways in which wives in early modern Europe "waged law" against their husbands and obtained access to the courts in order to pursue various strategies aimed at mitigating their legal situation, there is still little question that married women had greatly reduced legal capacity.[7]

The Muslim jurists, with only a few school-specific exceptions, took the contrary position that marital status held no ramifications for legal capacity for either spouse, and a husband had no right to manage or dispose of his wife's property. Al-Hilli, in his collection of Shi'i *fiqh*, discussed the case of a young wife whose husband made a bid to manage her property, on the basis that "he who safeguards her vulva, safeguards her money." Not so, opined al-Hilli, because "if she is mentally mature (*rashīda*), she is her own guardian, and if she is not yet *rashīda*, she has a guardian other than her husband, and there is no clear connection between the safeguarding of her money and the safeguarding of her vulva."[8] In other words, a husband's right to control his wife's sexuality did not give him the right to control her property, regardless of whether she had reached the age of full legal capacity. A woman's rights to sole control of all kinds of property she had acquired, whether through her own efforts or as dower and inheritance, were not affected in any way by her marriage.

But if her rights to manage and dispose of her property were identical to those of a male, certain legal doctrines introduced gender as key to the acquisition of property. As we have seen above (in chapter 2), the law specified that every wife should receive a dower (*mahr*) from her husband as part of a marriage contract; this dower, in the form of money, land, and/or personal items, became an undifferentiated part of the wife's private property and it

---

[6] Michelle Lamarche Marrese, *A Woman's Kingdom: Noblewomen and the Control of Property in Russia, 1700–1861* (Ithaca, NY: Cornell University Press, 2002), 48. See also Lee Holcombe, *Wives and Property: Reform of the Married Women's Property Law in Nineteenth-Century England* (Toronto: University of Toronto Press, 1983), 18–36.

[7] See the various papers in Nancy E. Wright, Margaret W. Ferguson, and A. R. Buck, *Women, Property, and the Letters of the Law in Early Modern England* (Toronto: University of Toronto Press, 2004).

[8] Al-Hilli, *Mukhtalaf*, 5:452.

could not be accessed or managed by any male relative, including her husband, as long as the woman had obtained her legal majority and was not under interdiction. The Qur'an had been clear on this point, noting that a bride must receive a dower and that dower property could not be accessed by anyone else unless the bride decided to share it of her own free will (4:4).

The privileged female access to property through the dower system was counterbalanced, however, by an inheritance law that discriminated against females. The Islamic law of succession strictly limited an individual's ability to bequeath his or her property at will: the law specified both the legal heirs and their shares, no more than one-third of the net value of an estate could be left as a bequest, and the legally designated heirs could not be beneficiaries of a bequest. The rules for inheritance had their origins in the survival of some preexisting tribal practices favoring male agnates which had then been greatly modified by the Qur'anic focus (4:11–12) on the marital ties and inheritance rights of spouses and a number of female relatives including mothers, daughters, and sisters. The resulting system of inheritance was both complex and comprehensive, and required a high level of specialized knowledge of the rules to work out inheritance shares in the context of varying configurations of survivors. For present purposes, however, it is particularly important to note two key aspects of the Sunni laws on inheritance, namely that most female heirs, including wives, mothers, and daughters, were slated to inherit one-half of the share of the corresponding male relation, and that, should a man or woman die without sons, certain other male heirs on the paternal side enjoyed inheritance rights that could greatly reduce the shares of closer female relatives and indeed all relatives on the maternal side. We can see the impact of these rules on how Ibn Taymiyya responded to one query on inheritance:

Question: A woman died and she left heirs including a daughter, a half-brother on her mother's side, and a male cousin on her father's side. What is apportioned to each one?

Answer: One half to the daughter, and the rest to the male cousin. And nothing to the half-brother on her mother's side, but if he attends the division of the inheritance, it is seemly to give him a small present. And the [presence of] the daughter cancels the claims of the maternal half-brother.[9]

Such an outcome, in which a paternal cousin has a stronger claim than a brother, and in fact stands to inherit a share of the estate equal to that of the

---

[9] Ibn Taymiyya, *Fatawa al-Nisa'*, 196.

only daughter, underscores the way in which the Sunni inheritance rules worked to limit the shares of females and those in the maternal line.

Under Shi'i jurisprudence, the 2:1 ratio held for many male and female shares, but unlike under Sunni law more distant male relatives on the paternal side had no special claims on inheritance and did not water down the rights of closer female heirs. Coulson seems quite correct in the emphasis he places on this difference: the fact that Shi'i jurists did not privilege the paternal line in their rule-making was a feature of inheritance law of key importance to women.[10] As al-Hilli pointed out in the following circumstances:

If one left behind the son of a paternal uncle, the daughter of a paternal uncle, the son of a paternal aunt, the son of a maternal uncle, the daughter of a maternal aunt, and the son of a maternal aunt ... [then] the children of the maternal uncle and the maternal aunt receive a third of the estate shared between them equally, and a third goes to the children of the paternal aunt, equal shares to the male and female, and the remaining third to the children of the paternal uncle, equal shares to male and female.[11]

In this kind of a scenario, when the deceased was survived by a number of cousins on both sides of the family, both paternal and maternal cousins would inherit, and their shares were not affected by their gender. The workings of Shi'i inheritance law thus tended, over time, to treat male and female, as well as paternal and maternal, heirs on a more equal footing, although the closest female heirs – wife, mother, daughters – were assigned one-half of the male share just as in Sunni law.

There are several features of both Sunni and Shi'i Islamic laws on inheritance worthy of note here: women were designated by law to inherit from many of their male relatives and could not be legally disinherited; women, although they often inherited one-half the share of their male relatives, enjoyed unfettered control of the family property they thus received; and finally, there were no constraints placed on the kinds of property women might inherit. We see some marked contrasts here to the rules for female dowers and inheritance in places like England and China. In England, the practice of primogeniture when it came to real property had become firmly ensconced in theory and practice by the early modern period: the eldest male child stood to inherit the family's real property while female children and younger males were typically allotted maintenance incomes. Although historians have pointed out some variations in this pattern, most

---

[10] See Noel J. Coulson, *Succession in the Muslim Family* (Cambridge: Cambridge University Press, 1971), chs. 2, 8.

[11] Al-Hilli, *Mukhtalaf*, 9:51.

significantly among classes, the fact remains that "property continued to be transmitted between men to secure patriarchal social structures."[12] By early Ming China, even daughters in sonless families had virtually no inheritance rights: by law, such families must practice "mandatory nephew succession" whereby the closest lineage nephew on the father's paternal side became the sole heir and the daughters received only a dowry. Although, in the later Ming and Qing periods, widows were able to acquire some rights to choose the heir from among the lineage nephews, women did not win the right to any significant share in family inheritance until the Republican Civil Code of 1929–30.[13] The absence of the concept of primogeniture in the Islamic law of inheritance[14] and its insistence on the inviolability, if not the full equality, of female shares in inheritance of all kinds of family property cannot be overemphasized. While, as we shall see below, these female rights to family property were sometimes honored in the breach, they endured in Islamic legal discourse over the centuries, providing a solid foundation for female acquisition of property.

The jurists' position that women were legal subjects with legal capacities little differentiated from those of men was clouded, however, by the view of female disability in the area of legal testimony. The Qur'an initiated the jurists' line of inquiry in a verse dealing with contracts:

> And call into witness
> two witnesses, men; or if the two
> be not men, then one man and two women,
> such witnesses as you approve of,
> that if one of the two women errs/ the other will remind her.   (2:282)

The implications of this verse were somewhat contradictory: on the one hand, it confirmed that the testimony of women on legal matters involving property carried weight in the court, but it also introduced some doubt as to a woman's ability to remember details of a transaction as well as a man. In their interpretations of this verse and of others, including Qur'anic verses 4:15 and 24:4 which discuss the need for four witnesses to prove the crime of illicit intercourse (*zinā'*), leaving the question of the gender of the witnesses open, most jurists arrived at a view of the matter that insinuated that women

---

[12] Wright, Ferguson, and Buck, *Women, Property, and the Letters*, 12.

[13] Kathryn Bernhardt, *Women and Property in China: 960–1949* (Stanford: Stanford University Press, 1999), 3–5.

[14] The one exception lies in the Shi'i rule that the eldest son inherit certain personal items of his father's, including his "clothing, sword, ring and copy of the Qur'an." See Coulson, *Succession in the Muslim Family*, 114.

were less trustworthy and less appropriate as legal witnesses than their male counterparts. At stake here was the status of women as legal actors who could play an authoritative role like that of men in court proceedings.

Al-Marghinani, a Hanafi, reviewed both the Shafiʿi and Hanafi positions as he understood them on the question of admitting female testimony as evidence:

> Shafiʿi said: The testimony of women is not accepted with men except in property and related matters, and the reason for this is the weakness of their intellect, and the deficiency of their accuracy, and their incapacity in ruling (*wilāya*), and so they are not suited for authority and [their testimony] is not accepted in cases of *ḥudūd* ... And for us [Hanafis], the foundation of competent [female] testimony rests on seeing, remembering, and communicating. The first provides the knowledge to testify, the second preserves it, and the third delivers it to the judge, and so a women's transmission of Islamic tradition was accepted. The shortcomings of her memory are corrected by joining with another [in the testimony]. Only the problem of judicial doubt (*shubha*) remains, and so female testimony is not accepted in cases where judicial doubt would nullify the outcome, and it is accepted in cases where rights are established notwithstanding judicial doubt. The refusal to accept the testimony of four women [in such cases] despite its support in analogical reasoning is calculated to limit their appearance in public space.[15]

Here al-Marghinani distinguishes the Hanafi from the Shafiʿi view of female limitations, suggesting that Shafiʿi's rather blanket dismissal of female intellectual capacity and authority was somewhat wide of the mark. He takes the position that women enjoy the basic human faculties required to take in, process, and relay information, and adds that their widely accepted role as transmitters of some of the hadith material central to the development of the Islamic community so attests. He allows, in a somewhat contradictory moment, that women may be more prone to lapses in memory, and therefore not ideal witnesses on their own, but this problem is easily addressed by adding another female witness. While Shafiʿi limited female testimony to property cases only, Hanafis were willing to accept female testimony in a broader range of cases (marriage contracts, divorces, manumissions, etc.), drawing the line only when it came to cases of *ḥudūd* and *qiṣāṣ* entailing prescribed corporal punishment. I will discuss *ḥudūd* crimes in more detail in chapter 5, but it is interesting to note here that al-Marghinani struggled a bit with the distinction. Why should women be acceptable witnesses in all cases except for those of *ḥudūd* and *qiṣāṣ*? He explains this anomaly through the concept of *shubha* (judicial doubt). *Shubha* refers to the possibility that an

---

[15] Al-Marghinani, *Al-Hidaya*, 3:1093.

illicit act (like extra-marital intercourse) may either resemble or appear to its participants to be a licit act (marital intercourse) in the event that they do not realize, for example, that their marriage is legally defective. It would be inappropriate to punish a couple for *zinā'* in these circumstances. This kind of judicial doubt, the resemblance of a licit act to an illicit act, if introduced into a case, can result in the dropping of prosecution in *ḥudūd* and *qiṣāṣ* crimes. But why would women be less discerning than men as witnesses in such cases? Al-Marghinani is not at all forthcoming on this point. He also makes short but interesting work of another apparent doctrinal anomaly, namely that two female witnesses can substitute for one man, but four women cannot substitute for the required two male witnesses. There is no attempt at legal reasoning here, but rather an appeal to social order in his comment that allowing four female witnesses as a regular practice would encourage too many women to come and go in public space. Elsewhere, however, he points out that a logical extension of the acceptance of women's ability to give evidence is the recognition that a woman could serve as a judge, at least in cases not involving *ḥudūd* and *qiṣāṣ* crimes.[16]

All the jurists seem to have accepted women as witnesses in property matters, at least if a male witness were also present, but certain hierarchies prevailed. In the case of conflicting evidence, Ibn Ishaq held that the testimony of two male witnesses took precedence over testimony by a male and two females.[17] Shiʿi jurists envisioned a more expansive role for female witnesses, allowing female testimony alone to support a plaintiff who is collecting a debt, as long as the plaintiff took an oath as well. Some Shiʿa were also open to the possibility that women could testify in all kinds of cases, including *ḥudūd* cases, although some of the penalties might be reduced if the case rested on a plurality of female witnesses.[18] The jurists also recognized that there were certain legally relevant facts that were likely to be known by women alone, such as matters related to childbirth. Establishing the paternity of the child by fixing the date of its birth, or ascertaining whether a baby were stillborn or had lived at least briefly outside the womb, had implications for inheritance and other legal claims. Although the jurists differed as to how many witnesses were required in these cases – Hanafis were satisfied with one or two and Shafiʿis insisted on four – they all acknowledged that female testimony alone provided sufficient evidence, often citing a hadith narrative for support.[19]

[16] *Ibid.*, 3:1078.   [17] Ibn Ishaq, *Abrégé*, 307.   [18] Al-Hilli, *Mukhtalaf*, 5:473–76.
[19] Al-Marghinani, *Al-Hidaya*, 3:1094.

How do we make sense of the many variations, in both the kinds of cases and the numbers of witnesses, in the jurists' positions on female testimony? Mohammad Fadel has proposed that these positions make sense if we think about legal disputes as "taking place across a public–private continuum." As long as the disputes lay primarily in the private sphere, and here he includes not only intimate female affairs at the far end of the private spectrum, but also most financial matters which are "essentially private," then female testimony appeared appropriate if not necessary. For disputes on the public end of the spectrum, however, and here Fadel includes not only assault and robbery but also marriage and divorce which "must meet standards of public recognition," only male testimony was relevant to this public space.[20] Fadel makes a second argument to the effect that the jurists had no difficulty in accepting women's capacity to speak in the "normative" register, that is, to make statements that "establish a universal norm or fact," but demurred when it came to "political" discourse in court which "would lead to some immediate, binding consequence."[21] It is the female connection with the private and, more importantly, male dominance of the public that renders female testimony in court so problematic: testimony is a political act inappropriate to woman's role in society.

These are intriguing arguments and certainly buttressed in part by juridical discourse: Fadel's characterization of property cases as "private," in the sense that they concern individual interests rather than the order and wellbeing of the wider society, helps us understand a jurist such as al-Marghinani who fully acknowledged women's capacity to testify in property cases but wanted to limit their presence in court for social reasons. There was a huge variety of opinions among the jurists, however, when it came to the issue of gendered capacity. For some jurists women were basically unreliable witnesses thanks to their inferior mental make-up, and could only be authoritative in instances where men, by definition, did not have access to the facts. For other jurists, male and female mental capacities were almost indistinguishable, and women's testimony was valuable in virtually every type of case, albeit in the two women to one man formula in many, although not all, instances. We are confronted yet again with a dizzying array of positions on a gender issue that bears directly on our sense of how Islamic law defined women's and men's roles in the legal system and in the wider society. The issue of female testimony was a malleable one,

---

[20] Mohammad Fadel, "Two Women, One Man: Knowledge, Power, and Gender in Medieval Sunni Legal Thought," *International Journal of Middle East Studies* 29, no. 2 (1997): 194.
[21] *Ibid.*, 188.

highly susceptible to social pressure, but in the hands of most jurists tinted with the notion of female disability. The equality between men and women when it came to the right to acquire and manage property was attenuated by this sense that women were not the equal of men as witnesses in court. But was this difference the result of innate weaknesses of reason and memory, or was it simply the product of a social order that limited the presence and the experience of women in public space? This ambiguity would prove to be critical to discussions of women, the law, and the courts in modern times.

The other major encroachment on the concept of Woman as legal subject came in the area of guardianship. Although adult males and females enjoy the same rights to enter into contracts pertaining to the management and disposal of property, they do not have identical capacities when it comes to entering into a marriage contract: there are elements of discrimination against women. The basic form of the marriage contract, as we have seen, is an offer of marriage and its acceptance. A man who has attained his legal majority may act independently and on his own behalf in the proposal of marriage which is a necessary part of the contract. A woman in her legal majority, however, may not always act independently or on her own behalf in her acceptance of this proposal. Unlike other types of contractual relationships (buying, selling, lending, borrowing, etc.), there are special rules for the marriage contract that vary among legal schools. Under Islamic law, the natural guardian (*walī*), who is the father, paternal grandfather, or nearest male relative, is charged with the protection of the interests of minor and other legal incompetents such as the insane, and is authorized to manage their property. In the case of the marriage contract, this guardianship is extended to adult females (but not males), whose *walī* must play a role in their marriage arrangements in most instances, in effect managing their person. In Hanbali, Shafi'i, and Maliki doctrine, and present (although not unanimous) in Shi'i doctrine as well, is the notion that the legal guardian, the father or grandfather of the woman, must play a role in the drawing up of the marriage contract: without the active presence of a guardian, or at a minimum his consent to the match, a woman's marriage would not be valid.[22]

Hanafi doctrine, at least what came to be the majority position, departed significantly from other legal schools, as summarized by al-Marghinani:

A free woman who is in her majority and of sound mind may enter a marriage contract by her own consent without a guardian whether she is a virgin or a *thayyib* [literally, a deflowered woman], according to Abi Hanifa and Abi Yusuf (may God have mercy upon them). And there is [another opinion] of Abi Yusuf (may God

---

[22] Al-Hilli, *Mukhtalaf,* 7:114–17.

have mercy on him) that there is no contract without a guardian. According to Muhammad [another of Abu Hanifa's disciples], the contract is conditional upon the guardian's consent. Malik and al-Shafi'i (may God have mercy on them) assert that a marriage is by no means contracted by a woman's own consent because marriage has its own aims and delegating to women would defeat these aims ... [For Hanafis] a woman disposes of her own rights because, if she is of sound mind and rational, she can dispose of property and also choose a husband. [23]

In this passage, al-Marghinani summarized current doctrines in his own Hanafi school as well as those of the Maliki and Shafi'i schools. The Hanafi majority opinion recognized the capacity of a woman in her legal majority to choose her own husband and to contract her marriage without the participation of her guardian, although minority opinions included the caveat that the guardian's consent was necessary to the validity of the contract in the sense that a guardian could void such an arrangement. Most Shi'i jurists also recognized the right of a woman in her majority to contract her own marriage but required the permission of the father or grandfather for its validity if she were still a virgin.[24] The Malikis and Shafi'is (as well as the Hanbalis and some Shi'a), however, required that the guardian actively participate in the making of the contract.[25] Why should a woman who is legally competent to enter contracts of all other kinds be subject to such restraint when it comes to the contract most central to her happiness and wellbeing?

The Hanafis saw no good reason why a female in her legal majority should not contract her own marriage: as a rational and mature person who was empowered to act on her own behalf in all other matters, why should a woman not control her own marriage? They were able to cite reports in support of this position that the Prophet said "The guardian has no authority over the girl" as well as a report that came through 'A'isha that the Prophet interceded on behalf of a girl whose father had arranged a marriage for her; the Prophet forbade her father to marry her off without her permission, and then gave her the authority to make her own marriage arrangements. The Hanbalis, Malikis, and Shafi'is, however, cite different hadith that report the Prophet saying "There can be no marriage without a guardian" along with the Qur'anic verse 4:25 "marry them with their people's leave" as textual authority for their position that virgin females must have a marriage guardian. These jurists justified such restraint on the basis that a woman's inexperience in the realm of men might lead her to make an undesirable match, resulting in

---

[23] Al-Marghinani, *Al-Hidaya*, 2:474–75.   [24] Al-Hilli, *Mukhtalaf*, 7:114–17.
[25] For Hanbali doctrine on the *walī*, see Ibn Hanbal, *Chapters*, 91–93.

harm to her and dishonor to her family.[26] There was more difference of opinion about whether a non-virgin woman (*thayyib*) was required to have a guardian, but most jurists who were not Hanafi or Shiʿi favored the involvement of a guardian in all women's marriages.

The power of the natural guardian over marriage arrangements did not, generally speaking, extend into other areas of a woman's life. Girls in their legal minority, just like boys, were under the control of a legal guardian who had the authority to manage their property as long as it was done responsibly and to the benefit of the minor. Most jurists seemed to agree that once a girl attained her legal majority, as signified by puberty and/or reaching the age of fifteen, she assumed full and unfettered control of both her person and her property as long as she had attained mental maturity. The Maliki school, however, developed a distinct position on this issue. Not only were mature females subject to their guardians' control in the matter of the marriage contract, but their property could also continue to be managed by their guardians for an extended period after their marriage, regardless of their physical or mental maturity. Females who had reached maturity could be retained under interdiction by their fathers until they married and four witnesses stepped forward to attest to their abilities to manage their own property. Even when both these conditions were fulfilled, a father might decide to continue the period of interdiction, up to one year according to Ibn Ishaq and up to as many as seven years in the opinion of other Maliki jurists.[27] When no longer under the tutelage of her father or other guardian, the married woman still lacked the ability to do exactly as she pleased, as we learn in the following:

The wife, the slave, and the debtor must seek permission to dispose freely of their property, and this applies in the case of a wife gifting more than a third [of her property] if her husband is not informed of it until such time as the marriage is ended by divorce or the death of one of them, and likewise such gifting by the slave if the master does not know of it until such time as manumission, and likewise the debtor if the creditor does not know until such time as the discharge of the debt.[28]

That a wife should stand in relation to her husband as a slave to a master or a debtor to a creditor when it came to certain acts, including her ability to donate more than one-third of her property or to act as a guarantor for more than one-third of a given sum, was understood by Maliki jurists as necessary

---

[26]   El Alami, "Legal Capacity," 193.

[27]   Muhammad ibn Ahmad Dasuqi, *Hashiyat al-Dasuqi ʿala al-Sharh al-Kabir*, 4 vols. (Cairo: Dar Ihyaʾ al-Kutub al-ʿArabiyya, n.d.), 3:298; Ibn Rushd, *Bidayat*, 4:1925.

[28]   Dasuqi, *Hashiyat*, 3:308.

to protect the husband, like the master or the creditor, from the material harm he might suffer. While the Maliki jurists were careful to specify that this was not a blanket interdiction, but rather one which applied only to a narrow range of actions, these opinions gave the husband a veto power over certain of his wife's property dealings. Cristina de la Puente, in discussing these Maliki positions, points out that they made serious inroads on a woman's juridical capacity by diminishing her "capacity to act" as a legal subject.[29] The extended tutelage of the natural guardian and the special powers of the husband constituted male encroachments on the rights of an adult woman to control her own property.

But did the jurists envision a situation in which the institution of guardianship might enhance a woman's legal capacity by, for example, allowing her to act as guardian for her children or other relatives? While females were not natural guardians – this was a role reserved to the father, grandfather, and, in their absence, other male relatives on the paternal side – they could be appointed as guardians if the occasion demanded. Islamic law allowed for the natural guardian or the court to delegate this role to another: the authorized stand-in guardian (the *waṣī mukhtār*) enjoyed many, although not all, of the powers of the natural guardian. The subject of the female guardian did not seem to occupy much of the jurists' time in the canonical works of *fiqh*. We find only oblique references to the female guardian in much of the literature. By the eighteenth century, however, some Hanafi jurists were discussing the powers of the female guardian in considerable detail:

Question: "Hind" was the guardian appointed by her deceased husband for his minor children by her, and she transferred guardianship to "Zayd," her cousin and worthy guardian as legally witnessed, and Zayd accepted that. Then she died leaving the above-mentioned children whose money was in her possession, and she left an estate. And the paternal uncle of the children contested that claiming that he, not Zayd, had the right of guardianship, and are his opposition and claims of no consequence?

Answer: Yes ... the agency and guardianship over a minor's property goes to the father, then to his delegate, then to the delegate's delegate ...[30]

Here not only could a mother acquire guardianship of her children, but she was also able to transfer powers of guardianship to a relative of her choice on

---

[29] Cristina de la Puente, "Juridical Sources for the Study of Women: Limitations of the Female's Capacity to Act According to Maliki Law," in *Writing the Feminine: Women in Arab Sources*, ed. Manuela Marín and Randi Deguilhem (London: I. B. Tauris, 2002), 100–01.

[30] Al-ʿImadi, *Al-ʿUqud*, 2:292–93.

her side of the family. Nor was her guardianship limited to the safekeeping of her children's property. Al-ʿImadi also addressed the question of her latitude of action:

Question: A mother was the guardian for her orphaned daughter, and the daughter owned a specified share in a house but no other property, and the daughter was in need of maintenance so the mother wanted to sell the share for a fair price for the purpose of maintaining her, is she permitted to do this?
Answer: Yes.[31]

It is much in keeping with the jurists' view of women as managers of personal property and witnesses in property cases that women would also be thought of, legally speaking, as fit guardians, at least as far as the property of minors was concerned.

When it came to the question of whether women could act as guardians for the purpose of arranging marriages, there was more hesitation. In the opinion of Ibn Rushd, Sunni jurists agreed that marriage guardians must be Muslim, in their majority, and male.[32] Later Hanafi jurists did not necessarily concur: by the eighteenth century, al-ʿImadi discussed the mother-guardian as a fully legitimate marriage *wālī*, although one who did not enjoy all the powers of the natural guardian:

Question: There is a woman, guardian of her orphaned daughter, who married her off to a suitable man with a fair dower, and the marriage was consummated. Then, as soon as she [the daughter] attained her majority, she chose annulment (*faskh*) and she testified to this in the court and appeared before the judge and asked for annulment in the legally prescribed fashion. The judge ruled for an annulment. If such is the case, does the annulment stand?
Answer: When the claim is presented fulfilling all legal conditions, then the above-mentioned marriage is annulled.[33]

So although a woman could assume the guardianship of her daughter, and arrange for her marriage while she was still a minor, the daughter did have the option of asking for an annulment when she came of age. The natural guardian, in the person of a girl's father or grandfather, on the other hand, not only could arrange such a marriage, but his arrangements were not subject to this "option of puberty," and could not be annulled in court. Still,

---

[31] *Ibid.*, 2:294.   [32] Ibn Rushd, *Bidayat*, 3:1255.   [33] Al-ʿImadi, *Al-ʿUqud*, 1:32.

some jurists thought that mothers could become guardians, for purposes of both property management and marriage. I cannot be sure at what point the jurists began to accept and develop the concept of the mother-guardian because of the absence of much discussion of the issue as far as I have been able to determine until rather late in the tradition, but it was certainly a feature of Hanafi legal discourse by the seventeenth century.[34]

In conclusion, we are left with the distinct impression that the jurists lived with a certain amount of doctrinal tension as far as the issue of Woman and Man as legal subjects was concerned. Women, like men, had substantial legal capacity as independent property owners and managers, but yet many jurists entertained reservations about the reliability of female testimony and their fitness as guardians. Were women the equal of men as subjects in law? The answer depended, for the jurists, very much on the category of legal act. Women could buy and sell, make bequests, lend and borrow, and otherwise dispose of property as they wished without being subject, in most instances, to male tutelage. But most jurists were less comfortable with the notion that women could have an equally authoritative legal voice in the affairs of others as witnesses or guardians. Whether this was a product of social context, specifically a disinclination to invite women into the public space of the court, or of deep-seated beliefs in the inferiority of women's mental powers, is difficult to determine because the discourse varied so widely among schools as well as individual jurists. Most jurists dealt with the issue of woman as legal subject not just as a legal question, but also a moral one (were women worthy in terms of their faculties to be full legal subjects?) and/or an anthropological one (were women in a position to acquire the requisite abilities to be full legal subjects?). Overall this is a juristic discourse marked by deep ambivalence about the role women could and should play in the legal system. The parameters of this discourse set the stage for the ways in which women acted as legal subjects prior to the modern period.

THE PRE-TWENTIETH-CENTURY LEGAL SUBJECT

While women had extensive property rights, in principle, under Islamic law, to what extent were they actually able to acquire and manage property in ways that lent these rights true solidity? Prescribed inheritance shares and required dower payments (*mahr*) represented prime opportunities for women to come into possession of property, so I first want to consider the evidence as to how often women could make such claims stick.

---

[34] See Tucker, *In the House*, 141–45.

Inheritance law, as we have seen above, assigned women shares in family property, but did families tend to honor the rights of all heirs? The information we have is contradictory. On the one hand, Nelly Hanna describes how inheritance law fragmented the fortune of an early seventeenth-century merchant family: Isma'il Abu Taqiyya had built an extensive commercial enterprise, but like other merchant families of the period it proved very difficult to maintain the integrity of the family fortune in the face of Islamic rules of inheritance. His three wives and ten daughters inherited pieces of his property and as a result his sole surviving son received only somewhat more than a tenth. Hanna notes, however, that other merchant families seem to have managed the inheritance challenge better by postponing partition of the estate and continuing to run the family business as a partnership of brothers and sisters, although in this latter case we may wonder if the sisters were being effectively disinherited.[35] Other studies also suggest that women had to resort to court actions to secure their legitimate inheritance because family members often played free and loose with their rights. Leslie Peirce reported on a number of such cases from her study of the Anatolian town of Aintab in the sixteenth century, including the following:

Selçük, Ayşe, and Magal(?), three sisters from the village of Seylan, bring a suit against the current owner of a vineyard of 750 vines that they inherited from their father when they were children. The owner claims that it was sold to him by their paternal uncle, Yusuf b. Hüseyin. Asserting that they have now reached their legal majority, the sisters deny the uncle's claim that they had given their uncle permission to sell (the uncle himself admitted that he sold it illegally). The current owner cannot provide proof that they had given their permission, the women take an oath supporting their claim, and the vineyard is restored to them. It is apparently left to the now former owner to reckon with the uncle.[36]

In fact, the records of the Islamic courts are littered with instances of inheritance disputes that pitted women against brothers, uncles, fathers-in-law, and brothers-in-law in particular. From sixteenth-century Anatolia to seventeenth-century Istanbul, to nineteenth-century rural Egypt, women went to court to assert claims that had been trampled by male relatives.[37] The goals of these male relatives appear, fairly consistently, to be connected

---

[35] Nelly Hanna, *Making Big Money in 1600: The Life and Times of Isma'il Abu Taqiyya, Egyptian Merchant*, 1st edn (Syracuse: Syracuse University Press, 1998), 41.

[36] Peirce, *Morality Tales*, 212.

[37] See *ibid.*, 211–16; Fariba Zarinebaf-Shahr, "Ottoman Women and the Tradition of Seeking Justice," in Zilfi, *Women in the Ottoman Empire*, 260–61; Judith E. Tucker, *Women in Nineteenth-Century Egypt* (Cambridge: Cambridge University Press, 1985), 46–50.

to the imperative of consolidating family property and protecting it from fragmentation through inheritance.

It is of some importance to note that women often succeeded in these inheritance claims. As long as the law was on their side, judges were apt to restore the property they had lost and reprimand their male relations. We can, of course, read this record in several different ways. The high incidence of inheritance disputes suggests that male relatives often disinherited women, rendering their inheritance rights a legal fiction. The fact that women could be successful in restoring their inheritance rights in court, however, demonstrates that judges were sympathetic to women's claims and further that women knew their rights under the law and trusted the court to uphold them. But we cannot know how many women were disinherited in silence, how many cases never entered the realm of the law at all. Nor is it easy to divine how many women willingly bartered their inheritance rights for other benefits, such as ongoing maintenance and protection from their brothers. Peirce points out how often men gifted houses to their sons, effectively removing that property from their estates before their death and disinheriting their daughters. It was rare, however, for a daughter to protest such a gift in court, and Peirce concludes that such acquiescence in her own disinheritance was her way of maintaining good relations with her brothers, an acquisition of "social capital" that might prove critical in the future when she was in need of a protector.[38] We also need to keep in mind the fact that inheritance was only one form of intergenerational transfers of property. Women might receive shares of family property *inter vivos* by way of trousseaux and other gifts, as we shall see below.

Although Islamic inheritance law did not differentiate among types of property, and all the legal heirs were entitled to their prescribed shares in family property, in much of the Ottoman Empire many females were not likely to inherit family land. The bulk of agricultural land was classified by the Ottomans as *miri*, state-owned land, over which individual landholders had rights of usufruct but not of full ownership. Property not owned outright as *milk* (fully private property) was not subject to Islamic laws of inheritance, and therefore the State could regulate the ways in which this land passed from one generation to another as it wished. Kenneth Cuno summarized the situation in the Balkans, Anatolia, and Syria:

the *qanūn*s [Ottoman laws] limited partibility in order to preserve households with their resources, including land, as viable units of production. This also entailed

---

[38] Peirce, *Morality Tales*, 227.

recognition of the traditions of patriarchal authority and patrilineal succession within peasant households. In the inheritance of usufruct rights priority was therefore accorded the sons of a landholder, who excluded all other heirs and received the land gratis, so long as they were capable of cultivating it and paying its tax. If a landholder was survived by a daughter and no son, then she could take the land upon payment of a fee (*tapu*), excluding her uncles, but only sons were supposed to inherit from women.[39]

Cuno notes that the situation in Egypt was a bit different insofar as the oldest capable male in the family rather than the sons usually received the usufruct of the family land, but throughout the Empire women were, generally speaking, residual heirs to land only in the absence of male heirs. The exclusion of agricultural land from the jurisdiction of Islamic inheritance law meant that women were not inheriting any part of what constituted the bulk of family wealth in rural areas. On the other hand, the court records suggest that women did inherit their shares in other types of family property, including money, household and personal items, and urban real estate: women are named as legitimate heirs to all these items. The evidence also demonstrates that women often chose to sell off the shares they inherited in real estate or in business equipment in order to acquire capital they used for business investments or the purchase of luxury goods. Peirce thinks that women chose to convert their assets to money or personal items since these liquid forms of wealth were much easier for them to control and manipulate. Most surveys of women's estate records tend to confirm this trend, since women's estates, at least among the well-to-do, tended to include lots of elegant (gold- and silver-embroidered) clothing, furs and jewelry, substantial household items such as weighty copper vessels, and money.[40] Women did also own urban real estate, but not in the proportions we might expect compared to the estates of their male kin.

Women also could acquire property at the time of marriage, through their *mahr*s, a form of property the courts held to be an essential part of the marriage contract and the exclusive property of the bride, and in the form of a trousseau (*jihāz*). Defrauding a bride of her dower was a serious moral offense: as the seventeenth-century jurist Khayr al-Din put it in the case of a village headman who took a girl's dower, "his eating of the dower is like filling his belly with fire and blazing flames," in reference to the Qur'anic

[39] Kenneth M. Cuno, *The Pasha's Peasants: Land Tenure, Society, and Economy in Lower Egypt, 1740–1858* (Cambridge: Cambridge University Press, 1992), 74–75.

[40] Peirce, *Morality Tales*, 225; also see Fatma Müge Göçek and Marc David Baer, "Social Boundaries of Ottoman Women's Experience in Eighteenth-Century Galata Court Records," in Zilfi, *Women in the Ottoman Empire*, 52–53.

verse 4:10.[41] The division of the dower into prompt (*muqaddam*) and deferred (*mu'akhkhar*) portions was apparently the standard practice by Ottoman times, when most marriage contracts so divided the dower, although in Rumelia the dower continued to be mentioned as a lump sum until the early eighteenth century.[42] The portions were roughly equal, although there was a tendency to make the prompt portion slightly larger on the grounds, no doubt, that life was uncertain when it came to collecting the deferred dower in the case of a divorce or the death of a husband. Previously married women were particularly likely to frontload their dower as a result, perhaps, of prior experiences.[43] The prompt portion of the dower might consist of gold and silver coins of known value and specified goods, including items of clothing, household furnishings, domestic slaves, and even farm animals in the case of peasant dowers, while the deferred portion was usually in coins alone. The dower was clearly an important source of property for women: after divorce or the death of their husbands they brought claims for payment of the deferred dower to court where they were usually successful in securing a favorable ruling.[44]

The dower was not the only standard marriage payment. In addition to the legally required dower, most couples also exchanged marriage gifts of food, jewelry, and clothing as part of the ceremonies leading up to the consummation of the marriage. The bride was equipped with a trousseau (*jihāz*) by her family composed of clothing and household furnishings. The latter could, in elite circles, constitute a serious exchange of property: chroniclers tell us that important political marriages among the 'Abbasid and Fatimid ruling circles entailed enormous trousseaux of costly jewels, clothing, and slaves.[45] In Mamluk times, similar trousseaux of elite brides tended to dwarf the *mahr*s they received, and constituted significant female shares in the natal patrimony.[46] Although such gifts and trousseaux were not part of the marriage contract under Islamic law, the courts and jurists were forced to engage questions relating to ownership, particularly when a woman died and her natal family attempted to reclaim the trousseau. In general, Ottoman-era jurists held that optional wedding gifts were the property of the receiver, and all trousseau items belonged to the bride and thus formed part of her estate. By so regulating customary practices, the courts and jurists further buttressed the rights of women to marriage payments.

[41] Al-Ramli, *Kitab al-Fatawa*, I:23.   [42] Ivanova, "Divorce," 115.
[43] Abdal-Rehim, "The Family," 103.   [44] Lutfi, "A Study"; Tucker, *In the House*, 72–73.
[45] Rapoport, "Matrimonial Gifts," 25–28.   [46] Rapoport, *Marriage, Money and Divorce*, 12–13.

Women could thus expect to acquire property of various kinds by way of inheritance and marriage payments. Although their rights to a share in family land might be offset by state and family strategies designed to resist fragmentation of family property, or they might cede their shares in family real estate or business operations in return for compensation in the form of material or emotional support, they retained rights to inheritance shares and dowers that allowed some of them to come into possession of significant amounts of property. Once they had acquired this property, how did they manage it? Some women, as noted above, chose to sell the real estate they received in order to acquire more liquid forms of property. Other women maintained an active presence in the real estate market, both selling and buying urban properties in ways and amounts little differentiated from their male counterparts, as was the case in the Aleppan real estate market between 1750 and 1850.[47] We need more systematic surveys of the major urban areas in the Empire in order to draw definitive conclusions, but there is enough current information to assert that women could be active real estate investors.

The impression we have that women did trade and manage real estate is further reinforced by the very active part women played in the institution of the waqf, the endowed property that came to play such a central role in Ottoman times. Significant amounts of urban real estate, as well as some agricultural land, came to be endowed property, the income from which was designated for a religious or charitable purpose. An individual could choose to establish a waqf with property he or she privately owned; such property was then alienated in perpetuity and its income was earmarked for the support of a mosque, school, hospital, soup kitchen, or public fountain, etc. During the Ottoman period, a variant type of waqf, the *waqf ahlī* or "family waqf," was widely recognized in which the income was directed toward individual beneficiaries named by the founder instead of or in addition to a charity; after the death of the beneficiaries and their designated descendants the entire income of the waqf finally found its way to the religious or charitable institution. In other words, an individual could insulate his private property from the play of inheritance law by naming beneficiaries of his or her choice: it was "a legal means to remove all or part of a patrimony from the effects of that law ... thereby limiting its fragmentation through inheritance."[48]

---

[47] Margaret L. Meriwether, "Women and Economic Change in Nineteenth-Century Syria: The Case of Aleppo," in *Arab Women: Old Boundaries, New Frontiers*, ed. Judith E. Tucker (Bloomington: Indiana University Press, 1993), 70.

[48] David S. Powers, "The Islamic Family Endowment (Waqf)," *Vanderbilt Journal of Transnational Law* 32 (1999): 1177.

In the copious waqf deeds we have from the Ottoman period, women appear as founders, managers, and beneficiaries of waqf property. But did this institution work to enhance or undermine female control of property? There is considerable disagreement among the historians who have studied the issue. Gabriel Baer first broached the subject through an examination of waqf in sixteenth-century Istanbul and argued that waqfs founded by women were of a small size and tended to weaken their control of property since they often named male beneficiaries and male managers, so that the waqf served to return control of property that women had inherited to men. Studies of other times and places, however, have reached different conclusions. In eighteenth-century Cairo, elite women endowed very sizeable waqfs and were able to retain control of this property as both managers and beneficiaries. In Aleppo in the same time period, women not only endowed waqfs but also were active as managers and beneficiaries of major waqf properties that had been founded by their ancestors.[49] These latter studies suggest that women's involvement with waqf property differed somewhat in degree but otherwise was strikingly similar to that of their male counterparts, except for the fact that as founders they tended to name both male and female heirs as beneficiaries as opposed to many male founders who favored males. Women were just as likely to be named managers of waqf property, and over time they also took their place as beneficiaries of waqfs founded not only by females but by males as well. Most researchers who have examined the court records are suitably impressed by the significant numbers of women for whom the institution of the waqf was a way to manage property.

But could the establishment of a waqf be a means to disinherit women? The variations in how families employed the instrument of the waqf to regulate the transfer of family property was strikingly demonstrated in Beshara Doumani's study of two towns, Nablus and Tripoli, in nineteenth-century greater Syria. While men who founded waqfs in Nablus routinely named their sons as beneficiaries and excluded their daughters, male founders in Tripoli almost always included their female children as beneficiaries, often assigning them shares equal to those of their brothers and thereby doubling the amounts the daughters would have received if the property had been left

---

[49] Gabriel Baer, "Women and Waqf: An Analysis of the Istanbul *Tahrir* of 1546," *Asian and African Studies* 17 (1983): 8–27; Mary Ann Fay, "From Concubines to Capitalists: Women, Property, and Power in Eighteenth-Century Cairo," *Journal of Women's History* 10, no. 3 (1998): 118–40; Margaret Meriwether, "Women and *Waqf* Revisited: The Case of Aleppo, 1770–1840," in Zilfi, *Women in the Ottoman Empire*, 128–52.

as a private inheritance. Doumani is not entirely sure about what underlies this dramatic difference: the men in these two towns obviously had very distinct notions about how family property should be distributed, but these ideas may have been influenced by differences in the material base of the two towns or perhaps by divergences in local culture, be it perceptions of family formation or legal discourse.[50] So, although this form of endowment no doubt served, at times, as an instrument for disinheriting women, most close studies have concluded that it also could protect their rights to family property while offering yet another field of endeavor for property-owning women and one in which their capacities as business managers were fully acknowledged. We do not yet have enough knowledge of the patterns of waqf endowments in a variety of times and places, however, to reach any final conclusions about the full impact of the institution on women's property holding.

We find further legal recognition of the female capacity to manage property in the realm of guardianship. In the Ottoman period, at least, the jurists' view that a woman, if properly appointed, could act as a guardian for her child or other minor had strong resonance in legal practice. Indeed, in the event of the death of a child's or children's father, their natural guardian, there often seems to have been a bias toward appointing their mother as their guardian. In a study of the period from 1818 to 1839 in Aleppo, for example, Meriwether found that women, usually the mothers, were designated the guardians for fatherless children more than 50 percent of the time. Mothers were routinely favored as guardians over paternal uncles or older brothers, even though natural guardianship devolved to male relatives on the paternal side in the absence of any formal designation of a different guardian. These female guardians oversaw sales and purchases of property for their wards, collected the income owed to them from rents and waqf properties, and settled any debts they had inherited.[51] They were not, therefore, simply titular guardians or temporary custodians of young children, but rather fully empowered managers of their children's property. In light of the extensive discourse in Islamic law about the importance of safeguarding the person and property of the orphaned child (fatherless but not necessarily motherless under Islamic law), the courts were apparently comfortable with entrusting women with this weighty responsibility. Nor does Aleppo stand out as a place where female guardians were commonplace: in Trabzon in 1846, for example,

[50] Beshara Doumani, "Endowing Family: *Waqf,* Property Devolution, and Gender in Greater Syria, 1800 to 1860," *Comparative Studies in Society and History* 40, no. 1 (1998), 23–27.

[51] Margaret L. Meriwether, "The Rights of Children and the Responsibilities of Women: Women as Wasis in Ottoman Aleppo, 1770–1840," in Sonbol, *Women, the Family, and Divorce,* 227–34.

the widow Zuleyha bint Osman was appointed guardian for her late husband's eight children who had inherited a sizeable estate.[52]

The Islamic courts did play more of a role in these guardianship arrangements than they would in the case of the natural guardian. In the eighteenth-century Jerusalem court records I have seen, the court routinely registered the fact of the guardianship and the arrangements made for child support, as in the following case:

The court recognizes the woman, Amna, daughter of al-sayyid Husayn, and her legal guardianship of her minor daughter, Khadra, daughter of the deceased al-sayyid Ibrahim … Amna has permission to spend from her [Khadra's] inheritance from her father for her needs. The judge fixes support (*nafaqa*) for meat, bread, fat, soap, bath fees, laundry, and other necessities at two *qita' misriyya*. The mother is authorized to spend this on her [Khadra] and to be reimbursed from the money the daughter inherited from her father. (17 Rabi' I 1146 H/1733 AD)[53]

Not only did the court register Amna as the legal guardian, but the judge also assigned an appropriate level of support for her daughter, based on the current understanding of what constituted the necessities of life, and authorized the guardian to spend this money from her daughter's inheritance. As a mother, Amna had no legal responsibility to provide material support for her daughter from her own funds; this responsibility was the father's and, after his death, that of the girl's relatives on the paternal side if there were need. As long as the minor had his or her personal resources, however, these could be tapped for support after the father's demise. Here the court stepped in to oversee the guardian, authorizing her to spend the child's inheritance but also regulating exactly how much and on what it could be spent. But does this mean that the mother had lesser powers over her ward's property than those of the natural guardian? In this case the mother's powers are not really at issue because she, and anyone else for that matter, needed court approval to spend down her daughter's inheritance for the purposes of the girl's maintenance. The mother had blanket authority, as guardian, to buy, sell, invest, and collect the income from her daughter's property, but she needed court authorization to consume it. Overall, the seemingly widespread practice of appointing mothers as guardians in the Ottoman period is one more instance of the society's view of women as appropriate and competent managers of private property.

There is less evidence, however, that women played much of a role as personnel or witnesses in the Islamic courts of the period. We have no

---

[52] Zarinebaf-Shahr, "Ottoman Women," 260.
[53] See Tucker, *In the House*, 144, for this case and further discussion.

evidence that women were ever judges, assistant judges, or scribes. Although women appeared in court for all kinds of notarial purposes and as plaintiffs and defendants in litigation, they were far more likely than men to be represented by agents they had appointed for the purpose of doing their business in the court. Their agents were usually accompanied by two witnesses who could testify to the fact that they were properly appointed by the woman in question, but these witnesses were not, in my experience working with court records from Cairo, Damascus, Jerusalem and Nablus, likely to be women. A common arrangement is the one by which a woman named Khadija registered her marriage in the Islamic court in Nablus in the eighteenth century without being present. Khadija was represented by an agent in the person of her brother, and her authorization of his agency was witnessed in court by another of her brothers and by her male cousin.[54] As a member of an affluent merchant family, Khadija typified the kind of woman most likely to do her court business through agents: women of elite circles tended to appoint agents to act for them in matters from marriage to routine purchase and sale transactions, while poorer women involved in modest transactions and disputes often appeared in court in person. In the case of Khadija, noting the familial identity of all agents and witnesses, we may well wonder about the degree to which elite women exercised a free hand in appointing their agents.

Nor did women often appear in court as witnesses in other contexts. Peirce notes in her extensive study of Aintab in 1540–1 that, "While women regularly came before the judge as plaintiffs, defendants, guardians, or bondswomen, only four times over the course of thirteen months did they serve as witnesses." This "near-ban" on women's testimony complicated and weakened many of the cases involving women since it was difficult to find appropriate male witnesses in many instances.[55] Ivanova reported a similar phenomenon in the Islamic courts of seventeenth- and eighteenth-century Rumelia (Bulgaria), where women often came to the court as litigants but acted as witnesses very infrequently, and then only in the kinds of cases for which male testimony would be virtually impossible to obtain. One of the latter was a case of an inheritance claim based on a childbirth narrative: a woman who had borne a son after the death of her husband brought two female witnesses to testify that the baby had breathed and moved before its death shortly after birth, therefore qualifying him as an heir in his father's estate and, more to the point, qualifying the woman as the baby's heir in turn.[56]

---

[54] Mahkamat Nablus (Nablus Islamic Court), s. 4, 269. [55] Peirce, *Morality Tales*, 191.
[56] Ivanova, "Divorce," 124.

The jurists had discussed this kind of case as one for which female testimony would suffice as evidence, and this seems to have been the practice in the Ottoman courts.

How do we reconcile the apparent contradictions of Islamic legal practice in the Ottoman period, namely that women retained well-defined rights to acquire property through inheritance and their dowers, played a significant role in managing this property whether as private real estate market or as waqf properties, and were regarded as fully competent guardians but, at the same time, were much more likely than men to be represented by agents and rarely testified in court? Woman, as legal subject, was indistinguishable from Man as far as her ability to enter into contracts was concerned and this signal legal fact was recognized in formal legal practice. But women were also enmeshed in an intricate array of legally regulated social relationships that colored their public personae. As we have seen in the chapters on marriage and divorce, gender occupied a central place in these relationships, defining reciprocal rights and obligations that differed for men and women. Women were subject to various kinds of male authority, albeit in ways that varied from one school of law to another, and the exercise of this authority could clash with their rights as adults endowed with freedom of action. Ottoman society struggled with this contradiction fully as much as the classical jurists had, and one indication lies in the ambivalent approach to female agency and authority in court. Although adult women were, in principle, fully qualified to act on their own behalf and even represent the interests of minors, they often resorted to the use of male agents in the court. Although adult women could own and manage property just like men could, their legal testimonies on these and related matters were not often welcome in court. At the end of the day, we are left with the impression that women could and did act as legal subjects, but were continually confronting a moral and anthropological context that privileged male authority and the male voice.

REFORM AND THE LEGAL SUBJECT

The late nineteenth- and early twentieth-century reformist jurists engaged these questions of the female legal subject with an eye to explaining, and minimizing, the differences between men and women as legal actors. They were united in the view that a woman, in her legal majority, had the right to dispose of her property as she wished, and they did not depart in any dramatic fashion from the discourse of earlier jurists except perhaps in a greater firmness of tone:

A woman has unrestricted freedom to dispose of her property, and she has [rights] of ownership, sale, purchase, guardianship, agency and trade, independence in her earnings and income, and competence to conclude contracts without her husband's supervision, and the marriage contract has no effect on her property.[57]

Influenced perhaps by their growing awareness of European law, the Tunisian jurists surveyed by al-Tahir al-Haddad in the 1920s were quick to point out that a Muslim woman had extensive property rights impervious to challenge through a change in her marital status. Rashid Rida, the Egyptian reformer, spoke explicitly to the contrast between the absolute rights Muslim women enjoyed over their property and the many strictures French women faced as a result of their husbands' prerogatives.[58] Unlike European women, a Muslim woman was fully empowered to manage her property. In this regard, the new commercial codes did not in any way contradict the spirit of the religious law, even if they removed such commercial transactions from the purview of the Islamic courts. Maliki jurists like al-Najjar, however, did retain the Maliki position that women should be supervised when it came to donations:

she has [the right] to make gifts and endowments and to give alms and other charitable donations which do not exceed the economic limit by way of prodigality and squandering, and that is a third [of her property] as in the sound tradition that a third is a substantial amount. She cannot exceed a third except with the agreement of her husband because this constitutes care for her interests and she consults [him] in order to guard her property and prevent it from being squandered.[59]

This Maliki position endured not only in discourse but in legal practice as well in much of North Africa because the giving of gifts and donations remained under the supervision of the Islamic court.

The reformers also turned their attention to the more troubling issue of inheritance, specifically the justification for the Qur'anic injunctions (4:11–12) that fixed the share of a daughter at one-half that of a son and of a wife at one-half that of a husband. Why should women receive a lesser share of family property? Rida argued that the inheritance rules must be viewed in the larger context of property relations, with full regard for all the material demands that are placed on the male:

If a man died leaving two children, a male and a female, and he left 3,000 *dinars* for example, 2,000 to the male and 1,000 to his sister. And if he [the son] marries, he must give his wife a *mahr*, and provide a house for her, and support her with his

---

[57] The words of the Maliki mufti Belhasan al-Najjar, in response to questions posed by al-Haddad in the 1920s, and published in al-Haddad, *Imra'atuna*, 105.

[58] Rida, *Huquq*, 20.   [59] Al-Haddad, *Imra'atuna*, 105–06.

funds whether she is poor or rich, and in this situation the 2,000 are for him and his wife, and so his share in actuality is equal to or less than the share of his sister. Then if he has children, he must maintain them and the mother is not responsible for anything. And in this situation, his inheritance is inferior to that of his sister. If she marries, as is usually the case, then she gets a *mahr* from her husband and her housing and maintenance are his responsibility, so that she receives the proceeds of the inheritance from her father and they benefit her only. So if the two heirs had only what they inherited as their property, the property of the woman would always be greater than the property of the man.[60]

The reformers did not challenge the laws on inheritance, which they generally held, in any case, to be part of the immutable Qur'anic legacy. Rather they argued that inheritance law did not discriminate against women because it was just one part of a complex set of rules governing transfers of property within the family. Indeed, when a woman's many property entitlements (*mahr*, maintenance, and the absence of any material responsibility to her family members) were taken into account, women stood to acquire more property through the operation of Islamic rules for property transfers than did men. This particular vision of equity was based on a notion of Woman as wife and mother, who would make up for her lesser inheritance shares by collecting her dower and support payments. The reformers' vision did not embrace the possibility that some women might not be anxious or able to marry, nor did it allow for changes in the level of support married women might be able to expect. They certainly did not anticipate sociological shifts, in the direction of a token dower, a minimal trousseau, or expectations of greater female contributions to family support, which were to develop in many places in the course of the twentieth century as we shall see below. Without parallel moves to increase the female's inheritance share, the net result could be the concentration of family wealth in male hands.

The problem of Woman as legal subject was most acute in the area of testimony. The reformers wrestled with the Qur'anic formula of two women to one man and the implications it held for female competency. Both Rida and al-Haddad took the position that the Qur'anic verse 2:282 was not a pronouncement on the limitations of Woman as a legal or moral subject, but rather a recognition of certain anthropological realities bounded in space and time. Al-Haddad cited her lack of instruction and her inexperience in business matters at the time of the revelation as key to the correct interpretation of the verse. Rida concurred, and leveled criticism at those interpreters who hold that women are liable to err or forget because of

---

[60] Rida, *Huquq*, 21.

defects in rationality and religion or their innate temperament. Rather, according to Rida, it was their lack of familiarity with business transactions that affected their memory, because it is in the nature of human beings to remember details of those things with which they are most familiar.[61] Implicit in these arguments, of course, is the idea that women might acquire the experience necessary to be full and equal witnesses although both reformers stop a bit short of drawing this conclusion, leaving it to the reader to conclude that as historical context changes, so could the formula for male and female witnesses. By the late twentieth century, an eminent Islamic jurist could make this argument in a very explicit fashion, stating that the requirement that a female witness "be reminded" by another woman could fade away, because "once society passes beyond that stage and women are allowed to participate more fully in its affairs, and in transactions in particular, there should no longer be a need for such arrangements."[62]

Various states also took up the task of legal reform beginning in the mid-nineteenth century in such a way as to limit the jurisdiction of Islamic courts when it came to some matters related to property and the legal subject. Over the course of the later nineteenth and twentieth centuries, most states developed legal codes and courts to deal with both criminal and commercial affairs. The shariʿa courts retained jurisdiction over "family law," including marriage, divorce, child support, and custody, as well as certain aspects of the law that were viewed as closely associated with religious precepts, such as inheritance and waqf. Most standard commercial transactions, however, such as sales and purchases, investments, loans, etc., came under the aegis of new European-influenced codes and national secular courts in much of the Middle East and North Africa (with the exception of Saudi Arabia and some other of the Gulf States) as well as the Indian subcontinent.[63] The changes in commercial law would not have much of an impact on women's property dealings, in the sense that women retained the right to enter into contracts as independent individuals and make commercial transactions as they wished without interference from male relatives. Many aspects of the law most central to women's acquisition and management of property, however, including the rules for *mahr*, inheritance, waqf, and other donations, remained under the aegis of Islamic law, albeit in the newly codified form.

[61] Al-Haddad, *Imraʾatuna*, 17; Muhammad Rashid Rida, *Tafsir al-Qurʾan*, 10 vols. (Beirut: Dar al-Maʿrifa, 1970–), 3:124.

[62] Taha J. al-ʿAlwani, "The Testimony of Women in Islamic Law," *American Journal of Islamic Social Sciences* 13 no. 2 (1996), 174.

[63] See Coulson, *A History*, ch. 11.

The Ottoman Law of Family Rights (1917) dealt with issues of *mahr* or dower in ways that appeared to enforce a woman's rights to her dower by: specifying that the dower was her property to do with as she wished and that she could not be required to use it to buy her trousseau (art. 89); noting that any deferred part of the dower would become payable immediately in the wake of a divorce or the death of either spouse (art. 82); and prohibiting her relatives from receiving "any dirham" in a marriage arrangement (art. 90).[64] The later codified versions of Islamic personal status law promulgated by successor states in the region tended to follow along the same lines, with a few significant dilutions of these dower rights. In Jordan, for example, article 64 of the 1976 law allowed the natural guardian, the father or paternal grandfather, of a virgin bride to take possession of her dower even if she had reached her legal majority. The Kuwaiti law of 1984 (art. 56) contained a similar provision that her natural guardian could receive her dower in her stead as long as she had not reached the age of twenty-five. On the question of when a woman could lay claim to the deferred part of the dower, both the Syrian code of 1975 (art. 55) and the Libyan code of 1984 (art. 20) cited customary practices that might trump the rule of immediate payment at the time of death or divorce.[65] In all these instances it is the prerogatives of the family and local custom that receive formal acknowledgment at the expense of strict adherence to the principle of the bride's uncontested control over her dower.

The practice of the courts in the twentieth century around issues of dower has also been influenced by the anthropological setting. In her study of dower in post-Islamic revolution Iran, Ziba Mir-Hosseini notes that although the law ties the payment of dower to the consummation of the marriage, most marriage contracts make the dower payable "upon request" of the wife. Women make such requests in very specific circumstances, usually as a way to prevent an unwanted divorce by making it clear to the husband that he will have to pay the entire dower if he chooses divorce, or alternately as a strategy to obtain a divorce from an unwilling husband by demanding the dower as the first step in negotiations. It is the rare case, however, in which a woman will actually take possession of her dower.[66] Annalise Moors' study of Jabal Nablus in Palestine makes a similar point about the diminishing weight of the dower in property transfers. Over the

---

[64] This and subsequent discussions of the OLFR are based on the Arabic version published in Sadr, *Majmuʿ at al-Qawanin.*

[65] This and the following discussion of modern codes in the Arab World are based on versions of those codes in El Alami and Hinchcliffe, *Islamic Marriage.*

[66] Mir-Hosseini, *Marriage,* 72–83.

period covered by her research (1920–90), the prompt dower shrank in significance, often reduced to a token payment. At the same time, women were increasingly less likely to collect the deferred dower upon divorce or the death of their husbands; in the former case, women bartered the deferred dower to receive a *khul'* divorce, and in the latter case they voluntarily relinquished their claims to dower property in favor of their sons.[67] While these practices undermine the importance of the dower as a method for female acquisition of property, they do meet the letter of the law insofar as the dower is still a required component of the marriage contract. The discernible trend here toward the trivialization of the dower as a source of property for women certainly bears watching.

Inheritance is the other legal entitlement a woman can rely upon to acquire property. The stipulation of one-half of the male's share to close female relatives, including wives and daughters, has rarely been challenged. Inheritance law has remained under the purview of the Islamic codes and courts, and inheritance rules have proved to be largely impervious to reform, not surprisingly so because of their clear Qur'anic origins. In a few areas, however, reforms have addressed certain glaring inequities. In Tunisia, a series of changes to inheritance law in the 1950s introduced three important reforms into the preexisting Maliki law of inheritance. First, the children of a predeceased daughter, who had previously been ineligible as heirs in any form, could now be named as beneficiaries of a bequest of up to one-third of their grandfather's property. Second, in the absence of agnatic heirs (male relatives on the paternal side), the inheritance shares agnates would normally claim were to be "returned" to other heirs, including wives and daughters. Prior to this reform, in the absence of a son and agnatic heirs, the state would claim these shares. Third, and most significantly, daughters and granddaughters could exclude agnatic relatives of the deceased, including the brother, paternal uncle and their descendants, as heirs: the old system by which a daughter would have to share her father's inheritance with a paternal uncle, for example, was replaced by a system that clearly privileged heirs in the nuclear family.[68] Other countries have also passed ordinances to ensure that orphaned grandchildren born to either a son or a daughter get a share of inheritance, generally by instituting a compulsory bequest so that the grandchildren in question receive a share in the estate on the grounds that this property would have come their way had their parent not predeceased their grandparent. In addition to Tunisia, the nations of Egypt, Syria, Morocco, Kuwait, Jordan, Iraq, and Algeria had passed such

---

[67] Moors, *Women, Property, and Islam*, chs. 5–6.   [68] Charrad, *States and Women's Rights*, 229–30.

legislation between the 1940s and the 1980s, legislation that represents a strategy of using the rule that up to one-third of an estate can be left as a bequest to redress perceived inequities in the law of inheritance. Moves to adjust inheritance law have occasioned some opposition. A Pakistani ordinance (1961) authorizing orphaned grandchildren to collect the share of the inheritance that would have belonged to their parents came under attack from the Federal Shariat Court in 2000 on the grounds that inheritance law was fully set out in the Qur'an and therefore sacrosanct.[69] As of this writing, the final fate of this ordinance is still uncertain. Taken as a whole, the reforms of inheritance law are rather modest, focused as they are on correcting what are widely perceived to be anomalous situations that seem to belie the spirit of the law. They have been helpful to women, and to many men as well, but they have stopped far short of contesting the half share concept that constitutes the central discriminatory feature of the law.

And it is not always guaranteed that a woman will, in any case, lay successful claim to her one-half inheritance share. Especially where land is concerned, other family members may attempt to persuade a woman to renounce her share in order to keep the patrimony intact for the greater good of the family, a pattern we have seen historically which certainly persists into the modern period. A woman may trade her shares in family inheritance for ongoing protection from her brothers, or she may simply not be able to ward off the inroads of more distant relatives if she is left an orphan and/or a widow.[70] In some areas of legal pluralism, such as northern Nigeria where Islamic law coexists with customary law, women may not be allowed to inherit land and other capital goods at all, despite formal law to the contrary.[71] So while the criticism of Islamic inheritance law as discriminatory against women is well taken, the failure to apply the law faithfully usually results in an even less satisfactory outcome for them.

Unlike inheritance regulations, the institution of the waqf has proven far more amenable to change and reform in the course of the twentieth century. In most countries, waqf as a way of managing property has been seriously eroded by two pervasive trends: an increase in direct state control of the waqf institution, and the related restriction or even elimination of the family

---

[69] See Lucy Carroll, "The Pakistan Federal Shariat Court, Section 4 of the Muslim Family Law Ordinance, and the Orphaned Grandchild," *Islamic Law and Society* 9, no. 1 (2001): 73–75.

[70] See Moors, *Women, Property, and Islam*, 48–76 and Erika Friedl, *Women of Deh Koh: Lives in an Iranian Village* (Washington, DC: Smithsonian Institution Press, 1989), 183–99, for accounts of women who variously bartered and struggled for their inheritance rights.

[71] Andra Nahal Behrouz, "Transforming Islamic Family Law: State Responsibility and the Role of Internal Initiative," *Columbia Law Review* 103, no. 5 (2003), 1153.

waqf. As part and parcel of the development of centralized control, most waqf property is now administered by 'ulama' employed by the state under the control of a designated ministry or department. Many countries, including Syria, Egypt, Tunisia, Libya, the United Arab Emirates, Lebanon, Kuwait, and Pakistan, have either abolished or greatly restricted the family waqf in ways that limit the duration and/or the beneficiaries of the endowment.[72] Whether these have been positive developments in the history of women and property depends, in large measure, on how we think about the role waqf has played. For those who view waqf endowments as instrumental in the disinheritance of women, the decline of the family waqf is hardly a matter for regret. If we focus, however, on the ways in which women utilized the waqf institution to manage their property, or even how men might privilege female relatives when they set up a family waqf, then the gradual disappearance of the family waqf could have some negative effects. In any event, the significance of the family waqf for property management, for men and women alike, is now largely a thing of the past.

When I turn to the broader question of how the reformed codes treated the problem of the gendered legal subject in terms of legal capacity, I still find considerable ambivalence. The area of guardianship in marriage illustrates a certain lack of will to embrace the vision of the adult woman as a fully empowered legal subject. In some cases, reformed codes reinforced the powers of the guardian: in Malaysia, Algeria, and Morocco, where the Shafi'i and Maliki schools had been dominant, reformed codes enshrined those schools' understanding of the power of the guardian. The guardians of women who had not been previously married were to play an essential role in their marriage arrangements: the codes insisted on the presence and consent of the guardian. Although the court (in Algeria) might overrule a guardian who refused a beneficial marriage proposal for his ward, the father-guardian reserved his right to oppose the marriage of his virgin daughter. The holdover of these guardianship rules in areas where Shafi'i or Maliki doctrines held sway is not particularly surprising, but we also encounter the requirement of consent of the marriage guardian in other codes, such as the Jordanian, where we would not expect to find it given the largely Hanafi milieu, and in the Iranian Civil Code (art. 2374) where the interpreters of the Shi'i position took a relatively conservative stance. Iraq, Lebanon, and

---

[72] See Lucy Carroll, "Life Interests and Inter-generational Transfer of Property Avoiding the Law of Succession," *Islamic Law and Society* 8, no. 2 (2001), 255–64; and Franz Kogelmann, "Some Aspects of the Transformation of the Islamic Pious Endowments in Morocco, Algeria, and Egypt in the 20th Century," in *Les fondations pieuses (waqf) en Méditerranée: enjeux de société, enjeux de pouvoir*, ed. Randi Deguilhem and Abdelhamid Hénia (Kuwait: Kuwait Awqaf Public Foundation, 2004), 343–93.

Syria, on the other hand, clearly followed the Hanafi lead in allowing a mature woman to enter a marriage without the participation of her guardian, although the guardian may object and request an annulment after the fact if the groom is not suitable. Almost all codes explicitly require the consent of a woman to whatever arrangements are made, and therefore the traditional juristic aversion to coercion has the full force of law. Morocco, before the legal reforms of 2004, was a partial exception here, since the judge, if it was feared that a woman might engage in "immoral" behavior, had the right to compel a woman to marry "in order that she be under the marital authority of a husband" (Code of Personal Status, Morocco, article 12). Guardianship in marriage has thus survived in almost every code as a legitimate institution, and one to which women, but not men, are subject. The coercive power of the guardian has been the object of modification, but the principle of family control of female marriage arrangements remains largely unchallenged and, in some cases I would argue, actually expanded into new or contested territory.

Nor has the issue of female testimony been settled in a definitive manner in the reformed codes. Most of the modern legal codes which deal with civil matters have adopted European procedural rules that are silent on the issue of the female witness and, in any event, put much less stress on witnessing in court procedure. In the reformed codes of personal status, however, the distinction between the capacities of male and female witnesses has endured in some, although not all, codes despite the position of many modern jurists that women's disabilities as witnesses were linked to specific historical circumstances. In reformed codes in Jordan, Libya, and Yemen, for example, a valid marriage contract requires proper witnesses, either two men or one man and two women, whereas the reformed codes of Algeria, Morocco, Iraq, and Lebanon do not specify the gender of the two required witnesses.[73] The fact that a woman's legal capacity as a witness can still be a contested area was made clear by the controversy surrounding the proposal made by lawyer Asma Khadr in 1998, as part of the discussion of personal status law in a future Palestinian state, that references to gender be dropped from the requirements for witnesses.[74] And, in some circles, the notion that women make poor witnesses because of sex-linked mental deficiencies has yet to die out. Abou El Fadl cites a fatwa delivered by the Saudi jurist Ibn Baz in 1990, as part of his work with the Permanent Council for Scientific Research

---

[73] See El Alami and Hinchcliffe, *Islamic Marriage*, 67, 82, 152, 185, 198, 251.
[74] Welchman, *Beyond the Code*, 363.

and Legal Opinions, which discusses the issue of female witnessing, and particularly the requirement for two female witnesses in the place of one male, in the following terms: "Thus, the Prophet explained that their [women's] intellectual deficiency is in the fact that their memory is weak, and that their testimony needs the corroboration of another woman."[75] Abou El Fadl is also careful to note that the Council is an official body and its fatwas carry real weight in the Saudi legal system. Despite the attention Saudi jurists have paid to this issue, there is less focus in recent times on the entire issue of witnessing, no doubt because of the greatly reduced role of the witness in most legal systems. The subject comes up primarily in connection with the witnessing of the marriage contract and, as we have seen above, opinion is divided, with many codes having abandoned the entire idea of gender as a factor in witnessing.

Both the discourse and the codifications of modern reform, then, have by and large embraced the idea of women as equal legal subjects. There is little departure from past theory and practice here. But did the modern reformers deal with the problem of the ambivalences of the legal subject? Did they grapple with the problem of how women were to be equipped to enter the legal system on a truly equal footing with men? The developments of the modern period made some of women's legal entitlements, like inheritance and *mahr*, no easier to claim. And while only a minority still seemed to think of women as mentally deficient, many jurists and courts were quick to uphold the power of the family over women when it came to matters of family relationships. The concept of the independent female legal persona continued to be trumped, in practice, by the reality of family and societal pressures limiting women's realization of their rights and capacities under the law.

RECENT DEVELOPMENTS

Some of the most interesting and far-reaching discussions of women's rights under Islamic law are taking place in regions where a certain level of legal pluralism or "interlegalism" prevails. In Indonesia, jurists and activists alike find themselves in a dynamic situation of shifting jurisdiction in which change and challenge characterize the judicial system. Indonesia, with its overwhelmingly Muslim population, emerged from colonial control with a tripartite legal system, composed of colonial law (in the French–Dutch

---

[75] As quoted in Abou El Fadl, *Speaking in God's Name*, 277.

tradition), customary law (*adat*) which varied from region to region, and Islamic law which had been limited, in principle, to cases of marriage and divorce. In the postcolonial period, a series of government decrees interpreting the rules and expanding the jurisdiction of Islamic law culminated in the 1991 Compilation of Islamic Law dealing with all matters related to marriage and inheritance. In most areas of the country, Islamic courts exist side-by-side with general courts and have been increasing their activity and reach largely at the expense of customary law. This situation has occasioned open and extensive discussion about what type of Islamic law can and should be applied in Indonesia.

The issue of inheritance, and specifically female inheritance rights, has been one of the flashpoints in the debates that have arisen. In his study of the Gayo highlands in Sumatra, John Bowen describes how the ascendance of Islamic rules transformed local inheritance practices: rather than privileging the claims of the lineage and allowing the disinheritance of daughters who married outside the village in accordance with local *adat*, the Islamic courts enforced the principle of inheritance shares for all children, albeit in the two to one male-to-female ratio, regardless of whether they remained in the village or in the lineage. In this context, the application of Islamic rules extended inheritance rights to many women, and some men, who under customary law would have forfeited shares in family property because of marriage outside the community. But some members of the Gayo community also argued that the application of Islamic rules, with its two to one ratio, introduced a new form of gender discrimination. Gayo customary law, they claimed, was gender-blind, based as it was on a standard of equal bilateral male/female inheritance. Offspring who married out of the village and were lost to the land and lineage, be they males or females, could not be endowed with that same land, but descendants who remained part of the village community, both males and females, were entitled to equal shares.[76]

The notion that Indonesian society has a "sense of justice" that provides the foundation for basic gender equality in its legal systems, including the Islamic rules of inheritance, was developed by Indonesian jurists in the course of the 1950s and 1960s. Professor Hazairin of the University of Indonesia Law School "argued that Islamic inheritance law contains general and universal principles, notably the principle that both women and men inherit property, and also specific rules. These rules derive from the Arab culture within which early jurists wrote, and in a different time and place

[76] John R. Bowen, "The Transformation of an Indonesian Property System: 'Adat,' Islam, and Social Change in the Gayo Highlands," *American Ethnologist* 15, no. 2 (1988): 279–86.

may be discarded."[77] Hazairin stopped short, however, of overturning the rule on half-shares for females because of its explicit Qur'anic support (4:11). Yahya Harahap, a Supreme Court justice, pushed the argument further in the 1990s by inviting jurists to consider the reason underlying the revelation on inheritance shares. If, for example, the purpose of the verse was to allow women to inherit alongside men in a social context where women had been systematically disinherited, then the "eternal norm" is one of female inheritance but the exact share is contingent and open to reform. Islamic inheritance rules could therefore be brought into line with the prevailing Indonesian sense of justice and practices of gender equality inherent in much of the *adat*.[78]

Indonesian judicial activists couch their arguments in similar terms. In 2004, Musdah Mulia, the Director of Religious Research and Social Affairs at the Department of Religious Affairs and a well-known advocate for gender equality, headed up a working group for the department charged with reviewing the Islamic Law Compilation (ILC) of 1991. The resulting critique of the ILC focused on the ways in which it contradicted "universal basic principles of Islam" as well as founding ideas of civil society including gender equality, and argued for a revision of the ILC based on Islamic sources and the norms of Indonesian society. The rules of classical "Arab" *fiqh*, including inheritance rules, were developed in a different social and cultural space, one of patriarchy that distorted the original Islamic message of equality. A rereading of the texts in the spirit of this message, combined with attention to the traditions and conditions of present-day Indonesians, led the working group to advocate for a number of changes in the ILC, including a revision of inheritance rules to assure equal shares to sons and daughters.[79]

Whatever the eventual outcome of this critique, it represents an unequivocal call to action to change the Islamic inheritance rules which reforming jurists had been loath to challenge in the modern period. Whether the difficulties posed by the apparent certainties of the Qur'anic text have been entirely done away with is, no doubt, a matter of judicial opinion yet to be resolved. Indonesia, as of this writing, has not yet changed the inheritance rules of the ILC. But the critique of these rules as discriminatory, and

---

[77] John R. Bowen, "Quran, Justice, Gender: Internal Debates in Indonesian Islamic Jurisprudence," *History of Religions* 38, no. 1 (1998): 68.

[78] *Ibid.*: 72–73.

[79] Siti Musdah Mulia *et al.*, "Counter Legal Drafting to Islamic Law Compilation (ILC): A Pluralism and Gender Perspective," *International Centre for Islam and Pluralism Journal* 2, no. 3 (June 2005): 1–16.

therefore in violation of Islamic, Indonesian, and universal norms, has engaged the fundamental issues of Islamic law and gender.

Another legal issue under recent discussion in several countries speaks directly to the concept of female legal capacity. Two high-profile cases of conflict over the question of guardianship of adult women for the purposes of marriage were widely publicized in the 1980s and 1990s. The first, *Karimatu Yakubu v. Alhaji Yakubu Tafida Paiko*, was decided by the Nigerian Federal Court of Appeal on December 11, 1985. In this case, a woman (Karimatu Yakubu), who had been given a choice of two suitors by her father, chose one of them and became engaged. Subsequently, she had a change of heart, broke her engagement, and married the other suitor. Her father, Alhaji Yakubu, asked the court to annul her marriage on the grounds that she had married without his permission: the marriage transgressed his right of *ijbār* (compulsion) as her father-guardian under Maliki law. The Court of Appeal ultimately sided with Karimatu on the basis that her father had given her a choice of suitors at the outset, thereby implicitly renouncing his right of *ijbār* and giving her the latitude to make a choice on her own.

The case has been a subject of controversy from several angles. Some Nigerian Islamic legal scholars criticized the extent to which it diluted a basic right under Maliki law: "a fatal blow has been struck to Muslim father's [*sic*] right of *ijbār* but he has also been divested of the right to persuade his daughter to have respect for her own selection."[80] Another commentator took quite a different view of the matter at stake: Lucy Carroll noted that this Nigerian judgment indirectly confirmed the rule that under Maliki law an adult virgin could not marry without the permission and involvement of her guardian, and the father-guardian could actually compel his daughter to marry the man of his choosing. She found such a reading of Maliki law to be out of step with twentieth-century reformist developments in both Maliki and Shafi'i law that have insisted on the full and informed consent of a woman to any marriage, albeit expressed through her guardian, and the abolition of the father-guardian's right of compulsion.[81] It is clear from such a case, however, that the right of an adult woman to contract her own marriage or refuse a marriage arranged for her, in defiance of the wishes of her family, can still be opened to question and the exercise of discretion at the judicial level.

[80] Alhaji Ma'aji Isa Shani and Mohammad Altaf Hussain Ahangar, "Marriage-Guardianship in Islam: Reflections on a Recent Nigerian Judgment," *Islamic and Comparative Law Quarterly* 6, no. 4 (1986): 281.
[81] Lucy Carroll, "Marriage-Guardianship and Minor Marriage in Islamic Law," *Islamic and Comparative Law Quarterly* 7, no. 4 (1987): 279–300.

A similar case was that of Saima Waheed, decided by the Lahore High Court, Pakistan, on March 10, 1997, in which the issue was again whether an adult woman could marry against the wishes of her guardian. Although the Hanafi school, dominant in Pakistan, is clear on the right of an adult woman to arrange her own marriage, this case was still vigorously debated with reference to customary social norms. The majority opinion of the court did support the right of Saima Waheed to marry without the consent of her guardian, but a dissenting opinion held that marriage in Islam was not just a contract but also a sacrament and a social institution in which the rights of parents should be respected.[82] The permanent Council for Scientific Research and Legal Opinions (CRLO) in Saudi Arabia, the official institution responsible for issuing Islamic legal opinions, particularly weighty in a country with no reformed code where such opinions effectively do the interpretive work of the code, has also produced a set of opinions as to whether a woman should obey her parents' demand that she marry. In a series of recent responses to women who want to refuse their parents' choices because they plan to continue their education or marry someone else or just do not feel ready for marriage, the CRLO invariably told women to obey their parents' wishes regardless of the circumstances.[83] These opinions were not based on legal sources or legal reasoning in any discernible fashion but rather, as in the Saima Waheed case, conflated a certain view of social order (daughters acceding to their parents' wishes in all things) with legal requirements. The ongoing debate over guardianship in marriage appears to be more about the patriarchal push for family control of women's marriage arrangements rather than about the intricacies of legal thought on guardianship. Once again, legal thought and practice succumb to the exigencies of the social order.

CONCLUSION

Islamic jurists produced a discourse that embraced the idea of Woman and Man as subjects of law, at least at the level of a legal and moral commitment to treating women and men as equal and autonomous individuals who could manage and dispose of property as they saw fit, and who were fully empowered to act in a legal sense and a legal setting. Women had access to

---

[82] Shaheen Sardar Ali, "Is an Adult Muslim Woman Sui Juris? Some Reflections on the Concept of 'Consent in Marriage' without a *Wali* (with Particular Reference to the Saima Waheed Case)," in *Yearbook of Islamic and Middle Eastern Law*, ed. Eugene Cotran and Chibli Mallat (London: Kluwer Law International, 1996), 156–74.

[83] Abou El Fadl, *Speaking in God's Name*, 193–95.

property by way of dower, inheritance, gifts, endowments, or their own earnings, and they could buy, sell, rent out, gift, or endow their property without having to seek the permission or submit to the oversight of any male relative or official. The Maliki school stood out for the ways in which it diluted women's property rights by prolonging interdiction and vesting a husband with certain, albeit carefully delineated, powers of oversight of his wife's actions. In general, however, juristic discourse constructed women, like men, as independent legal actors. Although women were thus confirmed as legal subjects, they did not, in the eyes of the jurists, always display all the features or characteristics of the legal subject. The demands of the social setting could encroach on female autonomy: women were not entrusted with their own marriage arrangements in most legal schools, for example, and their testimony in court was not held to be as trustworthy as that of men. In both these arenas, Woman as family member (whose marriage will affect her male relatives and therefore must be vetted by them) and Woman as part of patriarchal society (whose behavior must be policed and restricted, thereby limiting her knowledge of and activity in the public sphere) trump the Woman as equal legal subject. The assumption that all women were to be wives and mothers, whose primary roles lay in the domain of domesticity, underpinned many of the discriminatory practices in the areas of marriage arrangements, inheritance, and the valuation of testimony, all practices that lent an air of ambivalence to the question of female autonomy.

Such ambivalence persisted throughout the Ottoman period, when jurists and courts affirmed women's legal rights to acquire, manage, and dispose of property as fully entitled legal adults. Women inherited and endowed property of their own, and served as managers of the property of others in their roles as overseers of waqf or guardians for minors. On the other hand, women were far less likely than men to represent themselves in court or to serve as witnesses in legal cases of all kinds, nor were they encouraged to do so by the legal system. These kinds of contradictions are only comprehensible in the context of the wider society of the time, where gendered visions structured social space and the place of both women and men along a public–private continuum. I find it rather remarkable, indeed, that legal practices of the time so firmly retained core notions about the fundamental legal equality of women in property matters, given the many social pressures to the contrary.

The reformist thinkers and the reformed codes reaffirmed women's property rights and their capacity to act as legal subjects. There was little "reform" here in the sense that women had always, in Islamic legal discourse, enjoyed full and independent access to their property. Where discrimination on the basis of gender had persisted, in matters of inheritance, testimony, and guardianship in marriage arrangements for example, the reformers by and large proved to be rather timid: they skirted these issues on most occasions. While some voices were raised in support of revisiting past interpretations in these areas, most reform projects eschewed engagement with what were seen, no doubt, as somewhat peripheral and sticky issues. In recent years, however, as debates over Islamic legal interpretations have moved to the forefront, especially in places where the expanded application of Islamic law is on the agenda, the issues of inheritance and marriage guardianship have been engaged. Are women to be fully equal legal subjects, without any questions about their legal capacities, or not? Can the law be reinterpreted in ways that bring it into accord with local realities and sensibilities on the one hand, and social developments on the other? These discussions go to the very heart of our understanding of law and society, and the tensions between the discursive Woman and Man of law and the discursive Woman and Man of the wider social space. How and by whom these tensions are to be resolved is surely one of the most important legal debates of current times.

5

Woman and man in gendered space: submitting

At present, most discussions of Islamic law, women, and gender gravitate toward a set of issues assumed to lie at the heart of gendered Islamic discourse: gender segregation and/or female seclusion and veiling, and strict rules and sanctions for sexual behavior are the hot topics of the day, the emblems of Islamic discrimination against, and oppression of, women. I want to emphasize at the outset, however, that this basket of issues was not much featured in traditional legal discourse and premodern legal practices. Jurists, and many Muslim societies, did hold some definite ideas about the gendering of social space, dress requirements, and the gravity of sexual transgressions, but by and large these are ideas developed on the margins of the legal discourse and judges and courts do not seem particularly active in their enforcement. This is an area where modern concerns – perhaps we could say obsessions – threaten to skew our understanding of Islamic law, and therefore I proceed to discuss these issues with the caveat that I will be paying them, relatively speaking, far more attention than did the jurists and courts of premodern Islam.

In addition, any discussion of space and sexuality in Islamic law is complicated by the problem of concepts and terms. Feminist historians and legal thinkers in the West, beginning in the 1960s, worked with the rich analytical approach of public and private domains, where the concept of "separate spheres" for men and women ruled, as essential to our understanding of the ways women were restricted and controlled. Modern legal codes in Europe and North America had confined women to a "private" sphere of domesticity and excluded them from a "public" sphere of production and politics by denying them the franchise, placing restrictions on their entrance into trades and professions, and rendering them dependent for most legal purposes on their male relatives. At the same time, by refusing to enter the private sphere, the law abdicated all responsibility for protecting women in the place where they were confined and most vulnerable, the home, thus subjecting them to unbridled patriarchal control of their property

75

and their bodies. This legally supported configuration of space was one of the keys to female oppression and, while challenged and partially dismantled in the course of the twentieth century, its legacy is still felt in the law.[1]

The separate spheres were not always so separate, of course, and historians have pointed out that the vision of public/male and private/female space embodied in the law accorded rather poorly with the life experience of many members of poor and minority populations in the West.[2] Similar arguments have been made for Muslim societies. The public/private dichotomy was first problematized in the pioneering work of the late Cynthia Nelson questioning the relevance of a private/public typology made in the West. Elizabeth Thompson has furthered this argument recently by noting that we discern rigid public/private boundaries only with difficulty in the discourses and practices of Islamic societies in the medieval and early modern periods. Certainly the picture of a public world of men engaged in affairs of business, politics, the military, and scholarship, and a private world of women busy with the bearing and raising of children and the other nurturing tasks of domestic space – in other words a gendering of space in which men and women are performing different, spatially distinct, functions – does not chime with the findings of social historical studies such as those of Leslie Peirce on both elite and more ordinary women of the Ottoman period, or of Mary Ann Fay on Mamluk women in eighteenth-century Egypt. These scholars all invite us to question public and private spheres as the predominant construct for gendering space.[3]

This is not to imply that there were no concepts of public and private in Islamic law. Although, as Mohsen Kadivar asserts, Islamic legal discourse does not use these terms, there was still a well-defined notion of the private as a space where the individual exercised control and was protected from the interference of others; Kadivar points to the principle of the absence of *wilāya* (guardianship), the idea that an adult should be able to exercise direct and unfettered control of himself and his property, as evidence for the law's

---

[1] Nadine Taub and Elizabeth Schneider, "Women's Subordination and the Role of Law," in *Feminist Legal Theory: Foundations*, ed. D. Kelly Weisberg (Philadelphia: Temple University Press, 1993), 10–11.

[2] Dorothy O. Helly and Susan Reverby, "Introduction: Converging on History," in *Gendered Domains: Rethinking Public and Private in Women's History: Essays from the Seventh Berkshire Conference on the History of Women*, ed. Dorothy O. Helly and Susan Reverby (Ithaca, NY: Cornell University Press, 1992), 14.

[3] Cynthia Nelson, "Public and Private Politics: Women in the Middle Eastern World," *American Ethnologist* 1, no. 3 (1974): 551–63; Leslie P. Peirce, *The Imperial Harem: Women and Sovereignty in the Ottoman Empire* (New York: Oxford University Press, 1993) and Peirce, *Morality Tales*; Elizabeth Thompson, "Public and Private in Middle Eastern Women's History," *Journal of Women's History* 15, no. 1 (2003): 52–69.

recognition and protection of the private. He also admits, however, that this private sphere of Islam is "smaller than the norm in the contemporary world" and substantial limits are placed on individual freedom by Islamic authorities in the interest of "commending good and prohibiting evil."[4] We have been privy above, in chapters 2 and 3, to the deep involvement of the law in the "private" affairs of families: the law does not stop at the threshold of the domicile, or even the bedroom, but rather aspires to regulate familial rights and obligations in an ongoing and systematic fashion. Just as Islamic discourse countenanced major legal interventions into the world of the domestic and familial, it also based many of those interventions on the principle that space was and should be gendered, that a cardinal principle of social organization was that of gender segregation spatially constructed. Such segregation was directly and consciously linked, not to a philosophy of separate spheres, but rather to the problem of human sexuality and the power of sexual attraction to disrupt society and threaten the unity and stability of Muslim communities.

In this chapter I explore how Islamic jurists constructed gendered space and sexuality through a set of doctrines dealing with prohibited male–female interaction, dress, and sexual transgressions. I then focus on the Ottoman period for a discussion of the extent to which premodern legal practices gendered space and dress, and policed sexuality in various communities. When we move into the discourses and practices of the modern period, the picture is greatly complicated by the extent to which these issues take on a symbolic quality as measures of authenticity and difference in the encounter with imperialism and colonialism. Finally, gendered dress and sexuality are some of the most hotly debated legal issues of the present time, inviting us to reflect on how the regulation of the body in space continues to fascinate us as it takes center stage in the drama of cultural encounter.

SPACE, SEXUALITY, AND THE ISLAMIC JURIDICAL TRADITION

Muslim jurists engaged the issue of space as an issue of male and female interaction: space was gendered in the sense that they thought some social boundaries between men and women should be maintained, and male–female interaction should be carefully regulated. They did not address the question of gendered space, however, in a systematic or comprehensive

---

[4] Mohsen Kadivar, "An Introduction to the Public and Private Debate in Islam," *Social Research* 70, no. 3 (fall 2003): 670.

fashion: we do not find in their work an overall vision of how space in a variety of contexts, such as the home, marketplace, or administrative buildings, is or should be gendered. In other words, there is no clear demarcation of a public space that belongs to men and a private space that belongs to women, and therefore no crisp male/female dichotomy in their views on the ideal spatial arrangements for Muslim communities. The issue of gendered space does arise, however, in the context of religious duties; as men and women seek to fulfill their religious obligations, to what extent does their presence in shared devotional space bring them into the kind of physical proximity that might threaten social order? How are women and men to fulfill their religious obligations in the space of the home, mosque, or pilgrimage? There is palpable tension here between the idea that men and women have the same religious obligations that would logically place them in shared ritual space, and the recognition of powerful sexual drives that demand sexual segregation for the wellbeing of the community and society. Prayer presented a unique set of dilemmas for the jurists: how to promote the path of virtue in a shared prayer-space fraught with the possibility for vice? In the process of dealing with the many tensions generated by the conflict between religious duties and the requirements of safeguarding social stability and harmony, the jurists moved seamlessly from issues of prayer to considerations of why and how male and female interactions in space should be regulated.

From the first, the duty of prayer presented problems in terms of contact between the sexes. If a woman called a man to prayer, should he heed the call and come to pray? At least some Shi'i jurists thought it was not recommended (*mustaḥabb*) for him to go, while others thought it was forbidden (*ḥarām*). For those who held it to be forbidden, the problem was the seductive quality of the female voice, which can lead the man to sin, and thus only men who are close (*maḥram*) relatives are permitted to hear the voice of the woman.[5] From the inception of the discussion of prayer, we are immediately plunged into the world of the *ʿawra*, the consideration of what part of a woman (or man for that matter) should be covered, hidden away from all members of the opposite sex who are not close relations, or, put otherwise, what part of the body, if displayed, might inspire lustful thoughts and interfere with one's devotions.

This preoccupation frames the question of whether women should come to pray in the mosque at all. Ibn Rushd opined that the congregational Friday prayer, while obligatory for male members of the community, was

---

[5] Al-Hilli, *Mukhtalaf,* 2:139.

not obligatory for women.[6] He did not dwell on the issue, however, and the reader is left to conclude that, while not obligatory, women are welcome at Friday prayer. Al-Marghinani was rather less sanguine about the issue:

the presence of them [women] at the prayers is not recommended, that is the young ones among them, for fear of *fitna* (disorder), but it is all right for old women to go [to the mosque] for the dawn, evening, and night prayers. And the two [Abu Hanifa's disciples, Muhammad and Yusif] said that they [old women] can go for all the prayers because there is no *fitna* in the absence of desire so it is recommended as on feast days. According to Abi Hanifa, there is lust, so *fitna* can occur except for the fact that the dissolute (sinful) men are more likely to be present at the noon, afternoon and Friday prayers; as for the dawn and night prayers, they are sleeping, and in the evening, they are busy with eating.[7]

So, according to al-Marghinani, the problem can be laid at the feet of a particular category of men, those who are dissolute sinners who will be lusting after all women, even the old ones. Fortunately these sinners are lazy (they will be sleeping through the dawn and evening prayers) and gluttonous (they will be eating during the evening prayer) so that they leave some space for women. It is they who will bring inappropriate thoughts and maybe actions into sacred space and it is against them that precautions must be taken. This is an important revelation: the *fitna* or disorder arising from uncontrolled lust and illicit sexual interactions does not originate with women per se, but rather is attributed to some disreputable men, even if it is a problem to be solved by restricting women's movements.

A similar approach shapes the views of the jurists about how to position men and women should women come to pray in the mosque. The majority of the jurists seem to agree that women should never position themselves for prayer in front of men. Women pray behind men: if there are many women, they form lines in back of the lines of men; if there is only one woman and one man, she should pray behind him. Logically enough, most agree that a woman could not lead congregational prayer because she would have to stand in front of men to do so. Furthermore, a woman is not a suitable prayer leader for men because God has ordained that women must pray in the back: they take their place behind the first rows composed of

---

[6] Ibn Rushd, *Bidayat*, 1:364.
[7] Al-Marghinani, *Al-Hidaya*, 1:148–49; see also Camilla Adang, "Women's Access to Public Space according to al-Muḥallā bi-l-Āthār," in *Writing the Feminine: Women in Arab Sources*, ed. Manuela Marín and Randi Deguilhem (London: I. B. Tauris, 2002), 82–83, for a discussion of the opinions of Ibn Hazm of Cordoba (d. 1064), a Zahiri jurist, who did not place any restrictions on women when it came to attending prayer at the mosque.

men and the second composed of boys.[8] There is some nuance in this picture. A few of the earlier jurists, such as Abu Thawr and al-Tabari, had thought women imams were permitted, a position buttressed by the hadith about Umm Waraqa whom the Prophet ordered to lead the prayers for the members of her household. Most jurists, like Ibn Rushd, ultimately opted, however, for the "known practice," that is, for women to stay behind men.[9] While the jurists do not delve much into the reasons behind this practice, we are left to conclude that women could pray behind men without having their prayer disturbed by lustful thoughts, but that at least some men could not be trusted to control themselves should they have the moving body of a praying woman in their sight.

The jurists also held a variety of opinions about what kind of clothing was required for prayer. They agreed that women, and men for that matter, were obliged to cover their *'awra*s, the lust-inducing parts of their bodies, for prayer, but they disagreed on what, precisely, constituted the *'awra*. Most Malikis and Shafi'is classified a woman's body, in its entirety, as *'awra*, with the exception of her hands and face. The majority Hanafi position also exempted her feet.[10] Many Hanbalis, on the other hand, held that every part of a woman, down to her toenails, was *'awra* and must be covered for prayer.[11] Al-Hilli noted the spread of opinion among Shi'i jurists, ranging from a similar opinion that all of a woman is *'awra*, so that she is required to wear a garment that covers her from head to toe in addition to a face veil, to the minimalist stance that a woman need only wear modest clothing, like that of a man, to cover her front and back.[12] There was also diversity of views, across both Sunni and Shi'i schools, about the male *'awra* and what parts should therefore be covered for prayer. While most jurists held that a man's *'awra* was the part of his body between his navel and his knees, others reduced it to as little as the genitalia alone. But could a man then pray, for example, with a naked chest and back? Most jurists agreed that covering the *'awra* alone met the basic requirements for prayer dress, but some dissented and called upon men to cover their torsos for prayer.[13]

In addition to prayer, the requirement that all Muslims undertake the pilgrimage to Mecca (the hajj) at least once in their lifetimes if at all possible

---

[8] Ibn Rushd, *Bidayat*, 1:346; al-Marghinani, *Al-Hidaya*, 1:147.

[9] Ibn Rushd, *Bidayat*, 1:339–40. Adang, "Women's Access," 81–82, notes that Ibn Hazm also thought that women should not stand in front of men in prayer, and therefore were not qualified to lead men in prayer although they might lead women.

[10] Ibn Rushd, *Bidayat*, 1:271; al-Marghinani, *Al-Hidaya*, 1:109.

[11] Ibn Taymiyya, *Fatawa al-Nisa*, 28–30.   [12] Al-Hilli, *Mukhtalaf*, 2:113–14.

[13] Ibn Rushd, *Bidayat*, 1:272–73.

also put the tensions between religious requirements and the regulation of male–female interaction on display. The jurists agreed that women, like men, are commanded to make the hajj, but they differed as to whether this duty overrode the hadith narrative that "It is not permitted for a woman, who believes in Allah and the Last Day, to travel without a *mahram*." Malikis and Shafiʿis tended to give precedence to the obligation of pilgrimage, and allowed women to make the hajj in the company of a trustworthy female companion if need be.[14] Some Shiʿi jurists also held that a woman could perform the pilgrimage without a *mahram* if neither her husband nor another close male relative could or would accompany her.[15] Most Hanafis, on the other hand, insisted that she be accompanied by her husband or another close male relative on her pilgrimage journey, if that journey exceeded three days, because one "fears *fitna*."[16] And Hanbalis were ready to entertain the possibility of travel without a *mahram* only in extreme circumstances, "If she has a defect, is menopausal, has despaired of marriage, and has no *mahram*, then she is permitted to travel with a trustworthy person."[17]

Although women shared with men the religious obligation to make the pilgrimage, the idea of a woman moving freely though space, particularly on a journey of some distance, gave the jurists pause. A woman without a chaperone invited trouble in the form of *fitna*. All jurists preferred that she be protected by a *mahram*, although there was substantial disagreement as to whether the absence of a *mahram* would prevent her from making the trip altogether. Once she secured a *mahram*, however, the jurists agreed that her husband could not prevent her from fulfilling this most sacred duty of Islam, for "his right [to her] does not have the upper hand over her religious obligations."[18] Still, a woman on the hajj clearly ran the risk of crossing forbidden boundaries in her interactions with men.

The jurists' discussions of such boundaries in the context of prayer and pilgrimage inevitably expanded to encompass ruminations on how men and women should behave in each other's presence in general. Ibn Taymiyyah staked out the Hanbali position: since all of a woman's body is ʿawra, she must cover herself with a *jilbāb* that conceals her head and body as well as a face veil in the presence of any man who was not a close relative (*mahram*) of hers. She could remove her veil only in front of her *mahram* relations.[19] Al-Marghinani outlined a rather different Hanafi position that a woman

---

[14] *Ibid.*, 2:790–91; al-Marghinani, *Al-Hidaya*, 1:339.   [15] Al-Hilli, *Mukhtalaf*, 4:348.
[16] Al-Marghinani, *Al-Hidaya*, 1:339–40.   [17] Ibn Taymiyya, *Fatawa al-Nisaʾ*, 85.
[18] Al-ʿImadi, *Al-ʿUqud*, 1:14.   [19] Ibn Taymiyya, *Fatawa al-Nisaʾ*, 29–30.

need not cover her face and hands in the presence of men, noting that her business dealings may require that she keep her hands and face free, but may show her feet, and perhaps even her forearms. All these parts of her body might "normally appear" in the course of her daily activities.[20] There are two very distinct visions of gendered space here: in the latter, women are part of a world of trade and other activities that bring them into everyday contact with unrelated men, while in the former they are secluded and cloistered away. But the underlying problem is the same: sexual desire hovers relentlessly, always threatening to introduce a note of desire and undermine the stability of human society.

Al-Marghinani acquainted us further with this world of desire in his elaboration on the male gaze. First, a man is permitted to look at a woman's face and hands, but only if he feels that he can do so without desiring her in keeping with the saying of the Prophet: "He who gazes upon the allures of a woman with lust will have hot lead poured into his eyes on the day of judgment." So al-Marghinani recommended that men avert their gaze from women if they anticipate any such problems. Second, there are some females who do not incite lust, namely young girls and old women; there is no harm in looking at them and touching their hands in greeting as long as they do not arouse desire. Third, some men will be called upon to look at women whom they may find desirable. This is the case, for example, in the context of the Islamic court where a judge or a witness may be required to look closely at a woman's face, but in this instance the need to secure justice and people's rights takes precedence over the dangers of lust. Judges and witnesses should only gaze upon a woman's face with pure intentions, however, and only to fulfill their judicial responsibilities, not to fulfill their desires. Men in other professions might even need to look at parts of a woman which are clearly ʿawra: al-Marghinani thought that a doctor, for example, is permitted to look at a female patient although he recommended that all of her body except the ailing part be covered and that the doctor avert his eyes as much as possible. Ideally, he continued, it is best to train women as doctors who could then minister to their own sex.[21] It is interesting to note that the male gaze could be equally problematic when directed toward a comely young man. The jurists assumed that many, if not most, men would look upon an attractive beardless youth with desire, and they proscribed this gaze as well although they did not ordinarily bar a "pretty youth" (*sabīḥ*) from public space.[22]

---

[20] Al-Marghinani, *Al-Hidaya*, 4:1487.   [21] *Ibid.*, 4:1487–88.   [22] See Tucker, *In the House*, 153–54.

If lust had no place in public space, it did have a place in marriage. The jurists agreed that a man could look with lust at the woman he intended to marry because sexual attraction is an important part of marriage and should be encouraged. And once married, of course, a man could gaze upon all of his wife's *'awra*.[23] Marital space was sexualized space where desire could be given free rein and where the sexes could intermingle without transgression.

Outside of this marital space, however, we do not have a juristic consensus on the issue of women's place, on what they should wear when in public, or indeed on whether they should be permitted to be there at all. It is worthy of note that the jurists did not devote much time or energy to this issue, and we search in vain for detailed expositions on how space should be gendered. There was a shared anxiety about unregulated male–female interactions, but the expulsion of women from public space was not the answer for most. In eighteenth-century jurisprudence, we find mention of a category of secluded women, the *mukhaddara*s, who did not leave their homes even for necessary business. The jurists took the position that they should be accommodated in court: they are allowed to testify from home through two trustworthy witnesses who can convey their words to the court, where they take full legal effect.[24] But while this special category of *mukhaddara* commanded recognition and respect, there was no recommendation that all women assume such a lifestyle. On the contrary, the legal literature is full of scenarios in which women's personal testimony in court occurred as a completely ordinary and approved activity. The secluded lifestyle was an option for women, but it was not required or even expected of most.

How can we conceptualize the jurists' views of gendered space and dress? They construct what we might term three zones of desire. In the first zone, rampant sexual desire can spell discord and social danger. In this zone of illicit desire, men interact with unrelated women of childbearing age who, by definition, draw their gaze and incite lustful feeling. It is therefore an interaction that calls for ultimate constraint in the form of gender segregation. The jurists regulate dress, physical proximity, and the gaze to minimize male/female contact in this highly gendered zone. The second zone could be considered a neutral zone in the sense that men interact with females who are considered undesirable; young girls, old women, and close relatives do not arouse sexual feelings and, as a result, the rules of dress, proximity, and gaze can be relaxed. In this desire-free zone interactions are

---

[23] Ibn Taymiyya, *Fatawa al-Nisa*', 31; al-Marghinani, *Al-Hidaya*, 4:1490.
[24] See al-ʿImadi, *Al-ʿUqud*, 1:317.

only lightly regulated. The third zone is the marital zone, a zone of lawful desire. Here sexual desire is celebrated and finds its home. All restrictions and rules are suspended and a man is encouraged to gaze, to touch, to act on his desire. But were these three zones hermetically sealed? Some jurists entertained the notion that the exigencies of life could allow for permeable boundaries. Some of the rules could be relaxed in the zone of illicit desire in the interests of justice, welfare, and economic necessity, and men were exhorted to control themselves in these contexts.

The jurists seemed to agree that much of the problem originated in male desire. They acknowledged that women have sexual drives: they might caution women to lower their gaze should they find themselves looking at men with desire. But overall it was the male sexual impulse that framed the problem even if the necessary restrictions fell most heavily on women. This particular contradiction – that men's inability to control their lusts necessitated the restriction of women – colored much of the discourse.

Ultimately there was no simple public/private dichotomy based on distinguishing male and female activities and assigning women and men to segregated physical space. Rather, we find that the jurists focused on space as a fluid site for interaction between men and women. It was thoughts, attitudes, and illicit acts that were at issue, not the fixing of rigid boundaries of public and private and the assigning of different tasks based on gender. The jurists focused their attention elsewhere, namely on the power of the human sexual drive and the threat it posed to social stability and harmony. The law, charged as it was with the promotion of the public interest, sought to control sexual activity through the regulation of interactions in space and prescriptions for dress, but should the safeguards against illicit sexual acts fail, the jurists elaborated the rules for punishing the resulting transgressions, including the crime of *zinā'* (unlawful sexual intercourse).

Zinā' belongs to a particular category of crime, the *ḥadd* crimes, crimes specified in the Qur'an, the punishment of which is considered to be a right of God, not of man. *Zinā'* is specifically mentioned (4:15 and 24:1–2) as a crime that requires punishment. According to Ibn Rushd, *zinā'* is "all sexual intercourse that took place outside of valid marriage, the semblance (*shubha*) of valid marriage, or lawful ownership (*mulk yamīn*). This is agreed upon on the whole by the 'ulama' among the scholars of Islam, though they differed about what kind of doubt did or did not avert the *ḥadd* penalty."[25] There are only five other *ḥadd* crimes: slandering another by accusing of *zinā'*, theft, highway robbery (banditry), drinking alcohol, and apostasy (for some

---

[25] Ibn Rushd, *Bidayat*, 4:2235.

schools). *Ḥadd* crimes have prescribed punishments that are based on material in the Qurʾan or, in some instances, on precedents established by the hadith.[26] Among *ḥadd* crimes, *zinā*ʾ has pride of place: the jurists discussed *zinā*ʾ first in the section on *ḥadd* crimes in their works of *fiqh*, and they generally gave it the most space and detailed treatment.

Ḥadd crimes in general, and *zinā*ʾ in particular, demand high standards of evidence. The jurists accepted two kinds of proof for *zinā*ʾ: confession and witness. A person could be found guilty and punished for *zinā*ʾ on the basis of confession of the crime to a judge, but the jurists advised the judge to exercise caution when hearing a confession. Hanafis imposed the most stringent standards for confession by requiring that the criminal make four clear confessions in four different court sessions, citing the hadith in which the Prophet heard the confession of a man named Maʿiz and turned him away three times before finally accepting his confession in their fourth meeting. For most Shiʿa, however, the four confessions could be made in a single session, and Malikis and Shafiʿis held that a single confession was sufficient proof of *zinā*ʾ.[27] Hanafis further stressed the responsibility of the judge to make sure that the crime of *zinā*ʾ had indeed been committed:

> It is preferable that the judge prompt the confessing party to retract, and say to him "[perhaps] you [only] touched or kissed," according to what the Prophet said to Maʿiz, "[perhaps] you only touched or kissed her." And it says in the text that it is desirable for the judge to say to him, "perhaps you married her or had intercourse with her by *shubha* (the semblance of a legal act) which is close to the first in meaning, and God [alone] knows.[28]

Here the judge is invited to be an advocate for the confessing party, to actively probe the confession in a search for extenuating information. And even after a confession has been fully made and accepted, there was still the possibility of retraction. The legal schools again diverged here, with some Shafiʿis holding that confession led inexorably to punishment with no possibility of retraction, while many Malikis, Hanafis, and Shiʿa allowed for the possibility that punishment be waived should the guilty party retract his confession on the basis that a retraction is just as likely a truth as a confession. Some jurists even held that, should a person who had confessed then flee during punishment, he should not be pursued and the

---

[26] For a discussion of *ḥadd* crimes and penalties, see Rudolph Peters, *Crime and Punishment in Islamic Law: Theory and Practice from the Sixteenth to the Twenty-First Century* (Cambridge: Cambridge University Press, 2005), 53–65.

[27] Al-Marghinani, *Al-Hidaya*, 2:737; al-Hilli, *Mukhtalaf*, 9:172.   [28] Al-Marghinani, *Al-Hidaya*, 2:739.

punishment should be dropped because flight constituted a retraction of his confession.[29]

The jurists applied similarly high standards of evidence to the testimony of witnesses. Four witnesses were required to prove the crime of *zinā'*, and they must be witnesses to the act of sexual intercourse itself; they could not make assumptions or deductions but must have witnessed the act of penetration and be able to say that they saw it "like a dipstick going into a jar of kohl." The judge, on his part, was further exhorted to examine the witnesses carefully:

And if they testify, the judge asks them about the *zinā'* – what and how and where and when and with whom – because the Prophet, peace be upon him, sought an explanation from Ma'iz as to the circumstances and the act itself, because it might be something other than penetrating the vulva, or the *zānī* (committer of *zinā'*) might have been in a non-Islamic land, or it might have been committed a long time ago, or there might be some doubt (*shubha*) that neither he nor the witnesses are aware of ... so he examines the case deeply.[30]

Al-Marghinani went on to say that the character of the witnesses should also be closely investigated: the judge should make both private and public inquiries into the reliability of the witnesses and their information in light of the seriousness of the crime and the severity of the punishment. The credibility of their testimony might be impugned in a number of ways. Witnesses "chose" to give testimony or to "protect secrecy," and therefore anyone who delayed giving testimony opened himself up to charges of unworthiness because there was no reason for him to change his mind about testifying unless he was engaged in settling scores rather than doing his duty as a Muslim. Any disagreement among the witnesses as to the particulars of the act also rendered their testimony void. If any one of the witnesses were blind, or had a history of slandering others, or lacked right-eousness, the crime of *zinā'* could not be proved. And perhaps the most chilling aspect of the law when it came to witnessing was the fact that should the witnesses fail to prove their case for any reason, they could be accused of the *ḥadd* crime of slander (*qadhf*), a weighty offense carrying a required punishment of eighty lashes.

Confession and witnessing were the only universally accepted forms of evidence for *zinā'*, but some jurists entertained the notion that out-of-wedlock pregnancy constituted legal proof. Many Malikis were ready to find such a pregnant woman guilty unless she could provide evidence of coercion in the

---

[29] Al-Hilli, *Mukhtalaf,* 9:167–68; Ibn Rushd, *Bidayat,* 4:2248.   [30] Al-Marghinani, *Al-Hidaya,* 2:738.

form of bleeding after intercourse or other bruises or injuries. If she claimed to have been married, she must be able to prove it. Hanafis and Shafi'is, on the other hand, do not seem to have been predisposed to accept pregnancy as evidence of *zina'*. If they discussed the issue at all, they tended to focus on the ways in which a woman's claim of coercion or marriage should be accepted at face value, citing the hadith in which 'Ali asked an unmarried pregnant woman named Shuraha if she had been coerced and, after she said no, then suggested that "maybe someone came upon you while you were asleep."[31] Another hadith reported that the Caliph 'Umar accepted the explanation of a woman that she was a sound sleeper. Certainly all agreed that coercion precluded conviction for *zina'* on the part of the coerced party, although the jurists disagreed on the evidence required. In addition to a woman's claim, witnesses might testify to coercion and some jurists held that if two of the four required witnesses testify to coercion, the woman, whether pregnant or not, would not be liable for *hadd* punishment.[32]

Once found guilty of *zina'*, whether by confession, witnessing, or, much less likely, the fact of pregnancy, the guilty parties faced one of two prescribed punishments, lashing or stoning. The lesser punishment of lashing was meted out to women or men who had never been married, and therefore who, at least technically, had been virgins when they committed the transgression. They were to receive 100 lashes in accord with the punishment specified in the Qur'an (24:1–2) for those who committed *zina'*. Women and men faced identical punishments in terms of the number of lashes and the fact that punishment should take place in public, but a man was to be whipped in a standing position either naked or in the state of clothing in which he had been apprehended while a woman remained clothed and in a sitting position in order to conceal her *'awra*. The blows should be moderate and avoid the face, head, and genital regions. Most jurists agreed that the punishment should be postponed if the weather were extremely hot or cold, or if the condemned were ill, on the basis that the intent was to discipline, not to execute.

Execution by stoning was the punishment reserved for those who had consummated a marriage and thus were sexually experienced. This punishment was not prescribed in the Qur'an but rather was based on several hadiths, including those in which the Prophet ordered stoning for perpetrators, among them the man Ma'iz, a woman from Juhayna, and a woman from the Ghamid tribe. Again, the punishment should be performed in public. Some jurists thought the condemned should be placed in a pit, the

[31] Ibn Rushd, *Bidayat*, 4:2249.   [32] Al-Hilli, *Mukhtalaf*, 9:140–41, 144.

man up to his groin and the woman up to her chest, while others found a pit unnecessary. The order of stoning was generally agreed upon: if the condemned had been found guilty by confession, the first stones should be cast by the imam followed by the public; if found guilty by witnessing, the first stones should be cast by the witnesses followed by the imam and then the public.[33] Whether we are dealing with flogging or stoning, public enactment was a central part of the punishment: this was a crime against God and against the harmony and order of the Muslim community. In designing punishment as public spectacle and community activity, the jurists underscored the community role in both proving and punishing this crime. Public and communal punishment also made the price paid by those found guilty abundantly and graphically clear, and could therefore serve as a caution against casual accusation, as the Caliph ʿAli reportedly said of the rule that the witnesses initiate the stoning: "Because a witness may be bold to witness, but then when confronted with the outcome may retract, and so this beginning may be the device for prevention [of *ḥadd*]."[34]

Some jurists included banishment as an additional punishment for *zinā'* in keeping with a hadith in which the Prophet prescribed 100 lashes and a year's banishment for an unmarried offender. The Shafiʿis held that those who received lashes for *zinā'* should also be exiled for one year. Most Hanafis, on the other hand, did not accept exile as a punishment, on the basis that sending the perpetrators away from the community would only encourage them to persevere in their crimes once they were free of family and community surveillance. Malikis and most Shiʿa thought that men, but not women, should be banished; women who were removed from the usual family protection and support faced greater temptations to commit *zinā'* and might even be forced into prostitution as an economic necessity.[35] So, for most jurists, banishment was a punishment to be used very judiciously since it might have the unintended consequence of further jeopardizing moral standards.

The general tone of discussion of *ḥadd* crimes and their penalties is one of caution and care if not reluctance. Although an individual might have committed an act of *zinā'*, circumstances still might avert the draconian punishments of flogging or stoning. A woman could counter the testimony of witnesses with her own claim of virginity. The judge should then investigate by ordering women to examine her and, if they supported her

---

[33] For detailed discussion of lashing and stoning, see *ibid.*, 9:173–77; Ibn Rushd, *Bidayat*, 4:2239–45; al-Marghinani, *Al-Hidaya*, 2:739–40.

[34] Al-Marghinani, *Al-Hidaya*, 2:740.   [35] Al-Hilli, *Mukhtalaf*, 9:152; Ibn Rushd, *Bidayat*, 4:2242.

claim, the *ḥadd* penalty was dropped for her and her partner. A male or female found guilty of *zinā'* could claim that he or she was still a minor or insane, and thus escape punishment for *zinā'*. Women and men alike could assert that they were coerced and most jurists held that involuntary acts of *zinā'* did not incur penalties. Anyone who could claim that the crime was committed in territory not under Muslim control eluded *ḥadd* punishment according to many jurists.[36] But the most sweeping provision for the suspension of *ḥadd* punishment lay in the doctrine of *shubha*. The Hanafis developed the doctrine of *shubha* or judicial doubt to encompass both an unlawful act that objectively resembled a lawful act, and an unlawful act whose perpetrator thought it lawful. The presence of *shubha*, or this kind of judicial doubt, cancelled any *ḥadd* penalty. In the case of *zinā'*, the semblance of an illicit relationship to lawful marriage (a relationship based on a defective marriage contract, for example), or the belief that an illicit relationship was lawful (a relationship a man and woman take to be a valid marriage even if it were not) constituted possible grounds for waiving the *ḥadd* penalty. The standard of evidence did not appear to be very high: Hanafis were willing to accept statements from the accused such as "you married me" or "I married her," even though there had been no legal marriage, as sufficient for establishing *shubha*. Although a man owed his partner monetary compensation in this case equivalent to the amount of a fair dower, the judicial doubt established by these claims voided *ḥadd* penalties.[37]

And finally, many jurists respected the power of repentance. One hadith reported that as Ma'iz was being stoned for *zinā'*, he ran from his executioners in an attempt to reach the Prophet, but he was pursued and stoned to death. The Prophet regretted this course of events, saying "Would that you had let him go, perhaps he would have repented and God would have forgiven him." In this spirit, some jurists thought that such repentance before or even during punishment on the part of a person who had confessed to his crime should halt *ḥadd* punishment. In cases of evidence brought by witnesses, on the other hand, the accused needed to have repented before the evidence was brought to the judge in order to avert *ḥadd* punishment.[38] The expiating possibility of repentance underscores the nature of crime and punishment in the context of *zinā'*: to repent is to recognize the wrongness of one's act, ask for forgiveness, and foreswear

---

[36] Al-Hilli, *Mukhtalaf*, 9:137, 157, 174; al-Marghinani, *Al-Hidaya*, 2:752–53.

[37] Al-Marghinani, *Al-Hidaya*, 2:748–52.

[38] Al-Hilli, *Mukhtalaf*, 9:161; Ibn Rushd, *Bidayat*, 4:2248; Ibn Taymiyya, *Fatawa al-Nisa'*, 291–92.

similar acts in the future. Timely repentance therefore achieves the goals of punishment in that it embraces and endorses God's commands and acts as a deterrent.

Zinā, as we have seen above, was the very specific act of sexual intercourse between a man and a woman. This precise definition does not mean, however, that the jurists accepted other sexual encounters as licit. There was widespread agreement that men and women who had sexual relations short of intercourse – kissing and hugging or being naked in bed together, for instance – were guilty of a crime. If four witnesses testified against them, they were liable for discretionary punishment as imposed by the judge, anywhere from ten to ninety-nine lashes according to some sources. This was not a *ḥadd* crime, however, and *ḥadd* penalties did not apply. In the case of same-sex relations, there was more disagreement. The Hanafis split among themselves, with some following the lead of Abu Hanifa who held that anal intercourse (*liwāt*) between two men was not *zinā* because it could not result in an illegitimate birth, while others adhered to the position of his disciples who found it, as an "act of forbidden lust with the object of ejaculation," analogous to *zinā* and fully deserving of *ḥadd* punishment.[39] Shi'a also disagreed among themselves, although the majority opinion leaned toward treating anal intercourse between males as *zinā*.[40] Lesbian sex was also criminalized, although in this case no one argued that it met the definition of a *ḥadd* crime. Shi'i jurists, however, prescribed harsh punishment: flogging for the first three offenses and execution for women who were caught in a compromising position a fourth time. Nor was pimping a *ḥadd* crime, but the jurists prescribed a graduated scale of corporal punishment: for the first offense, a pimp should be whipped, have his head shaved, and be subjected to public reviling; the second offense called for whipping and banishment; for a third offense he would incur more whipping; after a fourth offense he would be called upon to repent and be whipped if he did so, and executed if he did not; and should he repent and survive to commit a fifth offense, execution was his lot.[41] The message was clear: sexual acts performed outside of marriage were by definition illegal and incurred punishment, although they might or might not fall into the category of *ḥadd* crimes.

---

[39] Al-Marghinani, *Al-Hidaya*, 2:751–52.

[40] See Khaled El-Rouayheb, *Before Homosexuality in the Arab-Islamic World, 1500–1800* (Chicago: University of Chicago Press, 2005), 118–28, for a discussion of the variety of legal positions on the categorization and punishment of anal intercourse.

[41] Al-Hilli, *Mukhtalaf*, 9:175, 179–80, 189–90, 192–94, 196, 202.

The jurists viewed all sexual activity pursued outside of lawful marriage (or concubinage) as fraught with the potential for social disruption. The Qur'an had clearly outlawed one form of it, extramarital sexual intercourse, and the jurists developed the details. But while the jurists acknowledged the gravity of this crime, their discussions of how to prove and punish *zinā'* were tinged with reluctance. The standards of evidence were high, impossibly high in most instances. Confessions were to be accepted only after considerable scrutiny, and witnesses were discouraged from presenting evidence on both moral and practical grounds. The accused was also afforded many opportunities to claim extenuating circumstances and resort to legal loopholes. In brief, the jurists did not manifest much zeal when it came to the prosecution of *zinā'*; the severity of the prescribed punishments may well have worked against any judicial activism in the pursuit of perpetrators.

The jurists' approach to the gendering of space, the regulation of dress, and the criminalization of sexual activity were all connected to the specter of *fitna*, the lurking disorder that stalked the Muslim community thanks to the force and vitality of the human sex drive. It was the twin beliefs in the power of human sexuality and its potential for social disruption that animated legal discourse on male–female interaction. The jurists worked on rules to regulate this interaction in social space, prescribed forms of dress to minimize sexual appeal, and worked out the details of harsh public punishment for sexual transgressions (even if difficult to prosecute). Although jurists of various schools agreed on the broad outlines of the problem, the legal discourse on space and sexuality once again displays a diversity of views and interpretations: there is a broad spectrum of opinion here about the strictness of sexual segregation, the degree of covering, and the many important details related to proving *zinā'*. Once again, the jurists offer a rich variety of possibilities, leaving a fairly wide field of maneuver open to Islamic courts and judges.

THE REGULATION OF SPACE AND SEXUALITY PRIOR TO THE TWENTIETH CENTURY

Even a cursory look at some of the legal concerns and practices of the late medieval and early modern periods suggests that matters of the body and sexuality, while remaining on the judicial map, were not handled in a uniform or particularly focused fashion. Members of the 'ulama', conscious of their role as preservers of public morality, did raise the issue of male–female mixing in public from time to time. Ibn al-Hajj, a fourteenth-century *'ālim* in Mamluk Egypt, decried the loose social arrangements of his time: women were going to markets, mingling with their neighbors, singing and dancing at weddings, and participating with men in funeral processions and tomb visits. He denounced these activities in no uncertain terms, but there is no indication that his prescriptions for female seclusion carried any legal weight. A pair of 'ulama' brothers in eighteenth-century Mosul, Yasin and Amin al-'Umari, raised similar laments about women in public space, particularly women who participated alongside men in the 'Ashura' commemorations of the death of Hussayn at Karbala where passionate expressions of grief and longing might well give rise to inappropriate interaction.[42] Many men of religion harped on this theme from time to time, taking the practices of everyday life and popular religion to task for their violations of the ethos of Islamic morality in the area of sexual segregation. There was, of course, a strong class element here, as the ideal of the protected and secluded woman was clearly out of reach for the majority of the population even if they had embraced it in principle. But some men of privilege felt it their responsibility to uphold the standard of minimal mixing of the sexes and call upon legal authorities to set some firm limits.

The law and the courts did not always rise to the challenge. One exception that proves the rule was the infamous eleventh-century Fatimid Caliph al-Hakim, who instituted a regime of seclusion for women, forbidding them to visit markets, public baths, and tombs, but we have no evidence that such regulations endured or had any but a fleeting impact on the arrangement of urban space. By the Ottoman period, the jurists and the courts had settled into a mode of regulation of male and female interaction that addressed some of the more egregious violations and responded to the community's sense of appropriate social contact. Khayr al-Din, the seventeenth-century mufti from Ramla, issued a fatwa in one such instance:

Question: There is a man who offended by entering the house of his sister's husband in his absence and without his permission, and there was another wife present who was not related to him, so he intruded upon her. Then he took his sister by force along with her possessions to his house. Is he forbidden to do this, and is he the perpetrator of a sin against God, and should suitable punishment (*ta'zīr*) be imposed upon him? And if the owner of the property brings a claim against him for it, and he

---

[42] See Dina Khouri, "Drawing Boundaries and Defining Spaces," in Sonbol, *Women, the Family, and Divorce*, 173–87; and Huda Lutfi, "Manners and Customs of Fourteenth Century Cairene Women: Female Anarchy versus Male Shar'i Order in Muslim Prescriptive Treatises," in Keddie and Baron, *Women in Middle Eastern History*, 99–121.

Answer:

still has it, should the judge require him to present it [in court] in order to identify it for [the matter of] claim and the testimony? Yes, he is forbidden to do that and he is to be punished for his perpetration of this sin which is legally forbidden. A similar case was referred to our shaykh, the Shaykh Muhammad ibn al-Hanuti, and he gave his view in a fatwa that he [the accused] must return her and all the property to her husband when the case has been proved. *Taʿzīr* is required for the accused who took the wife and the property and entered the house of the husband without his permission, and [also] imprisonment to prevent him from entering people's houses without permission. That is the judgment of all without disagreement. As for the presence of the accused [in court], the *mutun*, the *shurūḥ*, and the *fatāwa* [types of legal texts] all deal with this and they all require the accused to be present, and God knows best.[43]

There was an apparent moral equivalence here of abduction and theft with failing to get permission to enter someone's house. The mufti repeatedly highlighted the gravity of this crime: the uninvited intrusion into another's home had resulted in the serious matter of contact with another man's wife, a transgression that called for intervention and punishment in order to prevent future offenses. Khayr al-Din made it clear that respect of domestic privacy was one of the imperatives of Islamic morality, and an offender might need to be jailed to learn his lesson about the inviolability of domestic space. The courts of eighteenth-century Aleppo also recognized this legal right: one judge viewed with favor the claim brought by a group of residents against a builder who had dumped dirt against the exterior walls of their houses and thus exposed their courtyards, and their women, to the view of passersby.[44]

On the other hand, community policing of unlawful contact between men and women could necessitate, and even excuse, a certain voyeurism, as we see in the following case from sixteenth-century Anatolia:

I, Arab, chief of the night watch, came to court and summoned three individuals named Sadeddin b. Haci Süleyman and Ayşe bt. Halil and her husband Haci Mehmed, and said: "This woman was seen coming out of Sadeddin's house at daybreak. They were not closely related. What business does she have in his house?" When the aforementioned Sadeddin was questioned, he answered:

[43] Al-Ramli, *Kitab al-Fatawa*, 1:84.
[44] Abraham Marcus, "Privacy in Eighteenth-Century Aleppo: The Limits of Cultural Ideals," *International Journal of Middle East Studies* 18, no. 2 (1986): 169.

"I owed her 90 akçes; she came to ask for it. Also, my little son was sick. The previous evening I had sent my son to ask for a [nugget of sandalwood]; I thought perhaps she had come to bring it." When Haci Mehmed was asked the question "What business did your wife have in his house?" he said: "It was I who sent my wife; I told her to go get the money."[45]

As the case continues, we learn that the woman "was seen" coming out of the house by two other men from the neighborhood who apparently reported the incident to the night watch, a local security patrol. The very presence of this case in court suggests that neighbors felt it their right to spy and report on each other's private dealings in the interests of community morality, while at the same time the court might dismiss the case, as it did in this instance, if a satisfactory reason existed for the contact between an unrelated woman and man.

Members of a community might take even more aggressive action. Residents of one neighborhood in eighteenth-century Aleppo broke into a local house, apprehended unrelated men and women visiting together, and subsequently prevailed upon the local qadi to expel the owners of the house from the neighborhood, presumably as proprietors of a house where the accepted standards of male–female contact were not being observed. An Aleppan qadi also closed down a local shop because the owner had allowed male and female customers to mingle in suspicious ways on the premises.[46] In seventeenth-century Jerusalem, the court reviewed the case of four men and one woman who had been discovered by several other men sitting together in the evening in a room which had been locked from the outside. Although the woman turned out to be the wife of one of the men, had a small child with her, and offered a plausible explanation for her presence in the room (she had been looking for her husband and someone had, perhaps playfully or maliciously, locked her in), her husband and one of the men were found guilty and punished with whipping and public humiliation.[47] There is little question that the muftis and the courts of the period included the regulation of both public and domestic space as within the reach of the law and that the issue of male and female interaction was one of the central concerns in that context. How vigorously they pursued the enforcement of legal norms regulating space is another matter, however, and we are left with the distinct impression that the legal system often functioned in a passive mode, listening to complaints about local violations of the rules for male

---

[45] Quoted in Peirce, *Morality Tales*, 170.   [46] Marcus, "Privacy," 165, 169.
[47] Dror Ze'evi, "Women in 17th-Century Jerusalem: Western and Indigenous Perspectives," *International Journal of Middle East Studies* 27, no. 2 (1995): 162–63.

and female interactions and prescribing punishment, but also standing ready to accept interactions that made sense to the ongoing conduct of social and economic business in a community.

The regulation of dress, particularly for women, occupied even less space on the legal agenda. The jurists of the Ottoman period discussed the category of the secluded and veiled woman (*mukhaddara* in Arabic and *muhaddere* in Ottoman Turkish). It cropped up principally as a concern: how will the secluded woman be able to realize her rights in court? Will her business be properly conducted if she is not present? The eighteenth-century mufti of Damascus, al-ʿImadi, considered the issue:

Question: A woman brought a claim against another woman, and both of them are secluded (*mukhaddarāt*), and each of them appointed an agent. Are these legal proxies?

Answer: Yes, the claim of an agent for the plaintiff against an agent for the defendant, both legally appointed, is legally sound, and it is not required for either [of the women] to be present, as is concluded from the words of our ʿulamaʾ.[48]

In this fatwa, the mufti accepted a woman's decision to avoid the public space of the court in the interest of preserving her seclusion and concluded that the legal instrument of proxy was adequate for the protection of her rights. Ebuʾs Suʿud, the eminent Ottoman mufti, addressed similar issues and insisted that the witnesses to a secluded woman's appointment of an agent must see her face in order to ascertain her identity. But, as Peirce points out, Ebuʾs Suʿud thought of the *muhaddere* as a category of social custom more than of Islamic law: he was willing to discuss and help define the category – a *muhaddere*, according to Ebuʾs Suʿud, does not let herself be seen by people outside her household for example – but he never suggested that the shariʿa had legislated either the category or the behavior. Ottoman *qanūn* did lend some official recognition to the *muhaddere* category. In the law book of Sultan Suleyman, the punishments for women who brawl are differentiated based on whether they are secluded: a non-*muhaddere* woman is to be flogged and fined while a *muhaddere* woman's punishment is visited upon her husband, who is to be scolded and fined. But the *qanūn* did not impose specific dress regulations.[49]

The Ottoman state did issue sartorial regulations from time to time that included prescriptions for female clothing. In 1726, for example, the Grand Vezir Ibrahim Pasha decreed that women's outerwear should meet

---

[48] Al-ʿImadi, *Al-ʿUqud*, 1:338–39.　[49] See Peirce, *Morality Tales*, 158–62.

some exact specifications as to the sizes of collars, scarves and headbands, prohibited "monstrously shaped headgear," and directed the police and the Islamic courts to enforce these regulations. The motivation may not have been purely one of moral imperative. In part, these regulations were geared to encourage women to return to wearing traditional clothing of local manufacture in order to revive the local economy. There is little evidence, in any case, that the new rules were strictly enforced.[50]

So, we are left with the distinct impression that, prior to the late nineteenth century, women's dress in general, and the practice of veiling in particular, were not matters that much engaged the attention of Islamic jurists and courts. Women (and men) no doubt dressed modestly, at least in large parts of the Islamic heartland, but a wide range of degrees of covering, reflecting differences in class and setting, appears to have been the norm. Urban women of the elite might lead a secluded life in which they only ventured outside their homes in full cover, but dress was an issue most jurists and courts were content to leave in the hands of local custom and individual choice.

Zinā', on the other hand, continued to maintain an active presence in the law and periodically demanded the attention of jurists and courts. Despite the precise definitions, standards of evidence, and punishments in the legal tradition, however, the laws and courts of the Ottoman period interpreted the law and even innovated in some unexpected ways. The Ottoman state developed a series of criminal codes, *qanūns*, that incorporated many aspects of the shariʿa but also added further definition of crimes and a wide range of punishments for transgressions. These codes were intended to be the law of the land for the empire, and were to be enforced in the Ottoman system of Islamic courts; they represented the state's interpretation and distillation of Islamic penal law, augmented by rules and punishments devised to further the state's purpose of bolstering public security and welfare.

These codes tended to ameliorate the punishments for *zinā'* while expanding the scope of the crime. While the Ottoman *qanūn* paid lip service to the penalties prescribed by the shariʿa, which might be imposed in any given case, it also instituted a broad range of alternative penalties, primarily fines. Sultan Sulayman's criminal code, for example, listed a series of graduated fines incurred by perpetrators of *zinā'*, to be calibrated by the status of the perpetrator, whether a virgin or not, and by his or her assets. In the case of consensual *zinā'*, only a recurrent offender, such as a habitual

---

[50] Madeline C. Zilfi, "Women and Society in the Tulip Era," in Sonbol, *Women, the Family, and Divorce*, 300.

prostitute, incurred stiffer penalties of flogging, ridiculing in public, or banishment. The law specified that a prostitute could have her face blackened or smeared with dirt and be led through the streets sitting backwards on a donkey, holding its tail instead of its reins. In the case of abduction or rape, corporal penalties also applied: a man could be castrated and a woman who ran off with a man could have her vulva branded. And while not specified in the criminal code, abduction of a minor came to be punished by indefinite servitude on Ottoman galleys. In brief, the Ottoman criminal codes effectively eliminated execution as a penalty for *zinā'*, prescribed only monetary fines for consensual sexual intercourse, and reserved a range of non-lethal corporal punishments for those who were violent or habitual offenders. At the same time, these codes addressed other types of sexual crimes, eliding them with the crime of *zinā'*. Same-sex intercourse between males was to be punished like *zinā'*, with the same system of graduated fines. If a youth were involved, he was to be disciplined (presumably to discourage such acts in the future) with flogging and fines if he was of age; if he was a minor, his father was to be fined. A man could be flogged and fined for having anal intercourse with his wife. If a man and a woman were seen together in a secluded spot, the judge could collect the fine for *zinā'* from both of them. And if a man kissed, molested, or spoke indecently to another man's wife, daughter, or son, he could face both flogging and fines. Men and women who pimped were to be publicly ridiculed, and 'ulama' who married their girls off to abductors were to have their beards cut off.[51] The criminal code thus produced a long list of illicit sexual acts, liaisons, and improprieties, all of which called for similar kinds of punishments. In the process, the crime of *zinā'* lost much of its weight and shed its draconian penalties. By the same token, however, the law criminalized a raft of sexual behaviors about which the shari'a had been more or less silent.

What we know of court practices in the Ottoman period reinforces the notion that *zinā'* had become a more elastic behavior and one unlikely to incur a *ḥadd* penalty. Accusations of *zinā'* were still a serious matter, presumably for social as much as legal reasons. Some individuals came to court to defend themselves against rumors of sexual impropriety. In eighteenth-century Aleppo, for example, one woman brought legal suit against a man for falsely claiming that he had sexual intercourse with her; another

---

[51] For a translation of relevant sections of the Ottoman criminal code, see Uriel Heyd and V. L. Ménage, *Studies in Old Ottoman Criminal Law* (Oxford: Clarendon Press, 1973), 93–103. See also Dror Ze'evi, "Changes in Legal-Sexual Discourses: Sex Crimes in the Ottoman Empire," *Continuity and Change* 16, no. 2 (2001): 219–42, for a discussion of the Ottoman criminal code.

case featured a father who sought to rebut rumors about his daughter's behavior by bringing four women to court to testify to her virginity.[52] A young pregnant woman might confess to "doing *zinā*'" in sixteenth-century Anatolia, but the court and its clients seemed to be much more concerned with the impact that such confessions and accusations had on the reputations of the parties involved than they were with exacting any kind of corporal punishment for the perpetrators.[53] And in eighteenth-century Damascus, the courts routinely dealt with neighborhood complaints about local prostitutes by expelling them from the quarter, treating them as "mischievous persons" rather than criminals in need of *ḥadd* punishment.[54] *Zinā*', whether brought to court by officials or private persons, was a cause for concern and condemnation, but did not precipitate the harsh punishments called for in the classical and medieval doctrines.

We get further insight into the handling of *zinā*' cases from reading the opinions issued by muftis in the Ottoman period. Muftis in the Arab lands, at least from the seventeenth century onwards, appeared to maintain the position that the traditional shariʿa, and not the modified form found in the *qanūn*, defined and governed the punishments for *zinā*', but they also were quick to highlight *shubha* (judicial doubt) as a mitigating factor. Even in fairly outrageous circumstances, a perpetrator of *zinā*' was able to wriggle almost free:

Question: There is a peasant who abducted the daughter of the son of the son of his nephew [*sic*], and she had been contracted to someone else. He took her virginity by force. What is his punishment?

Answer: If he does not claim *shubha* in relation to the punishment for *zinā*', and the crime is proved in a legal manner, then the punishment for *zinā*' is imposed on him. If he claims *shubha*, then the *ḥadd* punishment is averted and he owes her a fair dower because there is no sexual intercourse in the land of Islam without a dower or an indemnity [for a slave], and God knows best.[55]

Such was the routine treatment of *zinā*', even in a case of rape: a man, or woman, could protect himself from *ḥadd* punishment simply by asserting that he had thought his act was legal. He might have to compensate his

---

[52] Marcus, "Privacy," 176.   [53] See Peirce, *Morality Tales*, 351–74.

[54] Abdul-Karim Rafeq, "Public Morality in 18th Century Ottoman Damascus," *Revue des Mondes Musulmans et de la Méditerranée* 55/56 (1990): 181–83.

[55] Al-Ramli, *Kitab al-Fatawa*, 1:80.

victim or partner (in the case of a consensual act), but *ḥadd* punishment could be avoided by the simple act of claiming *shubha*. Although the muftis upheld the prescribed *ḥadd* punishments as applicable in theory, they also supported a doctrine that, in practice, rendered the actual implementation of *ḥadd* punishment highly unlikely.

Our impression that *ḥadd* punishments for *zinā* were remarkable for their absence in the period leading up to the twentieth century is reinforced by a notorious incident in the life of Muhammad ibn ʿAbd al-Wahhab, the religious reformer and founder of the puritanical Wahhabi movement that flourished in the Arabian peninsula for a period in the eighteenth century. According to his biographers, ʿAbd al-Wahhab heard the confession of a woman who had committed *zinā*, and, acting as the leader and judge of his fledgling religious movement, ordered her execution by stoning. This was an "unexpected event" of some moment, and one that got him into trouble with the local ruler who, bowing to pressure, expelled him from his home town of al-ʿUyayna. It was also an event that brought him the kind of recognition he sought as a clear-eyed and uncompromising leader who would strictly enforce religious dictates. As a sympathetic biographer remarked, in the wake of the stoning "his cause flourished, his power increased, and the *tawhid* [monotheism] was everywhere disseminated, together with the enjoining of virtue and the prohibition of vice."[56] Whether perceived by his supporters as a purifying assertion of Islamic legal principles or by his detractors as an aberrant act of cruelty, there is little question that the infliction of such a punishment astonished local observers and occasioned much comment among them. Stoning people for *zinā* was not, apparently, the normal way of handling such affairs in the Arabian peninsula.

So, the jurists and courts of the Ottoman period, in Anatolia and the Arab lands, recognized *zinā* as a serious crime, but they did not normally apply the punishments discussed by the medieval jurists. They preferred to follow the Ottoman *qanūn*, with its emphasis on fines and banishment, or the doctrine of *shubha* that effectively sidelined *ḥadd* punishment in favor of indemnities. Illicit sexual encounters were a source of community concern in many contexts, and people often turned to the legal system to enforce local standards of morality, but there was neither expectation nor discernible desire that *ḥadd* penalties be applied for *zinā*. As in the case of rules for

---

[56] As quoted in Hamid Algar, *Wahhabism: A Critical Essay*, 1st edn (Oneonta, NY: Islamic Publications International, 2002), 18; see also Masʿud ʿAlam Nadvi and M. Rafiq Khan, *Mohammad bin Abdul Wahhab: A Slandered Reformer* (Varanasi: Idaratul Buhoosil Islamia, 1983) for a sympathetic view based on the writings of his disciples.

spatial segregation and covering, the jurists and the courts did not typically give this issue a prominent place in their discourse or their actions. The prosecution and punishment of *zinā'* was not neglected altogether, but it was certainly not a defining issue in the Islamic law of the period.

REFORM, SPACE, AND SEXUALITY

The issues of seclusion and veiling acquired a new prominence at the end of the nineteenth century. Juridical treatises took up the questions of the veil (*al-ḥijāb*) and unveiling (*al-sufūr*) as distinct topics that demanded a special attention they had not received in earlier works when, perhaps, the jurists had just assumed that everyone was voluntarily adhering to the same modest dress codes. Islamic thinkers began to address these issues in new ways, as they had others, as part of their arguments for the relevance of the shari'a in modern times and the compatibility between Islam and social progress. The debates over seclusion and veiling were caught up with the much wider questions of female education, the central role women played in educating their children and running modern households, and the appropriateness of women acting in public life. In other words, these debates were legal debates, strictly speaking, only in small part; rather, they were wide-ranging discussions focused on the sociological challenges mounted by the demands of modernity to Islam and local custom. Nor were they debates to be quickly or easily settled, as Malak Hifni Nasif remarked in 1910:

> There remains the question of the hijab, and this is a very difficult question that has occasioned years of deep conflict of the pen with no conclusive outcome, as neither the "conservatives" (guardians of tradition) nor the "liberals" have prevailed.[57]

Indeed, in turn-of-the-century Egypt, a number of intellectuals had engaged the questions of seclusion and veiling in unprecedented ways. Qasim Amin, a French-educated jurist, raised the issues in two books he published, *Tahrir al-Mar'a* (1899) and *Al-Mar'a al-Jadida* (1901). He took a firm stand against female seclusion and face veiling, arguing that Islamic law did not require either practice, that seclusion of women had led to the downfall of Islamic civilization in the face of European might, and that, in any case, the impeccable public behavior of European women amply demonstrated that women could maintain their modesty without these encumbrances. His position sparked a number of reactions in juridical circles. Muhammad 'Abduh, who was rumored to have collaborated with

[57] Nasif, *al-Nisā'iyat*, 61.

Amin in the writing of *Tahrir al-Mar'a*, chose to sidestep the issue: when asked, in his capacity as Grand Mufti in Egypt, for a fatwa on whether veiling and seclusion were required by Islam, 'Abduh simply declined to give his opinion. Rashid Rida took the position that the veil should be retained but female seclusion should end, citing the fact that the women of early Islam were recorded as doing business, fighting, and learning and teaching alongside men. Malak Hifni Nasif held that Islamic law did, in fact, support the right of women to appear in public unveiled, but added that society was not yet ready for the unveiled woman.[58] Beth Baron has noted the prevalence of this stance among Muslim women writers in early twentieth-century Egypt, who championed the reform of marriage and divorce laws but shied away from calling for an end to veiling, in part because of the impulse to assert cultural authenticity in the colonial context.[59]

Legal opinion elsewhere was also mixed. In Tunisia, al-Tahir al-Haddad marshaled an array of arguments against the face-veil, some of which directly addressed the problem of *fitna*. The morality of society rested on the cultivation of conscience and confidence in girls, not the deployment of physical restraints that sapped their will. "Putting a veil on a woman's face to prevent prostitution resembles putting a muzzle on a dog's mouth to prevent bites," he commented, and we nurture weakness with the veil and seclusion that affects not only the individual woman but her family and the entire society as well.[60] The veil and seclusion also represent obstacles to healthy marriages: they preclude a meaningful choice of marriage partner and therefore closeness between the couple, and they place the entire burden of work and public life upon the man, impoverishing home life for husband and wife alike. Veiling stands in the way of a woman realizing her civil rights in court, encourages homosexuality and lesbianism, and, most importantly of all, prevents a woman from acquiring the worldly knowledge she needs to manage her house and educate her children for the good of society as a whole.

We hear very similar arguments from Jamil Sidqi al-Zahawi, an Iraqi legal scholar who taught in Baghdad, in an article he published in 1910. Zahawi called for an end to veiling, noting that the Qur'an does not prescribe the custom, and outlining the social costs of the practice. In his view, the veil actually promoted immorality by facilitating secret liaisons, and posed a

---

[58] See Juan Ricardo Cole, "Feminism, Class, and Islam in Turn-of-the-Century Egypt," *International Journal of Middle East Studies* 13, no. 4 (1981): 387–407. For Nasif's discussion of social conditions and the hijab, see Nasif, *Al-Nisa'iyat*, 61–65.
[59] Baron, *The Women's Awakening in Egypt*, 113. [60] Al-Haddad, *Imra'atuna*, 182.

barrier to female education. He thought that female ignorance jeopardized the wellbeing of the family and by extension the wider society.[61] The connections among unveiling, female education, and the role the mother was to play in nurturing citizens who would be up to the challenges of the modern world were as abundantly clear to Zahawi as they were to al-Haddad.

There were other voices, however. Al-Tahir al-Haddad did not speak for all the 'ulama' in 1920s Tunisia. When he queried six of the prominent Hanafi and Maliki jurists as to "what part of a woman's body should be covered in accordance with the moral practices of the *sunna*?" he received a range of answers. Three of them sided with al-Haddad and held that a woman need not cover her face or hands in public. Another thought that she is not normally required to cover her face but it might be necessary "if *fitna* is feared." Two took the position that she should cover everything except her eyes because, in the words of one, we are living "in a time when immorality is widespread."[62] The men who took the latter position did not engage the social and political issues raised in the anti-veil opinions, but contented themselves with references to how interaction of men and unveiled women threatened to result in *fitna*.

The differences of opinion among 'ulama' on veiling helps explain why it was not until 1937 that the Fatwa Committee of al-Azhar in Cairo finally took up the issue of the face-veil and declared that the Hanafi school of law was not opposed to unveiling and that the Maliki school did not consider veiling a religious requirement. This was, by all accounts, something of a rearguard action because the Egyptian women, mostly urban and middle to upper class, who had worn the face-veil in modern times had by and large abandoned it in the 1920s and 1930s, as had most Muslim women in other countries. There were places, of course, where the face-veil endured as a standard item of dress much longer: it was worn by many urban Moroccan women into the 1970s and is still required, as a matter of law, for women in Saudi Arabia.[63] In general, however, outside of some small ultra-conservative Islamist circles, most Islamic jurists eventually abandoned seclusion and the face-veil in the first half of the twentieth century. Just recently, however, we have seen a modest resurgence of the face-veil throughout the region as part of the early twenty-first-century Islamic piety movement.

---

[61] Khouri, "Drawing Boundaries," 179–80.   [62] Al-Haddad, *Imra'atuna*, 80–108.
[63] See Yedida Kalfon Stillman, *Arab Dress: A Short History, from the Dawn of Islam to Modern Times* (Leiden: Brill, 2000), 153–56.

At moments the state could step in to force the issue. When the modern state of Turkey emerged in 1923 after the collapse of the Ottoman Empire, the government took a consciously secular course and aspired to westernize its population. Part of the process entailed attention to dress with an eye to physically embodying the new regime in its citizens. Under Ataturk, the state banned the fez for men and promoted the wearing of a western-style brimmed hat. It also encouraged women to remove both the face-veil and the traditional headscarf in favor of western fashions. The state did not ban these items of clothing, but rather issued a number of rules and regulations that prohibited the wearing of them in a variety of locations, such as university campuses, and in certain occupations, such as government jobs, including judicial posts.[64] In the case of Turkey, of course, the state did not engage Islamic law on the issue but rather dismantled Islamic courts and institutions, sidelining Islamic law. Later in the century, in a few other countries, the state undertook to interpret Islamic law on the matter of women's dress and issued rules requiring either face-veiling (Saudi Arabia and Afghanistan under the Taliban) or head-covering (the Islamic Republic of Iran), but in general the subjects of dress and public presence, including issues of veiling and seclusion, did not form part of the reformed Islamic legal codes of the twentieth century.

The subjects of seclusion and veiling, always marginal in traditional legal discourse outside of the sphere of religious ritual, moved to center stage as part of the discursive project of asserting Islamic identities in the face of western pressures. The Muslim reformers of the late nineteenth and twentieth centuries weighed in on these issues, but sparingly and even reluctantly in some cases. It was the wider society – journalists, social reformers, and political activists – that debated appropriate dress and comportment for women in a context colored by colonialism and movements for national independence. The debate was in part a defensive one, responding to European criticism of the position of women in Islam, but it also acquired an assertive cast in which the bodies of Muslim women were made to signify cultural identity and difference. It is only within this framework, not as a matter of legal doctrine as such, that we can grasp why these issues came to loom large, and ever larger, toward the end of the twentieth century. I return to this question in the section on recent developments below, where we explore debates about the headscarf in France.

---

[64] Anna J. Secor, "The Veil and Urban Space in Istanbul: Women's Dress, Mobility and Islamic Knowledge," *Gender, Place and Culture: A Journal of Feminist Geography* 9, no. 1 (2002): 9.

Attention to *zinā'* followed a rather different trajectory. *Zinā'*, as a doctrinal matter, seemed to disappear in the main from Islamic legal discourse in the late nineteenth and early twentieth centuries. The reformers did not devote much time or space to the subject, most likely because, as we shall see below, *ḥadd* punishment for sexual and other crimes had generally fallen into abeyance. Al-Tahir al-Haddad engaged the issue more than most. He reviewed the Islamic ban on *zinā'*, noting that extra-marital sex was antithetical to healthy marriage: *zinā'* was based on "nothing but lust" while marriage was based on love, cooperation, and the joint project of bearing and raising children. *Zinā'* was to be abhorred, then, not just because it was outlawed in the Qur'an, but also because its practice stood in the way of healthy families and national progress. Al-Haddad discussed Islamic *fiqh* on *zinā'* in some detail, stressing the many mitigating aspects of its harsh penalties, including the high evidentiary standards, punishments for false witnessing, and the doctrine of *shubha*. He worried that Tunisian law, by adopting French laws that criminalized sexual intercourse only in the case of rape, might actually have encouraged people to have sexual relations outside of marriage, with all the attendant social ills of wrecked unions and neglected children. Many European countries, he asserted, have had second thoughts about the negative social impact of such uncontrolled sexuality. The answer, however, did not lie in a simple return to *ḥadd* punishments for *zinā'*:

In fact, enacting punishments is easier for us than instituting a system of upbringing that would promote virtue. And so we liked the exactitude of the punishment and thought that would deliver results. And our first and last thought [still] goes to *ḥadd* today. But if we return to Islam, it is our opinion that it inclines more towards civilizing behavior than towards elaborating laws.[65]

To back up his position that true Islam stands for programs to "civilize" Muslims and encourage them to correct their faults, rather than draconian punishments, al-Haddad pointed to the hadith in which the Prophet Muhammad refused to punish a drinker who was found praying behind him on the basis that the sinner's prayers would lead him to reform. So, this is the spirit of correction in Islam: teaching and persuasion, not corporal punishment, will inculcate Islamic values and behaviors.

Al-Haddad was writing in the 1920s, at a time when many states under colonial regimes, like his home country of Tunisia and its North African neighbors, had effectively abolished *ḥadd* penalties, and transferred all penal

[65] Al-Haddad, *Imra'atuna*, 43–44.

matters to state courts applying versions of French law. In Egypt as well, the court system was reorganized in 1883 so that criminal cases of all kinds were similarly judged under newly codified laws of European inspiration, and the Ottoman Empire removed jurisdiction over criminal affairs from the shariʿa courts in 1917. Not all states followed suit. Iran and Afghanistan revised their penal codes in 1924, but retained *ḥadd* crimes, including *zinā*ʾ, under the aegis of Islamic law. Saudi Arabia and the Emirates did not undertake legal reform, leaving cases of *zinā*ʾ to Islamic courts operating under a Hanbali version of the law. In Saudi Arabia at least, the courts have been fairly strict in their application of the rules of evidence, and have also been willing to entertain exculpatory claims: the courts have routinely accepted pleas of innocence based on the concept of *shubha*, and although some jurists took the position that pregnancy constituted evidence of *zinā*ʾ, pregnant women have been allowed to claim that they were raped or impregnated while asleep and thus escape punishment.[66]

Elsewhere, *zinā*ʾ, at least as a matter of criminal behavior to be punished by the prescribed *ḥadd* penalties, appeared to be well on its way to oblivion by the middle of the twentieth century. This trend was to be dramatically reversed, however, in the context of Islamization policies undertaken by several countries, beginning in the 1970s. Libya reintroduced *zinā*ʾ into its legal system in 1973, but with the specification that the penalty was to be flogging, not stoning, on the grounds that the Qurʾan (24:2) only mentions the former. Presidential decrees in Pakistan in 1979 made *zinā*ʾ, as proven by confession or eyewitnesses, punishable by lashing or stoning. The 1983 Sudanese Penal Code criminalized *zinā*ʾ and specified that Muslim offenders were to be punished by lashing or stoning. And finally, in Nigeria, twelve northern states had set up shariʿa courts and given them jurisdiction in penal matters, including *zinā*ʾ, by 2002. In all cases, the "Islamization" of law appears to have been tied to bids by central or provincial governments to lay claim to the mantle of Islam, to present themselves as the protectors and promoters of Islamic identity as a legitimating strategy.

Such moves could spark juristic dissent. In 1981, for example, the Federal Sheriat Court of Pakistan balked when called upon to back the laws on *zinā*ʾ and ruled that stoning was an illegal penalty because of the absence of Qurʾanic material to support the practice. It took the interference of the Pakistani President, Zia al-Huq, to bring the Court into line, namely by dismissing the presiding members of the Court and appointing new members willing to overturn the ruling and reinstate stoning. Elsewhere, many

---

[66] Peters, *Crime and Punishment*, 104–05, 138–39, 150.

jurists distanced themselves from Islamization policies for a variety of reasons, both doctrinal and practical, echoing the position of the Muslim Brothers in Egypt, who argued in the 1940s that the *ḥadd* laws and penalties should be suspended until such time as a just Islamic government was fully in charge and able to address social ills; it would not be fair, for example, to punish a couple for *zinā'* if they were not able to marry because of poor economic conditions.[67] Some leaders of the Islamic movement in northern Nigeria took a similar position in the face of legal Islamization in 2000/1, arguing that the restoration of full Islamic governance and Islamic society must precede legal change.[68]

Just as in the case of face-veils and headscarves, the legal regulation of sexuality came to represent a form of Islamic identity, albeit at a later date and in a somewhat different register. It was in the context of splashy Islamization programs that *zinā'* was reintroduced to legal practice, not as a sustained legal discourse but rather as a series of discrete laws passed by rulers and governments seeking to underscore their Islamic identities. These new rules concerning punishments for *zinā'* were not often enforced (actual stonings being few and far between), but they generated heated discussion and protest at home and abroad. Again, as we shall see below, the debates revolved more around the politics of identity and modernity of the late twentieth and early twenty-first century rather than around doctrinal matters per se. And, I would add, whether the issue was one of dress or of sexuality, it was the bodies of women that were pressed into the service of representing Islamic identities in the modern era.

RECENT DEVELOPMENTS

The issue of Islamic law and dress codes acquired a new global prominence in late 2003 when French President Jacques Chirac endorsed the recommendations of a government committee on secularism and religion, including a proposal for new legislation to ban the wearing of Islamic head covering, large crosses, and yarmulkes in French public schools in keeping with the French commitment to secularism (*laïcité*) in public life. After considerable debate, new regulations were indeed issued to take effect with the start of the school year in the fall of 2004. Although the regulations did not target Islamic dress alone, the "headscarf debate," as it came to be called,

---

[67] *Ibid.*, 154–71, 184.
[68] Allan Christelow, "Islamic Law and Judicial Practice in Nigeria: An Historical Perspective," *Journal of Muslim Minority Affairs* 22, no. 1 (2002): 198.

touched on sensitive issues in French and wider European society concerning the process and, indeed, very definition of assimilation of religious and ethnic minorities into European nation-states. What did it mean to be a citizen of a modern nation-state? How were individual rights to believe and practice one's religion to be reconciled with a collective national identity? The headscarf debate touched on a wide range of sociological and political matters relevant to changes in European demographics and unresolved questions about the relationship between culture, religion, and citizenship.[69] For our purposes, however, it is the legal questions that are of central interest. How did Muslim jurists interpret Islamic law on the subject and how did they view its requirements in the context of conflicting state law?

One of the most prominent jurists to weigh in on the issue was Muhammad Sayyid Tantawi, the Grand Imam of al-Azhar in Cairo. In late 2003, Shaykh Tantawi made a public declaration to the effect that wearing the hijab (in the meaning of headscarf) was a divine obligation for every Muslim woman. He was quick to add, however, that France, as a non-Muslim and sovereign country, had the right to ban its wearing in state schools. Muslim women who found themselves in this situation, i.e. constrained to remove their hijabs in order to abide by the rules of the country they inhabited, were to be regarded as forced by necessity to uncover and therefore were not disobeying the commands of their religion.[70]

Other Muslim jurists and organizations joined the discussion. In France, the "official" umbrella organization of French Muslims, the Conseil Français du Culte Musulman (CFCM) took the position that the hijab was indeed required by Islam, but students should not sacrifice their schooling in order to continue wearing it. The proposed state regulations were a great mistake, however, since they had the unfortunate effect of stigmatizing and demonizing Muslim religious practices. Among the constituent groups within the CFCM, however, there were some nuances of opinion.

Fouad Alaoui, Secretary General of the Union of Islamic Organizations of France (UOIF), asserted that the headscarf debate was not as much about the obligation of Muslims to respect the laws of their countries as about the right to religious freedom as guaranteed by the fundamental principles of the French Republic on the one hand and international conventions for human rights on the other. Muslim women wore the hijab as an article of

---

[69] See John Richard Bowen, *Why the French Don't Like Headscarves: Islam, the State, and Public Space* (Princeton: Princeton University Press, 2007).

[70] Subhy Mujahid, "French Women Can Remove Hijab If Forced: Tantawi," *Islam Online* (December 30, 2003), www.islamonline.net/English/News/2003–12/30/article09.shtml.

belief, and any regulation interfering with this form of religious practice was an infringement upon their freedom to practice their religion. The hijab was not a religious "symbol," but rather a central religious practice. The UOIF and its officials repeatedly stressed both the religious obligation and the free choice involved: Islamic doctrine prescribed head covering for women, and most girls who wore a headscarf did so as a result of a personal decision based on religious commitment. There were a few girls, no doubt, who wore the scarf as a result of family pressure, but the image of the headscarf as symbol of the oppression of women was belied by the active agitation for the hijab on the part of Muslim students themselves. The UOIF was willing to entertain a compromise in the form of allowing Muslim girls to wear a small scarf or bandana if they chose, just as Christians were permitted to wear a small cross or Jews a small Star of David. The insistence on these regulations in their present form of prohibiting all head covering, however, was deemed discriminatory against Muslims, who were far more likely to suffer consequences than were the adherents of other religions.

Other constituent groups of the CFCM were even less adamant about the headscarf as a required religious practice. Dalil Boubakeur, speaking on behalf of the Institut Musulman de la Mosquée de Paris, asserted that hijab was recommended by Islamic law, but was not, in fact, an absolute obligation: neglecting to wear it was not a sin, and in any event there was no punishment prescribed in Islamic law. The Conseil de Coordination des Musulmans Turc de France, also a constituent group, viewed the hijab as a tradition as much as a religious prescription and bemoaned the tensions created by the regulations and by the CFCM engagement with the issue. The best course lay in a refusal to participate in a divisive debate of very secondary importance to Islamic law and society today.[71]

The European Council for Fatwa and Research (ECFR), whose mission is to provide religious guidance to Muslims throughout Europe, also weighed in on the proposed regulation from a broader European vantage point. In early 2003, the Council reacted with respectful disagreement to Shaykh Tantawi's statement:

---

[71] Union des Organisations Islamiques de France, "Réaction du secrétaire général de l'UOIF aux declarations de Cheikh Tantaoui au sujet du foulard islamique," www.uoif-online.com/mod-ules.php?op=modload&name=News&file=article&sid=162; Union des Organisations Islamiques de France, "Les filles qui portent le voile aiment la France," www.uoif-online.com/modules. php?op=modload&name=News&file=article&sid=166; Union des Organisations Islamiques de France, "L'UOIF s'adresse aux députés de la nation," www.uoif-online.com/modules.php? op=modload&name=News&file=article&sid=178; see also Franck Frégosi, "La position des acteurs islamiques: champ religieux officiel et contre-champ islamique," in *La politisation du voile: l'affaire en France, en Europe et dans le monde arabe*, ed. Françoise Lorcerie (Paris: L'Harmattan, 2005), 53–64.

Wearing the hijab is a matter of worship and a Shari'i (religious) obligation and not just a religious or political symbol. It is something that the Muslim woman regards as an important part of her legal practice of the teachings of her religion. The commitment is not confined to any public place, whether it is a place of worship or one of the official or other institutions, for the teachings of Islam, by their nature, do not allow contradiction or fragmentation in the life of the committed Muslim, which is something agreed upon by all the old and modern schools of Islamic thought, and recognized by the specialists among Muslim scholars all over the world, including the stance of His Excellency the Shaikh of al-Jami' al-Azhar, who clearly declared that the Islamic Hijab is a Shari'i obligation and not a "religious symbol." As to the saying attributed to him that France as a sovereign state has the right to enact the laws and legislations it deems suitable, it is valid and acceptable internationally. But we think that it would have been beneficial also for His Excellency to add that such right should comply with the conventions of human rights, international treaties and the UN Convention, and that it cannot be imagined that the sovereignty of a state justifies enacting laws that oppose human rights and the personal and religious freedoms.[72]

Later in the year, the ECFR issued a fatwa affirming that, based on Qur'anic verses 24:31 (on covering adornments) and 33:59 (on the wives of the Prophet not displaying themselves outside), the wearing of hijab was a religious obligation for adult Muslim women. The significance of the headscarf debate was underscored yet again a year later, at the twelfth ordinary session of the ECFR ending in January 2004, when Shaykh Yusuf al-Qaradawi, the Council's President, identified the French proposal as one of the most important issues of the year, and the ECFR devoted the first of the five resolutions it issued that year to the right of Muslim women to wear the hijab.[73]

There were subtle differences in the jurists' positions on the law, exhibiting an ongoing diversity in Islamic legal opinion. Some chose to emphasize the hijab as an incontrovertible religious obligation based on scripture, and therefore a duty on which all schools of law and jurists putatively concurred. Others recast the debate in the language of universal human rights and constructed the wearing of a headscarf as a right, as a religious observance that must be permitted for those women whose personal beliefs so dictated. Despite an inevitable tension between obligation and right, few disputed the fact that some covering for women was a standard Islamic practice.

---

[72] European Council for Fatwa and Research (ECFR), "The Statement on the Problem of Hijab in France," January 2003.

[73] See the ECFR fatwa of December 14, 2003, "France: Hijab under Attack," available from Islam Online, www.islamonline.net/servlet/Satellite?pagename=IslamOnline-English-Ask_Scholar/FatwaE/FatwaE&cid=1119503547428; European Council for Fatwa and Research (ECFR), "Final Statement of the Twelfth Ordinary Session," January 2004.

The question of how to live out the precepts of Islamic law in the modern world, particularly for Muslims who found themselves under the legal authority of state powers that might impose regulations that made it difficult or impossible to do so, emerged as the critical, and unresolved, issue. Jurists varied in their approach. Some took the Tantawi position that Islamic law allowed members of minority Muslim communities to adhere to the law of the land in which they found themselves, even if it prevented full observance of their religion: state sovereignty trumped religious obligation in cases of necessity. Others, like the jurists of the ECFR, underscored the absolute religious obligation of the hijab and simultaneously the universality of the right to practice one's religion: the state is required to respect the religious practices of its citizens. Still others, and here we find many of the French Muslim jurists, seemed eager to find a modus vivendi that would allow Muslims who so desired to live out their religious beliefs in ways that had a minimal impact on their surroundings: the state is called upon to negotiate a compromise, to meet its more devout Muslim citizens half-way.

The wearing of hijab as a right to religious practice resonated in the international human rights community. Human Rights Watch deemed the French law discriminatory on the grounds of its potentially disproportionate impact on Muslim girls, and further viewed it as "an infringement on the right to religious practice" because "for many Muslims ... it [wearing the hijab] is about religious obligation."[74] The United Nations Commission on Human Rights sent Asma Jahangir, a Special Rapporteur on Freedom of Religion or Belief, to France one year after the implementation of the law to assess its effects. Jahangir divined a "positive element" in the law insofar as it "takes into account the autonomy of a female child who may be subjected to gender discrimination at a stage when she is unable to realize the consequences of being lured or forced in wearing headscarf" but hastened to add that "the law also denies the right to those teenagers who have freely chosen to wear a religious symbol in school as part of their religious belief."[75] Although it proved difficult to establish how many Muslim girls had been negatively affected by the ban, in the sense of being barred from attending public school, Jahangir evinced concern about other consequences of this high-profile law which had ushered in an open season in France on women

---

[74] "France: Headscarf Ban Violates Religious Freedom," *Human Rights Watch News* (February 27, 2004), http://hrw.org/english/docs/2004/02/26/france7666.htm.

[75] UN Commission on Human Rights, "Special Rapporteur on Freedom of Religion Ends Visit to France" (Geneva: September 30, 2005), www.unhchr.ch/huricane/huricane.nsf/view01/AA8F269703D694EAC125708C00455C34?opendocument.

wearing the hijab, normalizing the public humiliation and stigmatization of women wearing headscarves in public spaces.

Muslim women were far from silent on this issue. As debate heated up in early 2004, there was a wave of demonstrations across Europe and the Middle East in which hijab-wearing women protested the French law. In a London demonstration in front of the French Embassy on January 11, slogans captured the theme of the right to religious practice:

> Education is – our right
> For hijab – We will fight
> One voice – Our choice
> In hijab – We rejoice.

The protesters also presented a letter addressed to President Jacques Chirac from the International Islamic Women Organization and the Islamic Human Rights Commission in the UK in which the French government stood accused of outright discrimination against Muslim Frenchwomen:

Your government's and institutions' actions have violated their rights to an education, work, free movement and free religious expression ... the Islamic dress is a mandatory part of the Islamic faith. The French state's attempts to force women to abandon their religious practice is the very antithesis of freedom and equality. If anything it evidences a fanatical desire to control women's minds and bodies ... Not only are these actions anti-Islamic they are misogynist.[76]

The discourse of human rights in general and women's rights in particular was thus employed to turn the tables on French claims that the headscarf ban liberated Muslim girls from the tyranny of their families and communities; on the contrary, asserted activist Muslim women, the law was yet another instance of manipulation of women's bodies for political ends. In demonstrations, public forums, letters and petitions, many Muslim women vociferously made the point that they wished to make their own decisions about the hijab.

Regardless of the level of female activism on this issue, I do not want to lose sight of the fact that it was, of course, female dress – not male dress – that was the flashpoint here. The subtext of gender was omnipresent. French "secular" discourse constructed the veiled Muslim woman as oppressed and robbed of her autonomy while the opposing Islamic legal discourse focused on covering parts of the female body as religious practice while maintaining a quasi-total silence on the male body. The formal legal discourse was largely a male affair where the voices of the male jurists

---

[76] Innovative Minds, "Protest against French Hijab Ban, Sunday, 11th January 2004, French Embassy, London," www.inminds.co.uk/french-hijab-ban.html#t17.

monopolized the debate. They did not use this occasion to address the starkly gendered differences in the rules and practices of Islamic dress as contained in the fact that there was no required "Islamic dress" for men at issue in French public space. It was the Muslim woman, at the end of the day, whose appearance was to represent Islamic cultural practices, a point upon which both the supporters and the critics of the headscarf ban could agree.

It was also the fate of women, not men, that engaged international attention in the heated debates and campaigns that accompanied some of the "Islamization" of law programs. While several states have instituted Islamic penal laws in the later twentieth and early twenty-first centuries, including laws prescribing draconian punishments for *zinā*, no legal practices have drawn as much negative attention as those of the Northern States of Nigeria, and particularly the two notorious cases of Safiyyatu Husseini and Amina Lawal.

Husseini and Lawal were defendants in separate cases prosecuted under Shariʿa Penal Codes. The application of some version of *ḥadd* laws had a long history in the region. The Sokoto Caliphate had launched a campaign of Islamic reform in the nineteenth century, and at least one scholar thinks that Islamic law was routinely applied in northern Nigerian criminal matters in the late nineteenth and early twentieth centuries as part of a program of assertion of state authority.[77] The British colonial administration introduced a criminal code in 1904, but shariʿa law was still applied in the predominantly Muslim northern states: *zinā*, for example, could be prosecuted under Islamic law although punishment was restricted in practice to fines and imprisonment for women and unmarried men, and flogging for married men only. In 1960, a new penal code of English inspiration was introduced for the northern region, but a few special "Islamic" provisions, among them the criminalization of *zinā* for Muslims, were included. Then, in a context of social and political upheaval and associated calls for moral retrenchment, twelve northern states established special shariʿa courts and promulgated shariʿa penal codes between 2000 and 2002.[78]

Cases of *zinā* soon surfaced. Safiyyatu Husseini, a divorced woman from the state of Sokoto, became pregnant, and her brother reported this out-of-wedlock pregnancy to their local Sharia Implementation Committee in late 2000, which brought charges against her in the Lower Sharia Court. After a police investigation, the case was referred to the Upper Sharia Court, where her lover was acquitted (since he refused to confess in court and there were no witnesses to the act of *zinā*); Husseini, on the other hand, was found

---

[77] Christelow, "Islamic Law," 187–88.   [78] See Peters, *Crime and Punishment*, 121–25, 169–71.

guilty on the grounds that she had initially confessed and, in any case, her pregnancy and the subsequent birth of her child Adamah provided absolute proof of her guilt in keeping with the Maliki rules of evidence. She was sentenced to be stoned. In Katsina state, another divorced woman, Amina Lawal, was similarly convicted and sentenced in March 2002, on like evidence of confession, pregnancy, and the existence of her daughter Wosilat, while the man she identified as the father of her child refused to confess and thus was found innocent. In both cases, the women's executions were postponed so that they could have time to nurture their babies.

The postponements allowed for the elaboration of their legal defenses. Local women's groups took an interest in these and other cases of women tried for sexual crimes under the new penal codes. BAOBAB for Women's Human Rights, a Nigerian organization, was particularly active in identifying these cases and assisting in the appeals process. It helped put together and fund Husseini's legal defense team which then subjected the shari'a penal codes and procedures to close scrutiny. Husseini's lawyers pointed to the many contradictions and omissions in the code as well as its procedural flaws: the proactive investigation of Husseini by the police was not in keeping with standard Islamic procedure that prohibits such a search for evidence; Husseini should have been permitted to retract her confession; her pregnancy was not proof of her guilt because Maliki law recognizes a gestation period of up to five years and therefore the child could have been fathered by her ex-husband; the judge, in omitting to explain *zinā'* to her and failing to ascertain if she were an adult Muslim with a legal prior marriage, had not followed Islamic procedural guidelines; the possibility of *shubha* was not considered; and finally, the reported act had occurred before the new penal codes were signed into law. Husseini was ultimately acquitted on this last technical point, as was Lawal on the basis of procedural and evidentiary problems, including the fact that she too had not been allowed to retract her confession and the judge had not considered the possibility of a "sleeping fetus" of long gestation. Their sentences also occasioned discussion of the constitutionality of the penal codes when it came to the stoning of women found guilty by way of pregnancy. It was argued that the law discriminated against women in contradiction to equal treatment as prescribed in the Nigerian Constitution (section 42,1), and that stoning violated the prohibition on cruel, degrading, and inhuman punishment (34,1).[79]

---

[79] For discussion of these two cases, see *ibid.*, 171; Silvia Sansoni, "Saving Amina," *Essence* 33, no. 11 (2003): 156–59; Ogbu U. Kalu, "Safiyya and Adamah: Punishing Adultery with Sharia Stones in Twenty-First Century Nigeria," *African Affairs* 102 (2003): 389–408; BAOBAB, *Sharia Implementation in Nigeria: The Journey So Far* (Lagos: BAOBAB for Women's Rights, 2003), 4–17.

Both of these cases achieved international notoriety and prompted public outcry. Nigerian embassies in Europe were deluged with petitions and protests, and both the Pope and the US House of Representatives went on record condemning Husseini's sentence. Several contestants withdrew from the Miss World Pageant scheduled to be held in Nigeria in a high-profile criticism of Lawal's sentence, and feminist groups in Europe and North America helped organize an e-mail petition campaign calling for Lawal's acquittal that garnered over 5 million signatures. The external pressure was perceived by supporters of Husseini and Lawal inside Nigeria as a mixed blessing: all this attention generated resources and political pressure to address the cases, but it also risked provoking a backlash in the North and a renewed resolve to carry out the punishments under the shari'a penal codes. In casting the issue as a cultural clash, as an enlightened attack on traditional oppressive practice, the internationalization of these *zinā'* cases made it increasingly difficult for local women to speak up out of fear of being branded as inauthentic or, in extreme instances, as allies of neo-imperial projects.[80]

BAOBAB, for example, preferred to focus on the ways in which the shari'a penal codes failed to realize the promise of justice and fairness embedded in the Islamic tradition. It was the flawed interpretation of shari'a, not the shari'a itself, that should be on trial. The organization chose its issues carefully, aiming its critique at the shortcomings of the penal codes in principle and practice, and situating its analysis within an Islamic legal tradition, in keeping with its goal of correcting "the impression that women's human rights cannot be discussed in relation to Sharia implementation and practice in particular and religion in general."[81] Three aspects of the way *zinā'* was handled drew BAOBAB's attention. First, it questioned the proactive approach taken by family members who informed on women and by police who then detained and interrogated them. According to Islamic doctrine, a case of *zinā'* should be opened only if four witnesses to the act initiate the proceedings or the guilty party confesses. Second, the judge accepts a person's confession only if she makes it voluntarily, has the benefit of counsel, and repeats it on four separate occasions. In addition, the confession can be retracted at any time, whether before or after sentencing. Third, the far from unanimous Maliki argument that pregnancy

---

[80] For a discussion of the complexities of the discourse on Islamization projects, see "Saving Amina Lawal: Human Rights Symbolism and the Dangers of Colonialism," *Harvard Law Review* 117, no. 7 (2004): 2365–86.

[81] BAOBAB, "National Discussion on Sharia and Women's Human Rights in Nigeria Series Two," www.baobabwomen.org/activities.htm.

constitutes proof of *zinā'* has no basis in the Qur'an or hadith literature, and should therefore be ruled out of order as evidence in *zinā'* cases.[82]

The BAOBAB report on the shari'a penal codes was also quick to point out that it has been women, and poor women in particular, who have been charged and convicted of *zinā'*. Men have been far more likely to run afoul of some of the other provisions of the penal codes, such as drinking alcohol and theft, but *zinā'* has devolved into a woman's crime. So once again it appears to be women's bodies that have been called upon as signifiers for both sides, as symbols of the subjection of Muslim women in western discourse, and as bearers of the moral standards of Islamic rules on sexuality. Men have often slipped both literally and figuratively out of the picture, eluding both the practice and the discourse of the law.

CONCLUSION

The discourse of the jurists on the gendering of space, dress rules for women, and the regulation of sexual activity spoke to an abiding belief in the need to control male–female interactions in the interests of the social stability and harmony of the Muslim community. The power of the human sexual drive threatened this community with *fitna*, and therefore the jurists worked out rules to minimize sex appeal and institute harsh penalties for sexual transgressions. I did not find a uniformity of opinion on these matters: the strictness of sexual segregation, the degree of covering required in dress, and many of the details concerning evidence and punishment of sexual crimes were matters on which jurists could and did disagree. We do see some convergence in the tendency of the jurists to discuss these issues more in relation to women than to men. Even though sexual desire affected both sexes, the burden of minimizing sexual contact fell on women and on controlling their bodies. It would be incorrect to leave the impression, however, that these sorts of issues occupied much space in the minds and treatises of the jurists. While certainly present in the juristic discourse, they were neither particularly prominent nor weighty, and there was rarely any sense that judicial activism was required or particularly desirable in relation to such matters.

Legal practice in the Ottoman period supports the view that the law occupied itself relatively little with interaction in public space or dress codes. We have evidence that Muslims of different regions and classes dressed and interacted with varying degrees of modesty and freedom. In general, these

---

[82] BAOBAB, *Sharia Implementation*, 17.

differences did not occasion legal action, with a few notable exceptions that prove the general rule that the courts left matters of costume and comportment to the play of local custom. The courts did recognize *zinā*ʾ as a serious crime, but their willingness to entertain the defense of *shubha* under most circumstances on the one hand, and the Ottoman *qanūn*'s preference for fines and banishment on the other, effectively rendered *ḥadd* punishments for *zinā*ʾ obsolete. There is no indication that any of these issues were signature ones for the courts, or that they occupied an important place in the construction of community identity and culture for most of the Ottoman period, although we cannot rule out the possibility of sporadic enforcement and punishment by extra-judicial government authorities when it suited their purposes.

The legal reformers of the late nineteenth and early twentieth centuries took up the matters of female dress and behavior, notably the issues of the veil and seclusion, rather reluctantly if at all. Debates about Islamic culture and the need to assert and maintain authentic identities in the face of the European onslaught inevitably reached the ears of the jurists, but they chose by and large to avoid taking detailed positions on these issues. The reforming jurists usually maintained cordial relations with state authorities who were engaging the project of modernity and looking to women's bodies to model the modern; but the jurists were also the putative upholders of Islamic tradition. In this complex environment it was no doubt easier to focus on the issues that appeared more critical to equipping Muslims for the modern era, female education in particular, and limit one's remarks about the veil. When it came to *zinā*ʾ, the replacement of Islamic penal law in most places with penal codes of European design rendered the matter moot for many jurists, and we see little evidence of any nostalgia for *ḥadd* penalties among early twentieth-century thinkers. It was only toward the end of the century that jurists were forced to react to the Islamization programs that placed *zinā*ʾ and associated *ḥadd* punishments on their mental maps.

Recent developments in the law, at least those that capture attention on a global scale, have moved the issues of Islamic dress and *zinā*ʾ to center stage in public consciousness. The hijab has posed interesting questions about the relation of religious practice to citizenship, and *zinā*ʾ cases have pitted local campaigners for Islamic identity against interpreters of international norms. Muslim jurists have not chosen these issues for their doctrinal importance, but rather they have achieved prominence as part of the political maneuvering of various groups to stake claims to legitimacy by raising or lowering the banner of Islam. In ways that appear to be unprecedented, Muslim women have also engaged these issues by way of wide ranging activism, from organizing advocacy groups to street demonstrations, bringing a critical perspective to both western interpretations of their plight and local Islamization initiatives. Law on dress and sexuality, thanks to its significance for definitions of male and female, the ordering of society, and questions of culture and identity, promises to remain a central field of inquiry and action in the twenty-first century.

6

Conclusion

I began this investigation with an apparent paradox: many Muslim women cling to the notion that rights, privileges, and fairness for women and men alike can be best secured within an Islamic framework, despite the many examples in recent times of Islamic principles and laws being pressed into the service of misogyny. The question was further complicated for me by what I had read, as a historian, working with legal materials from the Ottoman period, many of which, despite their male authorship, exuded a sensitivity to the situations and concerns of women. In an attempt to explore the intersection of Islamic law with issues of gendered privilege and power, I turned my attention to some of the classical and medieval doctrinal debates, premodern practices, modern reforms, and recent instances of activism, all of which shaped and are still shaping the history of the law.

One of the questions I posed was that of discrimination. How has Islamic law treated women and men? Have women suffered certain legal disabilities as a direct result of their gender? The answer to such a seemingly simple question turned out to be fairly complex. There was no pretension of equality in many of the rules for contracting and living a marriage. Most legal schools allowed women to contract a marriage only under the tutelage of a male relative, a disability which survives into the contemporary era in some iterations of the law despite a history of legal reforms and activism focused on its elimination. Nor was the marital relationship constructed as one of equality; rather it was the complementarity of the marital bargain of *nafaqa* for absence of *nushūz*, or the husband's material support for the wife's obedience, that characterized judicial discourse, a discourse that existed in a certain tension with an Islamic ideal of marriage as a loving and collaborative relationship. The jurists, modern reformers, and present-day activists have approached the inequalities of the marital relationship with caution, wary of the dangers of disturbing such a balance by undermining a wife's right to maintenance, when she might not be in a position to support herself, in return for a spurious or socially unacceptable freedom of action.

The doctrines on divorce also legislated gender inequality, with men empowered to choose divorce without having to show grounds or seek judicial approval while women were constrained on both counts. The degree of inequality in divorce law did differ among legal schools – this is one area where doctrinal differences were striking in the varying degrees of latitude they provided for female-initiated divorce. But all schools insisted that men incurred financial obligations in the wake of divorce, for temporary maintenance of their ex-wives, for payment of any outstanding dower, and for support of all children born to the marriage, while women ordinarily left their marriages without financial burdens but also without any share of their husband's past earnings. The history of legal practice in the courts, at least in the Ottoman period, tells the story of how women asserted their rights to material support from their husbands and ex-husbands in ways that cushioned the harshness of discrimination. The general trend among reformers has been to attempt to set some limits on the man's unbridled freedom of action in divorce while simultaneously increasing women's options by expanding the grounds for judicial decrees of divorce (*faskh*) and permitting women to obtain no-fault divorces (*khul'*) without their husbands' permission. As was the case in marital arrangements, changes in divorce law carry some risks for women, who may end up bartering their rights to support for their freedom to act.

I found formal legal discrimination much less evident in property law. Women enjoyed legal standing as equal and autonomous individuals with rights to manage and dispose of their property as they wished, and their marital status had no bearing on their ability to buy, sell, gift, or endow their property. Discrimination crept in with rules allowing prolonged interdiction for females and some limited powers of oversight of their property by their husbands, but such doctrines remained strictly confined to the Maliki school. The one area in which women faced discrimination across the board was inheritance law, with its allotment of one-half of the male share to females, and because of its Qur'anic roots this is an area that has proved to be fairly impervious to change. But women did inherit some property, and they were, by all accounts, able to take good advantage of their property rights in the Ottoman period so that we often find them in Islamic courts, managing property they acquired through inheritance, *mahr*, gifts, or their own efforts. The absence of much formal discrimination carried over into many of the areas of the law concerned with space and sexuality. When it came to the problem of maintaining an orderly and moral society, the jurists identified the sexual drives of both men and women as threatening *fitna* (social disorder). It was the mutual attraction of the two that could lead to unbridled sexuality, and therefore the law concerned itself with the separation of the sexes on the one hand, and the punishment of illicit sexual intercourse on the other, to be doled out without regard for gender difference. This principle of equality came to be transgressed in the process of elaboration of legal rules that gave women the lion's share of responsibility, both actual and symbolic, for the dress and comportment that would minimize sexual attraction. Premodern Islamic courts, at least in the Ottoman period, did not concern themselves much with the regulation of dress and behavior, however, beyond the enforcement of community norms prohibiting the intermingling of unrelated men and women in private space. Sartorial regulations were few and far between, and the draconian punishments for *zinā'* largely fell into abeyance in favor of fines levied on both consenting partners. Various Islamization programs in recent times have introduced new kinds of discriminatory features, including evidentiary processes in the prosecution of *zinā'* that place special burdens on women. Indeed, law on matters of dress and sexuality has proven to be the area most vulnerable to manipulation for political ends, and the place where male–female difference has been highlighted in ways particularly prejudicial to women, a point I return to below.

A second question addressed the extent to which the law took the particular experiences of women, especially the "counter-autonomous" experiences of pregnancy, childbirth, and nurturing, into account as opposed to adhering strictly to a male norm. Certainly one can argue that, in the case of the rights and obligations of the marital relationship, Islamic law recognized the special reproductive contributions of women by requiring husbands to compensate their wives for their work in the household by way of personal maintenance, wages for nursing, and full child support. In the wake of divorce, the jurists were also attuned to specifically female vulnerabilities, discoursing at length on the divorcée's rights and holding the courts responsible for insuring that women received their due. We have ample evidence that Islamic courts, with some nudging from women themselves, rose to the challenge of enforcing the rules on compensation for both wives and children. This acknowledgment of female difference endured through the period of legal reform and was enshrined in modern legal codes in the regulations for marital support, even though changing social and economic contexts in which many women work outside the home and contribute to the family income have lent it, in places, an anachronistic flavor. I would submit that women continue to pay for the legal recognition of the female life-cycle rather dearly in the context of the *nafaqa–nushūz* bargain, and we have yet to see reforms that successfully uncouple a husband's authority and dominance from his material obligations.

In the context of property rights, attention to the specificities of the female experience introduced a note of ambivalence into the construction of the woman as legal subject. Women's unfettered ownership of their property and their person was infringed upon primarily where their identities as daughters, wives, and mothers intruded. Most legal schools did not entrust women with their own marriage arrangements, taking the position that a woman's marriage had too many ramifications for the material and social standing of her family to be left entirely in her hands. The Maliki school also empowered a husband to guard his wife's property against her excessive benevolence, in the understanding that her actions affected the wellbeing of the family household. The idea that women required special oversight by male relations, particularly in the making of marriage arrangements, endured into the modern period and was enshrined in a number of the modern codes, even in places where it constituted something of an innovation. In the area of dress and sexuality, the results of attention to female difference were even more far ranging as the jurists highlighted biological difference, most dramatically in their discussion of female and male *ʿawra*s in such a way as to impose greater restrictions in dress and comportment on women than on men. And although *zinā'* was, in principle, an equal opportunity crime, the development of the Maliki doctrine that out-of-wedlock pregnancy constituted evidence of unlawful intercourse turned that female experience into a major liability. Some of the recent campaigns for Islamization have seized on this legal strand of female difference and magnified its importance to the Islamic legal ethos so that women's distinct experiences become the grounds for outright exclusion and oppression. The requirements for "Islamic dress" fall much more heavily on women than on men in most contexts, and it is women, in general, who are being called upon to model the kinds of modest behavior, and in extreme instances absence from public space, that is supposed to represent Muslim morality.

The third question focused on Woman and Man as discursive constructs deeply embedded in all fields of knowledge that gender a given society, and the extent to which we can explore, and critique, legal gendering practices that are inextricably linked to a larger project. It is, of course, quite impossible to separate Islamic law from the intellectual, social, and political contexts in which it developed, and in which it played and plays only one of many discursive roles. But attention to the law helps lend some historicity to these discursive constructs by allowing us to focus on a process of juristic elaboration of the Woman, and the Man, of law. Islamic laws governing marriage constituted Woman as dependent, vulnerable, and weak, and Man as authoritative, worldly, and strong. The rules for divorce followed along by entrusting Man with the power to choose divorce while placing Woman under the guardianship of the court. The jurists did not speak with one voice, however, and their divergences over many of the details of gendered rights and obligations cleared the way for the nuances and caveats we encounter in the courts, and in the juristic literature, where the categories of Woman and Man acquired some elasticity. The mother as guardian, ubiquitous in the Ottoman era, illustrates the extent to which a woman could play a male role in certain situations, primarily those in which her fitness for the care and nurturing of her children extended to the safe keeping and management of their properties.

Tensions in discursive legal practices were nowhere more apparent than in the construction of the Woman as a subject of law, as an equal and autonomous individual with full power to act in a legal setting, a construction with an impeccable textual pedigree. But this Woman as legal subject ran up against the Woman of patriarchal society whose body and behavior must be policed and restricted in ways that infringed on her ability to know and to act, thereby, among other things, devaluing her testimony in court. This whiff of disability in relation to the female capacity for full participation in legal institutions has continued to tinge discussions of the suitability of women as lawyers, judges, or even full citizens of the modern state. And in the realm of regulation of sexual desire and sexual activity, although Man and Woman were held equally responsible for sexual transgressions, the burdens of minimizing dangerous contacts fell more heavily on women in the form of regulations of their dress and mobility. The patriarchal drive to control female sexuality repeatedly trumped the egalitarian impulse, as is nowhere more apparent than in the ways control and chastisement of the female body have surfaced as a key feature of Islamization campaigns in recent times. The very existence of these tensions, however, suggests that there is plenty of material, within the field of Islamic law itself, to contest any monolithic categorization of the male and female attributed to juristic discourse.

This wealth of material is perhaps the most striking feature of Islamic law in relation to gender issues, and the one most pregnant with possibilities for projects of rethinking and reform. The Islamic legal tradition incorporated multiple doctrinal schools, majority and minority opinions, and esteemed jurists who agreed to disagree on matters both large and small. Doctrines developed over time as jurists proved themselves ready and able to adapt the legal tradition to changing social realities. The law was not immune to the play of personal proclivities on the part of the jurists: we have clear instances where the impulse of misogyny colored interpretation, but we have other examples of firm adherence to principles of fairness and righteousness. The very nature of the law – its textual scope, its decentralized authority, its responsiveness to community issues, its sense of higher purpose – has insured a legacy of diversity and adaptability with the potential to insert moral principles into a modern legal system in a way that is neither discriminatory nor male-normed.

I have argued that, indeed, the Islamic courts proved to be flexible and eclectic in their practices, operating with an eye on both individual need and the social setting. I am not asserting that this system delivered perfect justice every time, but the evidence from the Ottoman period at least suggests a fairly high level of community confidence in the law as a guide to the good life and the court as a fair institution. By the late nineteenth century, a pervading sense that Muslim communities were falling behind the West and had not proven equal to the demands of modernity shook that confidence and ushered in a period of reinterpretation of the law by Islamic modernists who initially approached the question of reform as one of reinterpretation of some of the particulars of the law based on a close rereading of the relevant religious texts. While this project yielded some promising results, legal reform gradually became part of the modern states' programs of centralization and the emphasis shifted to codification and control of the courts. In the course of the twentieth century, the production of codes transformed the face of Islamic law: diversity of opinion and possibility has given way to a unitary standard, leading to an impoverishment, many would argue, of the vastness of the legal tradition and a diminution of the law's former flexibility on gender issues. Whether Islamic law retains any central identity or rather has devolved into fragmented sets of rules deployed for various purposes of politics and power are valid and important questions, but ones that lie beyond the bounds of this particular study.

But the impoverishment of formal legal discourse is only one part of the story. I have tried, throughout, to attend to the question of agency, to examine the extent to which ordinary women and activists approached the law and managed to shape its effects. Certainly women "waged law" in the sense that they came to court to assert their rights and collect their dues. We have ample evidence from the Ottoman period, for example, of women using the court to secure their maintenance payments, their dowers, and their inheritance portions. Their beliefs in their God-given rights, and their activities in support of these rights, no doubt helped prevent the lapsing of such entitlements in the face of patriarchal pressures. In the course of the twentieth and early twenty-first centuries, women activists have continued in this tradition of demanding rights in a form of agency practiced within

Islamic legal norms. They have also taken the more proactive stance of critiquing various aspects of the codified law. Legal advocacy groups in a number of countries, including Malaysia, India, Pakistan, Nigeria, Jordan, Egypt, and Morocco, among others, have organized and launched campaigns targeting polygyny, guardianship in marriage, prejudicial divorce laws, unequal inheritance, and *zinā* rules. They have taken care, by and large, to conduct these campaigns in the spirit of realizing the true intent of Islamic law, of countering the misinterpretations and faulty accretions that have distorted correct understandings and practices. Sometimes they have met with striking success, as in the extensive recent reforms of the Moroccan Mudawwana instituted in February 2004. Among the 110 amendments passed by the Moroccan parliament were reforms such as placing divorce and polygyny under judicial control, rescinding the wife's duty of obedience, giving husbands and wives equal responsibility for the family, and eliminating the requirement for guardianship in marriage arrangements. Women's groups in Morocco had worked toward these reforms for many years, although most observers agree that it was only in the context of royal support and the weakening of Islamist factions following terrorist attacks in Casablanca that such reform became politically feasible. And, as in the case of all legal reform, the jury is still out as to how successful the actual implementation of these reforms will be as they come up against entrenched institutions and bureaucracies.[1] Elsewhere activists have made only modest gains, usually on single issues, but local groups and individuals continue to chip away at various aspects of the law considered to be discriminatory or oppressive.

Women have also engaged questions of legal interpretation. It has not been easy for women to raise their voices on matters of interpretation of religious texts, but we are witnessing what can only be termed a systematic assault on the male monopoly of scholarly study of Islamic law. Several women scholars have focused recently on the Qur'an as the fount of discourse on gender, and argued that responsible and scholarly Qur'anic interpretation (*tafsīr*) leads inexorably to an egalitarian view of gender relations, and not the male dominance expressed in some aspects of the legal tradition.[2] As the number and sophistication of these works increase, they are entering into serious contention for the hearts and minds of

---

[1] See Stephanie Willman Bordat and Saida Kouzzi, "The Challenge of Implementing Morocco's New Personal Status Law," *Arab Reform Bulletin* 2, no. 8 (September 2004), www.carnegieendowment.org/publications/index.cfm?fa=view&id=15783.

[2] See Omaima Abou-Bakr, "Islamic Feminism? What's in a Name?," *Middle East Women's Studies Review* 15, no. 1 / 16, no. 4 (winter–spring 2001); Asma Barlas, *"Believing Women" in Islam: Unreading Patriarchal Interpretations of the Qur'an*, 1st edn (Austin: University of Texas Press, 2002); Zaynab

believing Muslim women and men alike, and they are acquiring the potential to supply the necessary foundations for more extensive legal reforms. A number of international organizations also marry this kind of research to activism, one example of which is the US-based organization Karamah: Muslim Women Lawyers for Human Rights, with its interest in such scholarly work and its programs for education and activism on behalf of Muslim women and men. Karamah has engaged issues ranging from *zinā'* laws to the headscarf to domestic violence as part of a commitment to "advance Muslim women's human rights globally" by serving as a resource center and a forum for discussion and outreach.[3] Women Living Under Muslim Laws, based in the UK, Pakistan, and Senegal, is another prominent international organization with an extensive array of publications on women's rights in relation to Islamic law, and activist programs for international alerts, exchanges of information, and training for the purposes of women's rights advocacy.[4] It would be premature to argue that these individuals and organizations have captured the field of legal interpretation on women's issues; on the contrary, they face considerable opposition from established jurists, fatwa councils, and other official bodies of the legal establishment. I think, nevertheless, that these are the people and groups to watch in the near future, in light of both their energy and commitment.

Islamic law has survived into the modern world largely because believing Muslims are convinced that it contains guidance for living a good and moral life in keeping with God's plan, and institutes a system of justice and fairness for Muslim communities. The question of gender, which I would frame as whether Islamic legal systems can live up to these promises by treating women and men with equal dignity and giving full play to the strong egalitarian tradition of the religion, represents the critical test for Islamic law today and one which is likely to decide its continued existence as accepted authority for Muslim women and men alike.

Radwan, *Al-Islam wa-Qadaya al-Mar'ah* (Cairo: al-Hay'a al-Misriyya al-'Amma, 1998); Amina Wadud, *Qur'an and Woman: Rereading the Sacred Text from a Woman's Perspective*, 2nd edn (Oxford: Oxford University Press, 1999).

[3] See website for Karamah, www.karamah.org.

[4] See website for Women Living Under Muslim Laws, http://wluml.org.

Glossary

adab	belles-lettres; culture; good manners
aḥsan / ḥasan	better/good, in reference to the evaluation of legal acts
ʿālim	see ʿulamaʾ
ʿAshuraʾ	the tenth day of the Islamic month of Muharram, a day of mourning sacred to Shiʿa
ʿawra: lit.	pudendum, genitals; that part of the body which is sexually stimulating.
bayt al-ṭāʿa	"house of obedience," in reference to a husband's right to force his wife to return to the marital household
bulūgh (noun), *bāligh* (adj.)	the state of sexual maturity which in Hanafi law also marks legal majority, cf. *khiyār al-bulūgh*
dinar	gold coin
dirham	silver coin
diya	financial compensation for wounds or loss of life; blood money for voluntary or involuntary homicide which the perpetrator can be required to pay to the relative of the victim as satisfaction
faskh (noun), *fasakha* (verb)	annulment of the marriage contract
fatwa	a legal opinion, usually delivered by a mufti that pronounces on specific points, often as a result of a petition or inquiry; cf. *shurūḥ*
fiqh	Islamic jurisprudence; a system or body of law
fitna	social discord, particularly as caused by illicit sexual desire; civil strife
ghursh, pl. *ghurush*	a unit of money; piaster

ḥadd, pl. *ḥudūd*	a fixed penalty, prescribed Islamic punishment; cf. *taʿzīr*
hadith	the traditions of the Prophet Muhammad; cf. *sunna*
hajj	the pilgrimage to Mecca; a male who has made the pilgrimage
ḥajr	interdiction or restriction of legal competence
Hanafi	a Sunni school of law
Hanbali	a Sunni school of law
ḥarām	legally forbidden, as in reference to an illicit act
ḥasan, see *aḥsan*	
ḥiḍāna	the care and custody of children
hijab	a veil or head covering of various styles and extents worn to preserve female modesty
hijri (abbrev. H)	denoting the Muslim era when used after a date
ʿidda	a legally prescribed period of waiting during which a woman may not remarry after being widowed or divorced, and during which her former husband and his estate must continue to support her
ijbār	coercion or compulsion, in reference to the right of a guardian to coerce his ward
ijmāʿ	consensus of Islamic scholars
ijtihād	interpretation of the law; independent scholarly reasoning on legal issues on the basis of the Qurʾan and the *sunna*
īlāʾ	a vow by a husband to abstain from sexual intercourse with his wife which can result in divorce after four months of abstinence
imam	prayer leader (Sunni)
ʿiṣmataha fi yadiha	"she became independent," an expression referring to the delegation of the power of divorce to the wife by the husband
jabr	coercion, usually resulting in the cancellation of the effects of legal acts performed under coercion
jihāz	the bride's trousseau, given her (not her husband) by her family

jilbāb	a long, loose-fitting woman's robe
kafāʾa	the legal concept of the mutual suitability of the spouses
khalwa	a period of privacy, perhaps quite brief, shared by a man and a woman, usually assumed to include intercourse
khiyār al-bulūgh	the "option of puberty" in reference to the right of a woman who had been married off as a minor to refuse the marriage upon reaching puberty, if someone other than her father or grandfather had made the marriage arrangements
khulʿ (noun), *khalāʿa* (verb)	divorce at the instance of the wife, who must pay a compensation or otherwise negotiate an agreement acceptable to her husband
liʿān	procedure in which a husband, under oath, accuses his wife of adultery and denies the paternity of any children to which she will give birth, answered by an oath of innocence sworn by his wife; the effect of the procedure is that their marriage is dissolved and that he is legally not the father of any children born by her afterwards
liwāt	sodomy, sexual relations between men
madhhab	a school of Islamic law
mafqūd	a person who is held to be legally missing
mahr	the dower; the gift or collection of gifts given to the bride by the husband, without which the marriage is not valid; cf. *mahr al-mithl, muʾakhkhar, muqaddam*
mahr al-mithl	proper brideprice, i.e. the dower estimated to be appropriate for a particular woman, taking her age, social status, family, etc. into consideration
mahram	unmarriageable; being in a degree of consanguinity precluding marriage
Maliki	a Sunni school of law
milk	private property, land, and moveables privately owned
miri	land classified as state-owned

muʾakhkhar	that part of the *mahr* (dower) to be paid at the time of termination of the marriage; the deferred dower
muʿajjal / muʾajjal	"prompt/deferred," in relation to dower
mubāraʾa	divorce by mutual consent of husband and wife
mufti	a jurisconsult, a learned man empowered to deliver formal legal opinions (fatwas)
muhaddere	a woman who lives a secluded lifestyle (Ottoman Turkish)
mukhaddara	a woman who lives a secluded lifestyle (Arabic)
mulk yamīn	legally owned or possessed
muqaddam	that part of the *mahr* (dower) to be paid at the time of the signing of a marriage contract; the prompt dower
mustaḥabb	recommended, commendable, in reference to acts the performance of which, while not required, are rewarded by God
mutʿa	compensation paid to a divorced woman; a temporary marriage contracted for a specified period of time
mutun	textbooks that sum up the doctrine of a legal school
nafaqa	legally required material maintenance and support based on bonds of kinship
nāshiza	recalcitrant or disobedient, used to characterize such behavior on the part of a wife
nikāḥ	marriage, marriage contract, matrimony
nushūz	the state of disobedience of a wife, following which the husband is not bound to maintain her
qadhf	calumny; defamation: the *ḥadd* offense of a false accusation of fornication
qadi	a judge in an Islamic court
qanūn	Ottoman legal codes
qiṣāṣ	retaliation for homicide or wounding
qisma	apportioning, division, as of an estate
qitaʿ miṣriyya	unit of currency; Egyptian coins
qiyās	legal arguments including analogy and deductive reasoning among others

rushd /rashīda	maturity of mind, as evidenced by the attainment of reason, good sense, and proper conduct
Shafi'i	a Sunni school of law
shari'a	the revealed or canonical law of Islam
shaykh	an honorific title denoting any of several possible positions
shubha	judicial doubt produced by the semblance of legal to illegal acts and/or the mistaking of illegal for legal acts by the perpetrators
shurūḥ	legal commentaries related to specific situations or problems; cf. fatwa
sufūr	the act of unveiling
sunna	the sayings and doings of the Prophet Muhammad, later established as legally binding precedents (in addition to the law established by the Qur'an); cf. hadith
tafrīq	annulment of the marriage contract
tafsīr	Qur'anic commentary
tafwīḍ	delegation of the power of divorce (*ṭalāq*) by a husband to his wife
takhayyur	"choosing," an eclectic method of legal reform whereby rules are chosen from different legal schools in the formulation of shari'a legal codes
ṭalāq (noun), *tallaqa* (verb)	to divorce a wife by 'repudiation'; the pronunciation of a formula of divorce by a husband resulting in a legally binding dissolution of a marriage
ṭalāq al-bid'a	"unorthodox divorce," in reference to pronouncements of divorce that do not adhere to prescribed procedures, including triple pronouncements. While criticized by the jurists, these pronouncements came to have full legal effect
ta'līq	conditional repudiation, conditional pronunciation of a *ṭalāq*
tarjīḥ	a methodology employed to deal with conflicting legal opinions by establishing the superiority of particular ones

ta'zīr	discretionary punishment, in contrast to *ḥadd* (fixed punishment)
thayyib	a non-virgin woman
'ulama' (pl.), *'ālim* (sing.)	the jurist-theologians of Islam, collectively
'unna	male impotence
wājib	legally required, as in acts or duties required under the law
wakīl	legal agent for another person
wālī	the legal guardian of a minor, particularly for the purposes of marriage arrangement; cf. *wilāya*
waqf	a religious endowment; private property entailed for religious or charitable purposes
waqf ahlī	"family waqf," or a waqf established primarily to benefit descendants
waṣī	the executor or guardian of a minor's property following the death of his or her natural guardian
waṣī mukhtār	a guardian who has been chosen by the natural guardian, usually the father, to replace him if and when he should die
wilāya	guardianship, cf. *wālī*
zānī	the committer of *zinā*
zinā'	unlawful sexual intercourse; fornication; adultery

Bibliography

PRIMARY SOURCES, DOCUMENTS, AND REPORTS

BAOBAB. "National Discussion on Sharia and Women's Human Rights in Nigeria Series Two." www.baobabwomen.org/activities.htm.

Sharia Implementation in Nigeria: The Journey So Far. Lagos: BAOBAB for Women's Rights, 2003.

Bukhari, Muhammad ibn Isma'il. *Sahih al-Bukhari.* Translated by Muhammad Muhsin Khan. 9 vols. Medina: Islamic University, 1974.

Dasuqi, Muhammad ibn Ahmad. *Hashiyat al-Dasuqi 'ala al-Sharh al-Kabir.* 4 vols. Cairo: Dar Ihya' al-Kutub al-'Arabiyya, n.d.

European Council for Fatwa and Research (ECFR). www.e-cfr.org.

"Final Statement of the Twelfth Ordinary Session." January 2004.

"France: Hijab under Attack." Fatwa issued December 14, 2003. Available from Islam Online: www.islamonline.net/servlet/Satellite?pagename=IslamOnline-English-Ask_Scholar/FatwaE/FatwaE&cid=1119503547428.

"The Statement on the Problem of Hijab in France." January 2003.

"France: Headscarf Ban Violates Religious Freedom." *Human Rights Watch News,* February 27, 2004. http://hrw.org/english/docs/2004/02/26/france7666.htm.

al-Haddad, al-Tahir. *Imra'atuna fi al-Shari'a wa-l-Mujtama'.* Cairo: al-Majlis al-A'la li-l-Thaqafa, 1999.

Ibn Hanbal, Ahmad ibn Muhammad. *Chapters on Marriage and Divorce: Responses of Ibn Hanbal and Ibn Rahwayh.* Translated by Susan A. Spectorsky. 1st edn, Austin: University of Texas Press, 1993.

al-Hilli, al-Hasan ibn Yusuf ibn al-Mutahhar. *Mukhtalaf al-Shi'a fi Ahkam al-Shari'a.* 10 vols. Qom, Iran: Islamic Sciences Research Center, 1991.

Ibn Ishaq, Khalil. *Abrégé de la loi musulmane selon le rite de l'Imam Malek.* Translated by G. H. Bousquet. Vol. 2. *Le statut personnel.* Algiers: La Maison des Livres, 1958.

Ibn Rushd, Abu al-Walid Muhammad ibn Ahmad ibn Muhammad ibn Ahmad. *Bidayat al-Mujtahid wa-Nihayat al-Muqtasid.* 4 vols. Cairo: Dar al-Salam, 1995.

Ibn Taymiyya, Ahmad ibn Abd al-Halim. *Fatawa al-Nisa'.* 1st edn, Cairo: Maktabat al-Qur'an, 1983.

al-ʿImadi as edited by Ibn ʿAbidin. *Al-ʿUqud al-Durriyya*. Vols. 1–2. Bulaq: n.p., 1300 H/1882–83 AD.

Innovative Minds. "Protest against French Hijab Ban, Sunday, 11th January 2004, French Embassy, London." www.inminds.co.uk/french-hijab-ban.html#t17.

International Women's Rights Action Watch. www.iwraw-ap.org.

Islam Online. www.islamonline.net.

Karamah. www.karamah.org.

Mahkamat Nablus (Nablus Islamic Court), sijill #4, 1134–38 H/1722–26 AD; #5, 1139–41 H/1728–9 AD.

Mahkamat al-Quds (Jerusalem Islamic Court), sijill #226, 1145–6 H/1732–34 AD; #230, 1151–2 H/1738–40 AD.

al-Marghinani, Burhan al-Din ʿAli ibn Abi-Bakr. *Al-Hidaya: Sharh Bidayat al-Mubtadi*. 1st edn, 4 vols. Cairo: Dar al-Salam, 2000.

Nasif, Malak Hifni. *Al-Nisaʾiyat: Majmuʿat Maqalat Nushirat fi al-Jarida fi Mawduʿ al-Marʾah al-Misriya*. Cairo: Multaqa al-Marʾa wa-l-Dhakira, 1998.

al-Ramli, Khayr al-Din ibn Ahmad. *Kitab al-Fatawa al-Kubra li-Nafʿ al-Birriyya*. 2 vols. in 1. Cairo, Bulaq: n.p., 1856–57.

Rida, Muhammad Rashid. *Huquq al-Nisaʾ fi al-Islam wa-Hazzihina min al-Islah al-Muhammadi al-ʿAmm: Nidaʾ ila al-Jins al-Latif*. Cairo: Maktabat al-Turath al-Islami, 1984.

   Tafsir al-Qurʾan. 10 vols. Beirut: Dar al-Maʿrifa, 1970–.

Sadr, Yusuf Ibrahim, ed. *Majmuʿat al-Qawanin*. Translated by ʿArif Afandi Ramadan. Beirut: Matbaʿat Sadr, 1937.

Shafiʿi, Muhammad ibn Idris. *Islamic Jurisprudence: Shafiʿi's Risala*. Translated by Majid Khadduri. Baltimore: Johns Hopkins University Press, 1961.

Shaltut, Mahmud. *Al-Islam: ʿAqida wa-Shariʿa*. Cairo: al-Idara al-ʿAmma li-l-Thaqafa al-Islamiyya bi-l-Azhar, 1959.

Sisters in Islam, and Association of Women Lawyers. "Memorandum on Reform of the Islamic Family Laws on Polygamy." (December 11, 1996), www.sistersinislam.org.my/memo/040197.htm.

al-Suyuti, Jalal al-din ʿAbd al-Rahman. *Al-Tawshih Sharh al-Jamiʿ al-Sahih*. 9 vols. Riyadh: Maktabat al-Rushd, 1998.

UN Commission on Human Rights. "Special Rapporteur on Freedom of Religion Ends Visit to France." Geneva: September 30, 2005. www.unhchr.ch/huricane/huricane.nsf/view01/AA8F269703D694EAC125708C00455C34?opendocument.

Union des Organisations Islamiques de France. "L'UOIF s'adresse aux députés de la nation." www.uoif-online.com/modules.php?op=modload&name=News&file=article&sid=178.

   "Les filles qui portent le voile aiment la France." www.uoif-online.com/modules.php?op=modload&name=News&file=article&sid=166.

   "Réaction du secrétaire général de l'UOIF aux declarations de Cheikh Tantaoui au sujet du foulard islamique." www.uoif-online.com/modules.php?op=modload&name=News&file=article&sid=162.

Women Living Under Muslim Laws. http://wluml.org.

SECONDARY SOURCES

Abdal-Rehim, Abdal-Rehim Abdal-Rahman. "The Family and Gender Laws in Egypt during the Ottoman Period." In Sonbol, *Women, the Family, and Divorce*, 96–111.

Abou-Bakr, Omaima. "Islamic Feminism? What's in a Name?" *Middle East Women's Studies Review* 15, no. 1/16, no. 4 (winter–spring 2001): 1–5.

Abou El Fadl, Khaled. *Speaking in God's Name: Islamic Law, Authority and Women.* Oxford: Oneworld, 2001.

Adang, Camilla. "Women's Access to Public Space according to *al-Muḥallā bi-l-Āthār*." In Marín and Deguilhem, *Writing the Feminine*, 75–94.

Ahangar, Mohammed Altaf Hussain. "Compensation in Khulʿ: An Appraisal of Judicial Interpretation in Pakistan." *Islamic and Comparative Law Quarterly* 13 (1993): 113–43.

Ahmed, K. N. *The Muslim Law of Divorce.* New Delhi: Kitab Bhavan, 1978.

Algar, Hamid. *Wahhabism: A Critical Essay.* 1st edn, Oneonta, NY: Islamic Publications International, 2002.

Ali, Shaheen Sardar. *Gender and Human Rights in Islam and International Law: Equal before Allah, Unequal before Man?* The Hague: Kluwer Law International, 2000.

"Is an Adult Muslim Woman Sui Juris? Some Reflections on the Concept of 'Consent in Marriage' without a *Wali* (with Particular Reference to the Saima Waheed Case)." In *Yearbook of Islamic and Middle Eastern Law*, edited by Eugene Cotran and Chibli Mallat, 156–74. London: Kluwer Law International, 1996.

Al-ʿAlwani, Taha J. "The Testimony of Women in Islamic Law." *American Journal of Islamic Social Sciences* 13, no. 2 (1996): 173–96.

Amin, Sonia Nishat. *The World of Muslim Women in Colonial Bengal, 1876–1939.* Social, Economic, and Political Studies of the Middle East. Leiden: Brill, 1996.

Anderson, J. N. D. *Law Reform in the Muslim World.* London: University of London Athlone Press, 1976.

"The Tunisian Law of Personal Status." *International and Comparative Law Quarterly* 7, no. 2 (1958): 262–79.

Arabi, Oussama. "Contract Stipulations (*Shurūṭ*) in Islamic Law: The Ottoman Majalla and Ibn Taymiyya." *International Journal of Middle East Studies* 30, no. 1 (1998): 29–50.

"The Interdiction of the Spendthrift (*al-Safīh*): A Human Rights Debate in Classical Fiqh." *Islamic Law and Society* 7, no. 3 (2000): 300–24.

Arberry, Arthur J. *The Koran Interpreted.* Translated by Arthur. J. Arberry. London: Allen & Unwin; Macmillan, 1955.

Baer, Gabriel. "Women and Waqf: An Analysis of the Istanbul *Tahrir* of 1546." *Asian and African Studies* 17 (1983): 8–27.

Barlas, Asma. *"Believing Women" in Islam: Unreading Patriarchal Interpretations of the Qurʾan.* 1st edn, Austin: University of Texas Press, 2002.

Barnett, Hilaire. *Introduction to Feminist Jurisprudence*. London: Routledge-Cavendish, 1998.

Baron, Beth. "The Making and Breaking of Marital Bonds in Modern Egypt." In Keddie and Baron, *Women in Middle Eastern History*, 275–91.

The Women's Awakening in Egypt: Culture, Society, and the Press. New Haven: Yale University Press, 1994.

Behrouz, Andra Nahal. "Transforming Islamic Family Law: State Responsibility and the Role of Internal Initiative." *Columbia Law Review* 103, no. 5 (2003): 1136–62.

Bentzon, Agnete Weis, Anne Hellum, Julie Stewart, Welshman Ncube, and Torben Agersnap. *Pursuing Grounded Theory in Law: South–North Experiences in Developing Women's Law*. Oslo: TANO Aschehoug, 1998.

Bernhardt, Kathryn. *Women and Property in China: 960–1949*. Law, Society, and Culture in China. Stanford: Stanford University Press, 1999.

Bordat, Stephanie Willman, and Saida Kouzzi. "The Challenge of Implementing Morocco's New Personal Status Law." *Arab Reform Bulletin* 2, no. 8 (September 2004). www.carnegieendowment.org/publications/index.cfm?fa=view&id=15783.

Bowen, John R. "Quran, Justice, Gender: Internal Debates in Indonesian Islamic Jurisprudence." *History of Religions* 38, no. 1 (1998): 52–78.

"The Transformation of an Indonesian Property System: 'Adat,' Islam, and Social Change in the Gayo Highlands." *American Ethnologist* 15, no. 2 (1988): 274–93.

Why the French Don't Like Headscarves: Islam, the State, and Public Space. Princeton: Princeton University Press, 2007.

Bultaji, Muhammad. *Makanat al-Mar'a fi al-Qur'an al-Karim wa-l-Sunna al-Sahiha: Dirasat Mu'assala Muqarana Mustaw'iba li-Haqiqat Manzilat al-Mar'ah fi al-Islam*. Cairo: Dar al-Salam, 2000.

Cammack, Mark, Lawrence A. Young, and Tim Heaton. "Legislating Social Change in an Islamic Society – Indonesia's Marriage Law." *American Journal of Comparative Law* 44, no. 1 (1996): 45–73.

Carroll, Lucy. "Life Interests and Inter-generational Transfer of Property Avoiding the Law of Succession." *Islamic Law and Society* 8, no. 2 (2001): 245–86.

"Marriage-Guardianship and Minor Marriage in Islamic Law." *Islamic and Comparative Law Quarterly* 7, no. 4 (1987): 279–300.

"The Pakistan Federal Shariat Court, Section 4 of the Muslim Family Law Ordinance, and the Orphaned Grandchild." *Islamic Law and Society* 9, no. 1 (2001): 70–82.

"*Talaq-i-Tafwid* and Stipulations in a Muslim Marriage Contract: Important Means of Protecting the Position of the South Asian Muslim Wife." *Modern Asian Studies* 16, no. 2 (1982): 277–309.

Charrad, Mounira. *States and Women's Rights: The Making of Postcolonial Tunisia, Algeria, and Morocco*. Berkeley: University of California Press, 2001.

Christelow, Allan. "Islamic Law and Judicial Practice in Nigeria: An Historical Perspective." *Journal of Muslim Minority Affairs* 22, no. 1 (2002): 185–204.

Cole, Juan Ricardo. "Feminism, Class, and Islam in Turn-of-the-Century Egypt." *International Journal of Middle East Studies* 13, no. 4 (1981): 387–407.

Conaghan, Joanne. "Reassessing the Feminist Theoretical Project in Law." *Journal of Law and Society* 27, no. 3 (2000): 351–85.

Connors, Jane. "The Women's Convention in the Muslim World." In Yamani and Allen, *Feminism and Islam*, 351–71.

Cornell, Drucilla. *Beyond Accommodation: Ethical Feminism, Deconstruction, and the Law*. Thinking Gender. New York: Routledge, 1991.

Coulson, Noel J. *Conflicts and Tensions in Islamic Jurisprudence*. Publications of the Center for Middle Eastern Studies 5. Chicago: University of Chicago Press, 1969.

A History of Islamic Law. Islamic Surveys. Edinburgh: Edinburgh University Press, 1964.

Succession in the Muslim Family. Cambridge: Cambridge University Press, 1971.

Cuno, Kenneth M. *The Pasha's Peasants: Land Tenure, Society, and Economy in Lower Egypt, 1740–1858*. Cambridge Middle East Library. Cambridge: Cambridge University Press, 1992.

de Bellefonds, Y. Linant. "Le 'Hul' sans compensation en droit hanafite." *Studia Islamica* 31 (1970): 185–95.

de la Puente, Cristina. "Juridical Sources for the Study of Women: Limitations of the Female's Capacity to Act According to Maliki Law." In Marín and Deguilhem, *Writing the Feminine*, 95–110.

Doumani, Beshara. "Endowing Family: *Waqf*, Property Devolution, and Gender in Greater Syria, 1800 to 1860." *Comparative Studies in Society and History* 40, no. 1 (1998): 3–41.

Dupret, Baudouin. "The Person and the Law: Contingency, Individuation and the Subject of the Law." In *Standing Trial: Law and the Person in the Modern Middle East*, edited by Baudouin Dupret, 9–38. The Islamic Mediterranean. London: I. B. Tauris, 2004.

El-Rouayheb, Khaled. *Before Homosexuality in the Arab-Islamic World, 1500–1800*. Chicago: University of Chicago Press, 2005.

El Alami, Dawoud S. "Law no. 100 of 1985 Amending Certain Provisions of Egypt's Personal Status Laws." *Islamic Law and Society* 1, no. 1 (1994): 116–36.

"*Mut'at al-Talaq* under Egyptian and Jordanian Law." In *Yearbook of Islamic and Middle Eastern Law*, edited by Eugene Cotran and Chibli Mallat, 2: 54–60. London: Kluwer Law International, 1995.

"Legal Capacity with Specific Reference to the Marriage Contract." *Arab Law Quarterly* 6, no. 2 (1991): 190–204.

El Alami, Dawoud Sudqi, and Doreen Hinchcliffe. *Islamic Marriage and Divorce Laws of the Arab World*. CIMEL Book Series. London: Kluwer Law International, 1996.

Engineer, Asghar Ali. "Reflection on the Abolition of Triple Talaq – What Next?" *Asian Human Rights Commission* 6, no. 28 (July 12, 2004). www.rghr.net/mainfile.php/0618/749/.

Fadel, Mohammad. "Two Women, One Man: Knowledge, Power, and Gender in Medieval Sunni Legal Thought." *International Journal of Middle East Studies* 29, no. 2 (1997): 185–204.

Fakhro, Munira. "Gulf Women and Islamic Law." In Yamani and Allen, *Feminism and Islam*, 251–62.

Farooqui, Mahmood. "Three Times Too Many." *Mid Day*, July 2, 2004. www. mid-day.com/columns/mahmood_farooqui/2004/july/86854.htm.

Fay, Mary Ann. "From Concubines to Capitalists: Women, Property, and Power in Eighteenth-Century Cairo." *Journal of Women's History* 10, no. 3 (1998): 118–40.

"Women and Waqf: Toward a Reconsideration of Women's Place in the Mamluk Household." *International Journal of Middle East Studies* 29, no. 1 (1997): 33–51.

Frégosi, Franck. "La position des acteurs islamiques: champ religieux officiel et contre-champ islamique." In *La politisation du voile: l'affaire en France, en Europe et dans le monde arabe*, edited by Françoise Lorcerie, 53–64. Paris: L'Harmattan, 2005.

Friedl, Erika. *Women of Deh Koh: Lives in an Iranian Village*. Washington, DC: Smithsonian Institution Press, 1989.

Gerber, Haim. "Social and Economic Position of Women in an Ottoman City, Bursa, 1600–1700." *International Journal of Middle East Studies* 12, no. 3 (1980): 231–44.

State, Society, and Law in Islam: Ottoman Law in Comparative Perspective. Albany: State University of New York Press, 1994.

Gleave, Robert, and Eugena Kermeli, eds. *Islamic Law: Theory and Practice*. London: I. B. Tauris, 1997.

Göçek, Fatma Müge, and Marc David Baer. "Social Boundaries of Ottoman Women's Experience in Eighteenth-Century Galata Court Records." In Zilfi, *Women in the Ottoman Empire*, 48–65.

Hallaq, Wael B. *Authority, Continuity, and Change in Islamic Law*. Cambridge: Cambridge University Press, 2001.

"Was the Gate of Ijtihad Closed?" *International Journal of Middle East Studies* 16, no. 1 (1984): 3–41.

Hamadeh, Najla. "Islamic Family Legislation: The Authoritarian Discourse of Silence." In Yamani and Allen, *Feminism and Islam*, 331–46.

Hameed, Sayeeda Saiyidain. "Windows of Opportunity." *Communalism Combat*, May 2001.

Hanna, Nelly. *Making Big Money in 1600: The Life and Times of Isma'il Abu Taqiyya, Egyptian Merchant*. 1st edn. Middle East Studies beyond Dominant Paradigms. Syracuse: Syracuse University Press, 1998.

"Marriage among Merchant Families in Seventeenth-Century Cairo." In Sonbol, *Women, the Family, and Divorce*, 143–54.

Haykal, Muhammad Husayn. *The Life of Muhammad*. Translated by Ismail R. al-Faruqi. Plainfield, IN: North American Trust Publications, 1976.

Helly, Dorothy O., and Susan Reverby, eds. "Introduction: Converging on History." In *Gendered Domains: Rethinking Public and Private in Women's History: Essays from the Seventh Berkshire Conference on the History of Women*, 1–24. Ithaca, NY: Cornell University Press, 1992.

Heyd, Uriel, and V. L. Ménage. *Studies in Old Ottoman Criminal Law*. Oxford: Clarendon Press, 1973.

Hirsch, Susan F. *Pronouncing and Persevering: Gender and the Discourses of Disputing in an African Islamic Court*. Language and Legal Discourse. Chicago: University of Chicago Press, 1998.

Holcombe, Lee. *Wives and Property: Reform of the Married Women's Property Law in Nineteenth-Century England*. Toronto: University of Toronto Press, 1983.

Hooker, M. B. *Islamic Law in South-East Asia*. East Asian Social Science Monographs. Singapore and Oxford: Oxford University Press, 1984.

Howard, I. K. A. "Mutʿa Marriage Reconsidered in the Context of the Formal Procedures for Islamic Marriage." *Journal of Semitic Studies* 20, no. 1 (spring 1975): 82–92.

Ibrahim, Ahmad. *Ahkam al-Ahwal al-Shakhsiyya fi al-Shariʿa al-Islamiya wa-l-Qanun*. 5th edn, Cairo: al-Maktaba al-Azhariyya li-l-Turath, 2005.

Imber, Colin. *Ebuʾs-suʿud: The Islamic Legal Tradition*. Jurists: Profiles in Legal Theory. Stanford: Stanford Unversity Press, 1997.

Ivanova, Svetlana. "The Divorce between Zubaida Hatun and Esseid Osman Aga." In Sonbol, *Women, the Family, and Divorce*, 112–25.

"Marriage and Divorce in the Bulgarian Lands (XV–XIX c.)." *Bulgarian Historical Review* 21, no. 2–3 (1993): 49–83.

Jalal, Ayesha. "The Convenience of Subservience: Women and the State of Pakistan." In Kandiyoti, *Women, Islam, and the State*, 77–114.

Jennings, Ronald C. "Women in Early 17th Century Ottoman Judicial Records: The Sharia Court of Anatolian Kayseri." *Journal of the Economic and Social History of the Orient* 18, no. 1 (1975): 53–114.

Johansen, Baber. "Legal Literature and the Problem of Change: The Case of Land Rent." In *Islam and Public Law: Classical and Contemporary Studies*, edited by Chibli Mallat, 29–47. Arab and Islamic Laws Series. London: Graham and Trotman, 1993.

Kadivar, Mohsen. "An Introduction to the Public and Private Debate in Islam." *Social Research* 70, no. 3 (Fall 2003): 659–80.

Kalu, Ogbu U. "Safiyya and Adamah: Punishing Adultery with Sharia Stones in Twenty-first Century Nigeria." *African Affairs* 102 (2003): 389–408.

Kandiyoti, Deniz, ed. *Women, Islam, and the State*. Women in the Political Economy. Philadelphia: Temple University Press, 1991.

Karmi, Ghada. "Women, Islam, and Patriarchalism." In Yamani and Allen, *Feminism and Islam*, 69–85.

Keddie, Nikki R., and Beth Baron, eds. *Women in Middle Eastern History: Shifting Boundaries in Sex and Gender*. New Haven: Yale University Press, 1991.

Khan, Sakina Yusuf. "Divorced from Reality – Amending the Triple Talaq Law." *The Times of India*, October 5, 2000.

Khouri, Dina. "Drawing Boundaries and Defining Spaces." In Sonbol, *Women, the Family, and Divorce*, 173–87.

Kian-Thiébaut, Azadeh. *Les femmes iraniennes entre islam, état et famille*. Paris: Maisonneuve et Larose, 2002.

Kogelmann, Franz. "Some Aspects of the Transformation of the Islamic Pious Endowments in Morocco, Algeria, and Egypt in the 20th Century." In *Les fondations pieuses (waqf) en Méditerranée: enjeux de société, enjeux de pouvoir*, edited by Randi Deguilhem and Abdelhamid Hénia, 343–93. Kuwait: Kuwait Awqaf Public Foundation, 2004.

Kuehn, Thomas. *Law, Family and Women: Toward a Legal Anthropology of Renaissance Italy*. Chicago: University of Chicago Press, 1991.

Layish, Aharon. "Customary *Khul'* as Reflected in the *Sijill* of the Libyan *Shariʿa* Courts." *Bulletin of the School of Oriental and African Studies, University of London* 51, no. 3 (1988): 428–39.

Lutfi, Huda. "Manners and Customs of Fourteenth Century Cairene Women: Female Anarchy versus Male Shar'i Order in Muslim Prescriptive Treatises." In Keddie and Baron, *Women in Middle Eastern History*, 99–121.

"A Study of Six Fourteenth Century Iqrars from Al-Quds Relating to Muslim Women." *Journal of the Economic and Social History of the Orient* 26, no. 3 (1983): 246–94.

MacKinnon, Catharine A. *Toward a Feminist Theory of the State*. Cambridge, MA: Harvard University Press, 1989.

Mahmood, Saba. *Politics of Piety: The Islamic Revival and the Feminist Subject*. Princeton: Princeton University Press, 2005.

Mahmood, Tahir. "Islamic Family Law: Latest Developments in India." In *Islamic Family Law*, edited by Chibli Mallat and Jane Connors, 295–320. Arab and Islamic Laws Series. London: Graham and Trotman, 1990.

Marcus, Abraham. "Men, Women and Property: Dealers in Real Estate in 18th Century Aleppo." *Journal of the Economic and Social History of the Orient* 26, no. 2 (1983): 137–63.

"Privacy in Eighteenth-Century Aleppo: The Limits of Cultural Ideals." *International Journal of Middle East Studies* 18, no. 2 (1986): 165–83.

Marín, Manuela, and Randi Deguilhem, eds. *Writing the Feminine: Women in Arab Sources*. The Islamic Mediterranean. London: I. B. Tauris, 2002.

Marrese, Michelle Lamarche. *A Woman's Kingdom: Noblewomen and the Control of Property in Russia, 1700–1861*. Ithaca, NY: Cornell University Press, 2002.

Meriwether, Margaret L. *The Kin Who Count: Family and Society in Ottoman Aleppo, 1770–1840*. 1st edn, Austin: University of Texas Press, 1999.

"The Rights of Children and the Responsibilities of Women: Women as Wasis in Ottoman Aleppo, 1770–1840." In Sonbol, *Women, the Family, and Divorce*, 219–35.

"Women and *Waqf* Revisited: The Case of Aleppo, 1770–1840." In Zilfi, *Women in the Ottoman Empire*, 128–52.

"Women and Economic Change in Nineteenth-Century Syria: The Case of Aleppo." In *Arab Women: Old Boundaries, New Frontiers*, edited by Judith E. Tucker, 65–80. Indiana Series in Arab and Islamic Studies. Bloomington: Indiana University Press, 1993.

Meyer, Ann Elizabeth. "Rhetorical Strategies and Official Policies on Women's Rights: The Merits and Drawbacks of the New World Hypocrisy." In *Faith and Freedom: Women's Human Rights in the Muslim World*, edited by Mahnaz Afkhami, 104–32. Gender, Culture, and Politics in the Middle East. Syracuse: Syracuse University Press, 1995.

Mir-Hosseini, Ziba. *Marriage on Trial: A Study of Islamic Family Law: Iran and Morocco Compared*. Society and Culture in the Modern Middle East. London: I. B. Tauris, 1993.

Mitchell, Ruth. "Family Law in Algeria before and after the 1404/1984 Family Code." In Gleave and Kermeli, *Islamic Law*, 194–204.

Modarressi, Hossein. *An Introduction to Shi'i Law: A Bibliographical Study*. London: Ithaca Press, 1984.

Moors, Annalise. "Debating Family Law: Legal Texts and Social Practices." In *Social History of Women and Gender in the Modern Middle East*, edited by Margaret Lee Meriwether and Judith E. Tucker, 150–55. The Social History of the Modern Middle East. Boulder, CO: Westview Press, 1999.

  Women, Property, and Islam: Palestinian Experience, 1920–1990. Cambridge Middle East Studies. Cambridge: Cambridge University Press, 1995.

Mujahid, Subhy. "French Women Can Remove Hijab If Forced: Tantawi." *Islam Online*, December 30, 2003. www.islamonline.net/English/News/2003–12/30/article09.shtml.

Nadvi, Mas'ud 'Alam, and M. Rafiq Khan. *Mohammad bin Abdul Wahhab: A Slandered Reformer*. Varanasi: Idaratul Buhoosil Islamia, 1983.

Nair, Manoj. "Two Women Recall 'Triple Talaq' Trauma." *Mid Day*, July 4, 2004. www.mid-day.com/news/city/2004/july/87030.htm.

Najmabadi, Afsaneh. "Hazards of Modernity and Morality: Women, State and Ideology in Contemporary Iran." In Kandiyoti, *Women, Islam, and the State*, 48–76.

Nasir, Jamal J. *The Islamic Law of Personal Status*. 2nd edn. Arab and Islamic Laws Series. London: Graham and Trotman, 1990.

Naveh, Immanuel. "The Tort of Injury and Dissolution of Marriage at the Wife's Initiative in Egyptian Mahkamat al-Naqd Rulings." *Islamic Law and Society* 9, no. 1 (2002): 16–41.

Nelson, Cynthia. "Public and Private Politics: Women in the Middle Eastern World." *American Ethnologist* 1, no. 3 (1974): 551–63.

Noorani, A. G. "The Big Idea: Reform, Reform, Reform." *Hindustan Times*, July 13, 2004.

Pearl, David. *A Textbook on Muslim Law*. London: Croom Helm, 1979.

  A Textbook on Muslim Personal Law. 2nd edn, London: Croom Helm, 1987.

Peirce, Leslie P. *The Imperial Harem: Women and Sovereignty in the Ottoman Empire*. New York: Oxford University Press, 1993.

  Morality Tales: Law and Gender in the Ottoman Court of Aintab. Berkeley: University of California Press, 2003.

Peters, Rudolph. *Crime and Punishment in Islamic Law: Theory and Practice from the Sixteenth to the Twenty-First Century*. Themes in Islamic Law. Cambridge: Cambridge University Press, 2005.

  "Idjtihad and Taqlid in 18th and 19th Century Islam." *Die Welt des Islams* 20, no. 3/4 (1980): 131–45.

Powers, David S. "The Islamic Family Endowment (Waqf)." *Vanderbilt Journal of Transnational Law* 32 (1999): 1167–90.

Radwan, Zaynab. *Al-Islam wa-Qadaya al-Marʾah*. Cairo: al-Hayʾa al-Misriyya al-ʿAmma, 1998.

Rafeq, Abdul-Karim. "Public Morality in 18th Century Ottoman Damascus." *Revue des Mondes Musulmans et de la Méditerranée* 55/56 (1990): 180–96.

Rahman, Fazlur. "Status of Women in the Qurʾan." In *Women and Revolution in Iran*, edited by Guity Nashat, 37–54. Boulder, CO: Westview Press, 1983.

"A Survey of Modernization of Muslim Family Law." *International Journal of Middle East Studies* 11, no. 4 (1980): 451–65.

Rapoport, Yossef. *Marriage, Money and Divorce in Medieval Islamic Society.* Cambridge: Cambridge University Press, 2005.

"Matrimonial Gifts in Early Islamic Egypt." *Islamic Law and Society* 7, no. 1 (2000): 1–36.

Rispler-Chaim, Vardit. "Nushuz between Medieval and Contemporary Islamic Law: The Human Rights Aspect." *Arabica* 39, no. 3 (1992): 315–27.

Roded, Ruth. *Women in Islamic Biographical Collections: From Ibn Saʿd to Who's Who.* Boulder, CO: L. Rienner Publishers, 1994.

Rostam-Kolayi, Jasamin. "Expanding Agendas for the 'New' Iranian Woman: Family Law, Work, and Unveiling." In *The Making of Modern Iran: State and Society under Riza Shah, 1921–1941*, edited by Stephanie Cronin, 157–80. RoutledgeCurzon / BIPS Persian Studies Series. London: RoutledgeCurzon, 2003.

Sansoni, Silvia. "Saving Amina." *Essence* 33, no. 11 (2003): 156–59.

"Saving Amina Lawal: Human Rights Symbolism and the Dangers of Colonialism." *Harvard Law Review* 117, no. 7 (2004): 2365–86.

Schacht, Joseph. *An Introduction to Islamic Law.* Oxford: Clarendon Press, 1964.

Secor, Anna J. "The Veil and Urban Space in Istanbul: Women's Dress, Mobility and Islamic Knowledge." *Gender, Place and Culture: A Journal of Feminist Geography* 9, no. 1 (2002): 5–22.

Shaham, Ron. *Family and the Courts in Modern Egypt: A Study Based on Decisions by the Shariʿa Courts, 1900–1955.* Studies in Islamic Law and Society. Leiden: Brill, 1997.

Shani, Alhaji Maʾaji Isa, and Mohammad Altaf Hussain Ahangar. "Marriage-Guardianship in Islam: Reflections on a Recent Nigerian Judgment." *Islamic and Comparative Law Quarterly* 6, no. 4 (1986): 275–82.

Siddiqui, Mona. "Law and the Desire for Social Control: An Insight into the Hanafi Concept of *Kafaʾa* with reference to the Fatawa ʿAlamgiri (1664–1672)." In Yamani and Allen, *Feminism and Islam*, 49–68.

Siti Musdah Mulia et al. "Counter Legal Drafting to Islamic Law Compilation (ILC): A Pluralism and Gender Perspective." *International Centre for Islam and Pluralism Journal* 2, no. 3 (June 2005): 1–16.

Sonbol, Amira El Azhary. "Adults and Minors in Ottoman Shariʿa Courts and Modern Law." In Sonbol, *Women, the Family, and Divorce*, 236–56.

ed. *Women, the Family, and Divorce Laws in Islamic History.* 1st edn. Contemporary Issues in the Middle East. Syracuse: Syracuse University Press, 1996.

Srivastava, Siddharth. "Triple Talaq on its Last Legs?" *The Day After* (July 2004), www.dayafterindia.com/july2004/societyhealth.html.

Stillman, Yedida Kalfon. *Arab Dress: A Short History, from the Dawn of Islam to Modern Times*. Themes in Islamic Studies. Leiden: Brill, 2000.

Tadros, Mariz. "Khul Law Passes Major Test." *Al-Ahram Weekly*, December 19–25, 2002.

"Rooster's Wrath." *Al-Ahram Weekly*, January 20–26, 2000.

"The Third Option." *Al-Ahram Weekly*, October 31–November 6, 2002.

"What Price Freedom?" *Al-Ahram Weekly*, March 7–13, 2002.

Taub, Nadine, and Elizabeth Schneider. "Women's Subordination and the Role of Law." In *Feminist Legal Theory: Foundations*, edited by D. Kelly Weisberg, 9–21. Women in the Political Economy. Philadelphia: Temple University Press, 1993.

Thompson, Elizabeth. "Public and Private in Middle Eastern Women's History." *Journal of Women's History* 15, no. 1 (2003): 52–69.

Tucker, Judith E. *In the House of the Law: Gender and Islamic Law in Ottoman Syria and Palestine*. Berkeley: University of California Press, 1998.

Women in Nineteenth-Century Egypt. Cambridge Middle East Library. Cambridge: Cambridge University Press, 1985.

Wadud, Amina. *Qur'an and Woman: Rereading the Sacred Text from a Woman's Perspective*. 2nd edn. Oxford: Oxford University Press, 1999.

Welchman, Lynn. *Beyond the Code: Muslim Family Law and the Shariʿa Judiciary in the Palestinian West Bank*. The Hague: Kluwer Law International, 2000.

"In the Interim: Civil Society, the Sharʿi Judiciary and Palestinian Personal Status Law in the Transitional Period." *Islamic Law and Society* 10, no. 1 (2003): 34–69.

West, Robin. "The Difference in Women's Hedonic Lives: A Phenomenological Critique of Feminist Legal Theory." *Wisconsin Women's Law Journal* 3, no. 81 (1987): 81–145.

Williams, Wendy. "The Equality Crisis: Some Reflections on Culture, Courts, and Feminism." In *Feminist Legal Theory: Readings in Law and Gender*, edited by Katharine T. Bartlett and Rosanne Kennedy, 15–34. New Perspectives on Law, Culture, and Society. Boulder, CO: Westview Press, 1991.

Wright, Nancy E., Margaret W. Ferguson, and A. R. Buck. *Women, Property, and the Letters of the Law in Early Modern England*. Toronto: University of Toronto Press, 2004.

Würth, Anna. "Stalled Reform: Family Law in Post-unification Yemen." *Islamic Law and Society* 10, no. 1 (2003): 12–33.

Yamani, Mai, and Andrew Allen, eds. *Feminism and Islam: Legal and Literary Perspectives*. Reading: Ithaca Press, 1996.

Yazbak, Mahmoud. "Minor Marriages and *Khiyar al-Bulugh* in Ottoman Palestine: A Note on Women's Strategies in a Patriarchal Society." *Islamic Law and Society* 9, no. 3 (2002): 386–409.

Zarinebaf-Shahr, Fariba. "Ottoman Women and the Tradition of Seeking Justice." In Zilfi, *Women in the Ottoman Empire*, 253–63.

"Women, Law, and Imperial Justice in Ottoman Istanbul in the Late Seventeenth Century." In Sonbol, *Women, the Family, and Divorce*, 81–95.

Ze'evi, Dror. "Changes in Legal-Sexual Discourses: Sex Crimes in the Ottoman Empire." *Continuity and Change* 16, no. 2 (2001): 219–42.

"Women in 17th-Century Jerusalem: Western and Indigenous Perspectives." *International Journal of Middle East Studies* 27, no. 2 (1995): 157–73.

Zilfi, Madeline C. "'We Don't Get Along': Women and *Hul* Divorce in the Eighteenth Century." In Zilfi, *Women in the Ottoman Empire*, 264–96.

"Women and Society in the Tulip Era." In Sonbol, *Women, the Family, and Divorce*, 290–303.

ed. *Women in the Ottoman Empire: Middle Eastern Women in the Early Modern Era.* The Ottoman Empire and Its Heritage. Leiden: Brill, 1997.

Zomeño, Amalia. "*Kafāʾa* in the Maliki School: A *Fatwa* from Fifteenth-Century Fez." In Gleave and Kermeli, *Islamic Law*, 87–106.

Suggestions for further reading

CHAPTER 1

Abou El Fadl, Khaled. *Speaking in God's Name: Islamic Law, Authority and Women.* Oxford: Oneworld, 2001.

Ali, Shaheen Sardar. *Gender and Human Rights in Islam and International Law: Equal before Allah, Unequal before Man?* The Hague: Kluwer Law International, 2000.

Anderson, J. N. D. *Law Reform in the Muslim World.* London: University of London Athlone Press, 1976.

Barnett, Hilaire. *Introduction to Feminist Jurisprudence.* London: Cavendish, 1998.

Bartlett, Katherine T., and Deborah L. Rhode. *Gender and Law: Theory, Doctrine and Commentary.* 4th edn. New York: Aspen, 2006.

Chamallas, Martha. *Introduction to Feminist Legal Theory.* 2nd edn. New York: Aspen, 2003.

Hallaq, Wael B. *The Origins and Evolution of Islamic Law.* Cambridge: Cambridge University Press, 2005.

Hirsch, Susan. *Pronouncing and Persevering: Gender and the Discourses of Disputing in an African Islamic Court.* Chicago: University of Chicago Press, 1998.

Mernissi, Fatima. *The Veil and the Male Elite: A Feminist Interpretation of Women's Rights in Islam*, translated by Mary Jo Lakeland. Cambridge, MA: Perseus Books, 1992.

Rahman, Fazlur. *Revival and Reform in Islam.* Oxford: Oneworld, 1999.

CHAPTER 2 (SEE ALSO CHAPTER 3)

Charrad, Mounira M. *States and Women's Rights: The Making of Postcolonial Tunisia, Algeria, and Morocco.* Berkeley: University of California Press, 2001.

El Alami, Dawoud. *The Marriage Contract in Islamic Law: In the Shari'ah, and Personal Status Laws of Egypt and Morocco.* New York: Springer, 1992.

Rapoport, Yossef. *Marriage, Money and Divorce in Medieval Islamic Society.* Cambridge: Cambridge University Press, 2005.

Shaham, Ron. *Family and the Courts in Modern Egypt: A Study Based on Decisions by the Shari'a Courts, 1900–1955.* Leiden: Brill, 1997.

Tucker, Judith E. *In the House of the Law: Gender and Islamic Law in Ottoman Syria and Palestine.* Berkeley: University of California Press, 1998.

Welchman, Lynne. *Beyond the Code: Muslim Family Law and the Shariʾa Judiciary in the Palestinian West Bank*. The Hague: Kluwer Law International, 2000.

ed. *Women's Rights and Islamic Family Law: Perspectives on Reform*. London: Zed Press, 2004.

CHAPTER 3 (SEE ALSO CHAPTER 2)

Ahmed, K. N. *The Muslim Law of Divorce*. New Delhi: Kitab Bhavan, 1978.

Mir-Hosseini, Ziba. *Marriage on Trial: A Study of Islamic Family Law*. Rev. edn. London: I. B. Tauris, 2000.

Peirce, Leslie P. *Morality Tales: Law and Gender in the Ottoman Court of Aintab*. Berkeley: University of California Press, 2003.

Sonbol, Amira El Azhary, ed. *Women, the Family, and Divorce Laws in Islamic History*. Syracuse: Syracuse University Press, 1996.

Zilfi, Madeline, ed. *Women in the Ottoman Empire: Middle Eastern Women in the Early Modern Era*. Leiden: Brill, 1997.

CHAPTER 4

Agarwal, Bina. *A Field of One's Own: Gender and Land Rights in South Asia*. Cambridge: Cambridge University Press, 1995.

Doumani, Beshara, ed. *Family History in the Middle East: Household, Property, and Gender*. Albany, NY: SUNY Press, 2003.

Dupret, Baudouin, ed. *Standing Trial: Law and the Person in the Modern Middle East*. London: I. B. Tauris, 2004.

Islamoglu, Huri, ed. *Constituting Modernity: Private Property in the East and West*. London: I. B. Tauris, 2004.

Moors, Annelise. *Women, Property and Islam. Palestinian Experiences, 1920–1990*. Cambridge: Cambridge University Press, 1995.

Powers, David S. *Law, Society and Culture in the Maghrib, 1300–1500*. Cambridge: Cambridge University Press, 2002.

Shatzmiller, Maya. *Her Day in Court: Women's Property Rights in Fifteenth Century Granada*. Cambridge, MA: Islamic Legal Studies Program, Harvard Law School, 2007.

Sonbol, Amira El Azhary. *Women of the Jordan: Islam, Labor, and the Law*. Syracuse: Syracuse University Press, 2003.

Tucker, Judith E. *Women in Nineteenth-Century Egypt*. Cambridge: Cambridge University Press, 1985.

CHAPTER 5

Afsaruddin, Asma, ed. *Hermeneutics and Honor: Negotiating Female "Public" Space in Islamic/ate Societies*. Cambridge, MA: Harvard Center for Middle East Studies, 2000.

Bowen, John R. *Why the French Don't Like Headscarves: Islam, the State, and Public Space*. Princeton: Princeton University Press, 2007.

El-Rouayhab, Khaled. *Before Homosexuality in the Arab-Islamic World, 1500–1800*. Chicago: University of Chicago Press, 2005.

Heyd, Uriel and V. L. Ménage. *Studies in Old Ottoman Criminal Law*. Oxford: Clarendon Press, 1973.

Moghissi, Hiadeh. *Feminism and Islamic Fundamentalism: The Limits of Postmodern Analysis*. London: Zed Press, 1999.

Musallem, B. F. *Sex and Society in Islam: Birth Control before the Nineteenth Century*. Cambridge: Cambridge University Press, 1986.

Peters, Rudolph. *Crime and Punishment in Islamic Law*. Cambridge: Cambridge University Press, 2005.

Sedghi, Hamideh. *Women and Politics in Iran: Veiling, Unveiling, and Reveiling*. Cambridge: Cambridge University Press, 2007.

Ze'evi, Dror. *Producing Desire: Changing Sexual Discourse in the Ottoman Middle East, 1500–1900*. Berkeley: University of California Press, 2006.

CONCLUSION

Ali, Kecia. *Sexual Ethics and Islam: Feminist Reflections on Qur'an, Hadith and Jurisprudence*. Oxford: Oneworld, 2006.

Barlas, Asma, *"Believing Women" in Islam: Unreading Patriarchal Interpretations of the Qur'an*. Austin: University of Texas Press, 2002.

Stowasser, Barbara, *Women in the Qur'an: Traditions, and Interpretations*. Oxford: Oxford University Press, 1996.

Wadud, Amina, *Inside the Gender Jihad: Women's Reform in Islam*. Oxford: Oneworld, 2006.

Index